From This
Broken Hill
I Sing to You

From This Broken Hill I Sing to You

God, Sex, and Politics in the Work of Leonard Cohen

Marcia Pally

t&tclark

LONDON • NEW YORK • OXFORD • NEW DELHI • SYDNEY

T&T CLARK

Bloomsbury Publishing Plc

50 Bedford Square, London, WC1B 3DP, UK

1385 Broadway, New York, NY 10018, USA

29 Earlsfort Terrace, Dublin 2, Ireland

BLOOMSBURY, T&T CLARK and the T&T Clark logo are trademarks of
Bloomsbury Publishing Plc

First published in Great Britain 2021

A catalogue record for this book is available from the British Library.

A catalog record for this book is available from the Library of Congress.

ISBN: HB: 978-0-5676-9477-5
PB: 978-0-5676-9476-8
ePDF: 978-0-5676-9479-9
ePUB: 978-0-5676-9478-2

Typeset by Newgen KnowledgeWorks Pvt. Ltd., Chennai, India

To find out more about our authors and books visit www.bloomsbury.com
and sign up for our newsletters.

CONTENTS

List of Figures vii
Acknowledgments ix
Foreword by Moshe Halbertal xiii

Introduction 1

1 Theodicy: Arguments with God about Evil,
  Suffering, and God Himself 15

2 Covenantal Theology and Its Place
  in Cohen's Work 33

3 From Covenantal Theology to Theodicy:
  Failing Covenant with God and Persons 61

4 Failing Covenant with God and Persons:
  Doubled Imagery in Cohen's Work 81

5 Those Who Did Not Fail Covenant: Moses and
  Jesus—Cohen's Jewish & Christian Imagery 93

6 The Double Bind That Is Not a Bond:
  Cohen and Women 103

7 Betrayal of God, Betrayal of Persons,
  Political Betrayals: Cohen's Trinity 129

Conclusion: *You Want It Darker* and
Thanks for the Dance—Cohen's Last Creed 147

References 161
Index 177

FIGURES

1   An image of the Star of David 91
2   The 1984 cover of *Book of Mercy* 91
3   The cover of the 2019 reissue of
   Let Us Compare Mythologies 92

ACKNOWLEDGMENTS

My first thanks goes to the students in my first seminar on the theology of Leonard Cohen, taught at Humboldt University-Berlin in 2018. Their insights, curiosity about Cohen, and sheer enthusiasm were part of what convinced me to continue my research into his theology and theodicy. The students and I are indebted to Prof. Dr. Rolf Schieder, who proposed the idea for the course, and to Prof. Dr. Torsten Meireis, who also contributed to our teaching.

I would like to thank the many people cited in the book who have spent much time with Leonard Cohen's work and written about it with insight and commitment. Parsing Cohen is not so much an academic pursuit as a passion and a grappling with genius that can't be wrestled down.

In particular, I would like to thank Prof. Catherine Keller, Prof. Moshe Halbertal, and Byron Belitsos for their careful attention to the manuscript and for their feedback and assistance. Thanks also to Prof. Susan Eastman for her early support. The book has greatly benefited from their contributions. Also helpful were comments by Prof. David Feltmate, editor-in-chief of the *Journal of Religion and Popular Culture*, who edited a 2020 article drawn from the book. Thanks as well to the anonymous reviewers whose feedback helped expand and improve the text.

Many thanks to my publisher T&T Clark/Bloomsbury Academic, to my editor Anna Turton, and to all the people at Bloomsbury for their help in bringing this manuscript to the public. Special thanks goes to Yannik Ehmer for especially precise work on the many reference and formatting details necessary in such a book.

For her support throughout the many stages of writing this volume, I thank Pamela Parker. I would like to express my gratitude also to my teachers at the Solomon Schechter School, who were my first guides to thinking about relationship with God and other persons, the two topics grounding this exploration into Cohen's theology and theodicy. Sending me to this school was a great gift from my parents, Nettie Rose Pally and Dr. Sidney Pally, and from my grandfather, Isaac Schachter, who insisted on this sort of education, even for girls. In particular, I would like to thank my mother, Nettie, whose soprano voice and piano-playing gave me a lifelong love of music, including Leonard Cohen's.

*

The author and publisher gratefully acknowledge the permission granted to reproduce the copyright material in this book.

Every effort has been made to trace copyright holders and to obtain their permission for the use of copyright material. The publisher apologizes for any errors or omissions in the above list and would be grateful if notified of any corrections that should be incorporated in future reprints or editions of this book.

Biblical quotations: All are taken from the NIV (New International Version) of the Bible.

SONG COLLECTIONS DISCUSSED IN THIS BOOK

Song Collections cited: (all lyrics in this volume are written by Leonard Cohen unless otherwise specified in the in-sentence parentheses where the song is mentioned).

Songs of Leonard Cohen. 1967. Written by Leonard Cohen. Produced by John Simon. Columbia Records.

Songs from a Room. 1969. Written by Leonard Cohen, Hy Zaret, and Anna Marly. Produced by Bob Johnston. Columbia Records.

Songs of Love and Hate. 1971. Written by Leonard Cohen. Produced by Bob Johnston. Columbia Records.

Live Songs. 1973. Written by Leonard Cohen and Dick Blakeslee. Produced by Bob Johnston. Columbia Records.

New Skin for the Old Ceremony. 1974. Written by Leonard Cohen. Produced by Leonard Cohen and John Lissauer. Columbia Records.

Death of a Ladies' Man. 1977. Written by Leonard Cohen. Music and production by Phil Spector. Warner Bros. (Columbia, reissue).

Recent Songs. 1979. Written by Leonard Cohen, John Lissauer, and Antoine Gérin-Lajoie-Traditional. Produced by Leonard Cohen and Henry Lewy. Columbia Records.

Various Positions. 1984. Written by Leonard Cohen. Produced by John Lissauer. Columbia, Passport.

Famous Blue Raincoat. 1986. Written by Leonard Cohen, Jennifer Warnes, and Bill Elliott. Produced by C. Roscoe Beck and Jennifer Warnes. Cypress.

I'm Your Man. 1988. Written by Leonard Cohen, Sharon Robinson, Jeff Fisher, and Federico García Lorca. Produced by Leonard Cohen, Roscoe Beck, Jean-Michel Reusser, and Michel Robidoux. Columbia.

The Future. 1992. Written by Leonard Cohen, Sharon Robinson, Frederick Knight, and Irving Berlin. Produced by Leonard Cohen, Steve Lindsey, Leanne Unger, Rebecca De Mornay, and Yoav Goren. Columbia.

More Best of Leonard Cohen. 1997. Written by Leonard Cohen, Sharon Robinson, and Federico Garcia Lorca. Complication album. Columbia.

Ten New Songs. 2001. Written by Leonard Cohen and Sharon Robinson. Produced by Sharon Robinson. Columbia.

Tour of 1979. 2001. Written by Leonard Cohen. Produced by Bob Metzger and Sharon Robinson. Sony Music Entertainment.

Dear Heather. 2004. Written by Leonard Cohen, Lord Byron, F. R. Scott, Redd Stewart, and Pee Wee King. Produced by Leanne Ungar, Sharon Robinson, Anjani Thomas, Henry Lewy, and Leonard Cohen. Columbia.

Blue Alert. 2006. Written by Leonard Cohen. Produced by Leonard Cohen. Columbia.

Old Ideas. 2012. Written by Leonard Cohen, Patrick Leonard, and Anjani Thomas. Produced by Ed Sanders and Patrick Leonard. Columbia.

Popular Problems. 2014. Written by Leonard Cohen, Patrick Leonard, and Anjani Thomas. Produced by Patrick Leonard. Columbia.

Can't Forget: A Souvenir of the Grand Tour. 2015. Produced by Mark Vreeken and Ed Sanders. Columbia Records.

You Want It Darker. 2016. Written by Leonard Cohen. Produced by Adam Cohen and Patrick Leonard. Columbia.

Thanks for the Dance. 2019. Written by Leonard Cohen. Produced by Adam Cohen. Columbia Legacy.

FOREWORD

Hineni

Moshe Halbertal

There are certain words and terms that derive their meaning not only from their current use but from the way they were employed in earlier and familiar contexts. Whenever such a word is spoken or written, it carries with it the echoes of its previous occurrences; it evokes the wealth and complexity of its past resonance. All the words we utter have been used before, but that doesn't mean that we are engaging in quotation. Nevertheless, when we use unique words that are charged with the aura of their previous utterances, we are unable to free ourselves from the burden and gift of quoting. An English speaker cannot merely state "I have a dream" without carrying with it the echoes of Dr. King's proclamation. One such word in Hebrew is *hineni* (here I am); any user of this word echoes its previous momentous appearances.

In all of Leonard Cohen's poems, *hineni* is the only word that appears in its original Hebrew. *Hineni* is repeated three times in one of Leonard Cohen's last songs "You Want It Darker," and the poem's recording ends with a chain of *"hineni"*s sung in a haunting melody and in the voice of the cantor of Cohen's synagogue in Montreal. The poem, written with Cohen's full awareness of his impending end, is an inverted self-Kaddish, the Jewish ritual prayer for the dead. In "You [God] Want It Darker," Cohen makes a direct reference to the opening line of the Kaddish, "Magnified, Sanctified, Be Great Thy Name," which are recited by relatives at the funeral of their deceased parents, children, or siblings. In Cohen's poem, while he faces his own death and recites Kaddish for himself, this line of praise to God turns into a proclamation of protest embedded in a tone of defiant resignation:

Magnified, Sanctified be thy Holy Name
Vilified, crucified in the human frame
A million candles burning for the help that never came
You want it darker

Hineni, hineni
I am ready My Lord

As Marcia Pally, in her beautiful conclusion to this book, notes, Leonard Cohen's *hineni* "here I am" (I am ready) carries with it the solemn echo of Abraham's response to God: "Now, after these things, God tested Abraham, and said to him: 'Abraham'; and he said: 'Here I am (*hineni*)'. And He said: 'Take now your son, your only son, who you love, Isaac, and go to the land of Moriah; and offer him there for a burnt-offering on one of the mountains which I will tell you'" (Gen. 22:1-2).

These two verses open the dialogue between God and Abraham as God commands Abraham to sacrifice his beloved Isaac. God calls "Abraham," and before God states his shattering request, Abraham answers "*hineni*"—here I am. Abraham's *hineni* expresses an attentive, alert readiness. The word *hineni* is a construct of two words—*hineh* (here) and *ani* (I am). In signifying the first person, I am, and in signifying presence, here, Abraham assures that no length of space or any gap in time will transpire between asking and responding: he is available, wholehearted and immediate. The "hereness" encompasses his full self. Abraham's readiness is magnified in his proclaiming "*hineni*" before God's command is actually stated. Abraham is ready for whatever will be asked of him though even the faithful Abraham could not have imagined how extreme the request would be—wasn't he promised to be a father of many nations? And Abraham, after receiving the most difficult of all requests—to sacrifice his beloved son—doesn't argue; he follows suit immediately, early in the morning.

The next dialogue within the passage is between Isaac and Abraham while they are walking alone on the road to the mountain. A second *hineni* appears, this time proclaimed by Abraham to Isaac, and this second *hineni* captures Abraham's terrible bind:

And Abraham took the wood of the burnt-offering, and laid it on Isaac his son; and he took the fire and the knife in his hand; and the two of them went together. And Isaac spoke to Abraham his

father, and said: "My father." And he said: "Here I am (*hineni*)
my son." And he said: "See the fire and the wood; but where is
the lamb for a burnt-offering?" And Abraham said: "God will
provide the lamb for a burnt-offering Himself, my son." So the
two of them went together. (Gen. 22:7-8)

Isaac calls Abraham "My father," and before knowing the content
of Isaac's request, Abraham answers "here I am (*hineni*) my son," in
the exact same manner he made himself fully available to God. Isaac
is worried. It is not out of mere curiosity that he asks, "But where
is the lamb for the burnt-offering?" Does Isaac dare to entertain the
thought that he might be the designated burnt-offering?

Abraham's two "*hineni*"s—to God and to his son—are now
positioned in direct conflict; Abraham cannot be fully loyal to both
of them. Abraham expects and maybe hopes that God will show the
way in which this contradiction will be resolved: "God will provide
the lamb for a burnt-offering Himself."

This biblical *hineni* as an expression of attentive, alert
presence and readiness is common especially within a hierarchical
relationship. *Hineni* is used in a person's response to God and in
a servant's response to his master (see, e.g., 1 Sam. 3:4; 14:7). But
such a stance of compliance and resolve, *within* the hierarchical
context, might express either a wholehearted embrace or a defiant
acceptance. In a very different manner from Abraham, Jeremiah
proclaims *hineni* as defiant acceptance. Jeremiah's *hineni* was stated
by him after he had declared a prophecy of doom and destruction
to the leaders of Judea and the people of Jerusalem. He offers them
a way out, a path to true repentance that will save them from the
impending ruin. Jeremiah is aware that in the past such a prophecy
was considered an act of treason among the political elite of the
besieged city of Jerusalem. He has become a marked man. And then
in a direct appeal to the nation's leaders Jeremiah says,

As for me, here I am [*hineni*] in your hands; do to me what seems
good and right to you. But know that if you put me to death,
you and the city and its inhabitants will be guilty of shedding the
blood of an innocent man. For the truth of the Lord has sent me
to you, to speak all these words to you. (Jer. 26:14-15)

Jeremiah's *hineni* is of a tone altogether different from Abraham's.
It means, "I know you might kill me, here I am, in your hands.

I am not going to fight you, nor am I planning to escape, I will accept your verdict. But know you will be shedding the blood of an innocent man who was sent to you by God." One wonders whether Cohen's *hineni* expresses an alert wholehearted readiness like that of Abraham or a defiant resignation like that of Jeremiah. Whatever that might be, Cohen proclaims *hineni, hineni*, I am ready.

But the complex resonance of the biblical *hineni* doesn't end here with the ambivalence added to it by Jeremiah's *hineni*. *Hineni* is proclaimed by God himself toward humans in what might be the deepest expression of biblical and Jewish religious sensibility. The ascription of *hineni* to God was conceived twice in the religious genius of Isaiah. The first occurrence of God's proclaiming *hineni* is in the chapter that condemns ritual fasting as a mode of approaching God. Isaiah reports the people's resentful grievance to God: "Why, when we fasted, did You not see? When we starved our bodies, did You pay no heed?" To this the prophet answers bluntly, "Because on your fast day you see to your business and oppress all your laborers!" (Isa. 58:3). In the following verses Isaiah proceeds to describe the proper path to approach God and to be seen by him:

No, this is the fast I desire: To unlock fetters of wickedness, and untie the cords of the yoke. To let the oppressed go free, to break off every yoke. It is to share your bread with the hungry, and to take the wretched poor into your home; when you see the naked, to clothe him, and not to ignore your own kin. (Isa. 58:6-7)

If the proper way of approaching God were to be followed, God's response would surely come, and God will then say *hineni*: "Then, when you call, the Lord will answer; when you cry, He will say: [*hineni*] here I am. If you banish the yoke from your midst, the menacing hand, and evil speech" (Isa. 58:9). The human mode of being ready and alert toward God's calling is reversed in Isaiah's prophecy. God says *hineni* to a human call.

Isaiah carries this reversal to its most radical extreme in his second ascription of *hineni* to God, in a prophetic moment in which God's longing for the human appeal is acutely expressed:

I responded to those who did not ask, I was at hand to those who did not seek me; said, [*hineni, hineni*] "Here I am, here I am" to a nation that did not invoke my name. I constantly spread out my hands to a disloyal people, who walk the way that is not good, following their own designs. (Isa. 65:1-2)

God was responding to those who didn't even seek him out; he was ready at hand and he said *hineni, hineni*. God's *hineni* surpasses that of Abraham's. Abraham made himself available after he was called though before the content of the request was articulated by God. In Isaiah's words, God has proclaimed *hineni* even before he was addressed at all, waiting attentively to be called, knowing full well that his availability to serve might be completely ignored. In God's search for his people, he spreads out his hands in a gesture known as praying. The full reversal of the human stance to God is completed: God calls *hineni, hineni*.

To be sure, *hineni* was ascribed to God in biblical literature prior to Isaiah, but never in the dialogical context of a response to a human quest. In prior occasions when it is ascribed to God, it serves as an opening of an announcement of God's plan. Here is just one such example in the Noah narrative: "And behold [*hineni*] I will bring the flood waters upon the earth to destroy all flesh under the sky in which there is breath of life; everything on earth shall perish" (Gen. 6:17). As an introduction to a statement of a divine plan, *hineni* doesn't signify a readiness to obey and follow but rather a resoluteness and immediacy of execution. I am here; it will happen. Biblical translators tend to translate such occurrences of *hineni* not as "I am here" but rather as "behold." Yet Isaiah's ascription of the human *hineni* to God is indeed "I am here, ready, open to you." It is a bold and most radical extension of the relational covenantal biblical religious thinking.

Marcia Pally has ingeniously uncovered in her book Cohen's ongoing struggle with his inability to adopt the stance of *hineni* in love and in life. He lacked the steadfastness needed to respond to the hands that were stretched out to him from the world. He failed to be fully there.

Cohen had arrived, toward the end of his life, at the place where he could say, I am here, *hineni*. It takes a life journey to come to this stance. But it is not devoid of defiance as well; Cohen's *hineni* echoes both Abraham's ready and open *hineni* and Jeremiah's defiant-resigned one. Cohen had poetic perfect pitch when it came to the religious quest; he was the last of the psalmists. Was he aware of God's *hineni* in Isaiah? Did his use of *hineni* in its Hebrew original carry the resonance not only of Abraham's and Jeremiah's "*hineni*"s but also that of God's? One might think so, since the only time in all the biblical uses of *hineni* that the word is repeated twice, *hineni, hineni,* it is stated by God to his people. And Cohen repeats his *hineni* twice. Is he answering God's *hineni*? Is he saying, I am here, and you, God? Do You want it darker? You do.

Introduction

"If you love only what cannot be snatched out of its lover's hand, you undoubtedly remain unbeaten." Augustine wrote these words in *On Christian Belief* (397, 88, XLVI.86.243) to explain his faith in loving God over worldly goods. If one directs one's love at what cannot be "snatched" away—at God and love itself—one will suffer neither longing nor loss. Thomas Aquinas, elaborating on the idea, held that the "theological virtues" of faith, hope, and most of all charity direct humanity toward God, who is the one Good that can satisfy all needs and desires. With this, we may come to a sense of inner unity and peace (Thomas Aquinas [1265–73] 1948: I-II.3.8; II-II.29.1,3; Porter 1990: 169).

Aquinas' insight may serve as an introduction to the novels, poetry, and songs of Leonard Cohen (1934–2016). Cohen's images of inner disunity and loss—of desire that is not unsatisfied but *unsatisfiable*—reach at once into the human intimate and to the transcendent. Contrary to the wisdom of Augustine and Aquinas, he was unable to stay constant to God and so find peace with himself. He stayed no more constant to the women he loved. This double restlessness was his persistent wound, investigated in over sixty years of art in a magisterial vivisection of his soul. Aubrey Glazer called Cohen's work a "circum/fession," both confession and circumcision, where "we cut a hole in our hearts as we spill our story onto the page" (2017: Kindle Locations 173–4). Or as Lou Reed said, "If we could all write songs like Leonard Cohen, we would" (Billingham 2017b: 7).

A great deal has been written about the "black romantic" and "poet laureate of despair" (Scobie 1978: 4; Worrell 2008: 1; respectively)— every joint smoked, drink imbibed, and woman bedded. This book has a far more modest focus on Cohen's theology and theodicy and limits itself to these aspects of Cohen's thought. It thus references Cohen's well-known life, interviews, career, and popular reception only as they shed light on these theological concerns. While a brief sketch of Cohen's life and career can be found at the end of this introduction as contextualization for his work, more detailed biographical treatments can be found in Kubernik (2014), Leibovitz (2014a), Nadel (1996), Reynolds (1990), and Simmons (2012). For a fine collection of interviews, see Burger (2014). In these and other works, Cohen's writing is explored for its sex, politics, darkness, and "a monotheism that never quite gave up the ghost" (Gitlin 2002: 97). Specific imagery has been interrogated: Elliot Wolfson (2006a) has written on Cohen's kabbalist tropes; Jiri Měsíc (2015) has looked at Cohen's use of Sufi and Islamic references; Doron Cohen has published a wealth of pieces that explore imagery drawn from Persian poetry to the Talmud (2016); and Fernando Toda has described Cohen's use of Wordsworth (1984).

Yet while Cohen's imagery has been richly investigated as the work of any great artist invites, the theology undergirding it has been less addressed. Měsíc and Glazer make valuable contributions, and it is to this effort that I hope to contribute. What are the *sources* of Cohen's much-mentioned "darkness," the inner strife and restlessness of "the poet laureate of pessimism" (Lisle 2004)?

At least one source is Cohen's reckoning with his failure— humanity's failure—to be constant to God and other persons, to act covenantally in the Jewish tradition into which Cohen was born and which he plumbed through his life. "Whatever we may make of Leonard's Judaism," biographers Lorraine Dorman and Clive Rawlins note, "he is a man seized by its traditions" (1990: 91). "The 'charged speech of the synagogue' and the 'absence of the casual' in it [Burger 2014: 164] gave Cohen a sense of the ritualized nature of a speaking that does more than merely describe the world" (Howes 2017: 96). Cohen's poetry came from many places; the synagogue was among the earliest. He later wrote, "How beautiful our heritage, to have this way of speaking to eternity" (Cohen 1984, poem 15).

What is this covenantal commitment that we fail? This is the subject of Chapter 2, but here we may say that God forged a bond of reciprocal love and commitment with humanity (through Adam and Noah) and with the biblical patriarchs "for the blessing of all humanity"—a *telos* thrice emphasized, once with each patriarch

(Gen. 12:3, 26:4, 28:14). It is a pledge between God and person *and* among persons. As each person reciprocates commitment to God and other persons, each of us is embraced by the divine. In the tradition of the Psalms, Cohen in *Book of Mercy* wrote, "We are made to lift my heart to you [God] … travel on a hair to you … go through a pinhole of light … and fly on the wisp of a remembrance" to you ("Not Knowing Where to Go," in Cohen 1994: 332). More than two millennia earlier, the psalmist himself said it this way: "I call out to the LORD … My steps have held to your paths; my feet have not stumbled" (Pss. 3:4, 17:5-6).

Max Layton, son of Cohen's mentor, poet Irving Layton, called Cohen "the greatest psalmist since King David" (Posner 2017: 516). Yet Cohen also saw that, though we are made as covenantal creatures, dependent on bonds with God and other persons, we breach them and bolt. Inconstancy, betrayal, and abandonment are the human condition. "I made a date in Heaven," Cohen wrote, "Oh Lord but I've been keepin' it in Hell" ("Got a Little Secret" Live at Auckland Soundcheck, *Can't Forget: A Souvenir of the Grand Tour*, 2015).

Like the prophets, who cried out as we forsook God and each other, Cohen the "bard-*kohen*" (bard-priest) understood the problem of human inconstancy and suffering as a religious one (Glazer 2012: 176). "The religious promise is very cruel," Cohen said in 2005, "that if you get enlightened you can live without suffering … because no one can live without suffering … It doesn't matter how advanced or fulfilled or enlightened an individual is" (Hesthamar 2005). In the mid-1990s, five years in a Zen monastery coming to terms with the human condition had not much improved Cohen's outlook. After leaving the monastery, he wrote:

After Years Of
Spiritual Rigour
You Did Not Manage
To Enlighten Yourself.

The most one can expect is that

A Certain Cheerfulness
Will Begin To
Arise Out Of Your Crushed
Hopes And Intentions. ("A Life of Errands,"
Book of Longing, 2007: 66)

Boring into this human condition, Cohen came to this theodical question: Why did God make us needy of him and others and yet founder in inconstancy? Why is it so difficult to sustain covenant, so easy to abandon, abuse, and be left with gaping loss? The problem of covenant *un*sustained is the theme of Cohen's theodicy. Beneath each interrogation of why humanity fails covenant is the more anguished question of why God created us so prone to fail it. Cohen's problem was not a crisis of faith—he never ceased believing in God—but the scandal that *God* makes it so hard for us to live by our beliefs. If one promise of Judaism—indeed, the central promise at Sinai—is covenant with the God of grace and compassion (*"el rachum v'chanun,"* Exod. 34:6), why are we so on-our-own to forsake and be forsaken? Why is each of us out there, dangling like "a bird on the wire," trying to be "free," having "torn everyone who reached out for me" ("Bird on a Wire," *Songs from a Room*, 1969)? In this song, Cohen says he'll repent, "I swear by this song / And by all that I have done wrong / I will make it all up to thee." Yet he breached this and so many promises over the next half century, each failure fueling the next song.

This returned him to the question: Why did God make us this way? The easy answer says that our suffering is self-inflicted. In his *Free Choice of the Will*, Augustine argues that God gave humanity free will to choose between good and evil, to sustain or abandon commitment to God and neighbor. This freedom makes our choices those of a responsible moral agent, not of a robot preprogrammed to be good. Yet given this freedom, a fallen humanity breaks covenant for the possibilities of advantage, wealth, and power. And so we wound the very relationships we need. The linchpin of the free will theodicy is that it transfers responsibility from God to (fallen) humanity. In modern theology, it is most associated with Alvin Plantinga's free will defense (1974a, 1974b). God, Plantinga argues, could surely end evil. But the important goal of allowing humanity to learn to make the moral choice requires that we be able to choose the immoral one. Without this option, there is no possibility of a moral act, only of a humanity that is God's puppet. God's desire for human moral agency necessitates the possibility that we choose evil, which it seems humanity frequently does.

Free will reasoning did not satisfy Cohen. His interrogation of it reprises many of the questions tackled also by contemporary theologians (Chapter 1). For instance, while human moral agency may require the freedom to choose evil, why do we choose it so often? Could God not have made us less prone to its worst excesses? Could we not retain free will but within a narrowed range of possible actions, a range that would eliminate the gross evils of war, torture, betrayal, abandonment, and injustice? After all, freedom to choose between (a) and (b) renders the choice a moral one even if neither is very awful. Yet instead, we have broad leeway and we breach covenant cruelly because breaching it is easy for us. Is this not, Cohen asks, our Creator's fault?

Cohen did not solve the religious paradox of being committed to a God who seeks our covenant yet made us able to "freely" break it. He gave us fourteen studio song collections plus touring albums, fourteen books of poetry, two novels, and sundry writings through which this paradox runs. It is this predicament that the present book traces, focusing on Cohen's lyrics with reference to his poetry and novels where helpful. That is, this volume is one treatment of *Cohen's* theodical questions and struggles (if not answers). It does not attempt to write a theodicy on its own or to employ Cohen to illuminate *other* investigations of theodicy, be they from antiquity or the present day. Rather, it seeks to describe my understanding of the theodical strains within Cohen's work.

There is no suggestion here that covenant and theodicy were Cohen's sole occupations. He had many, and as with all art, his work has been multiply interpreted. Other students of Cohen explore different themes and concerns. They understand images and metaphors differently as well. This book is not meant as an overview of all Cohen's concerns or approaches to his work. It is an effort to trace and illuminate specific theodical questions as they evolved over his life and writing. These questions are, biographer Sylvie Simmons writes, "the same old ideas that were on his first album, *Songs of Leonard Cohen*, and that have been on every Leonard Cohen album since" (2012: 522). Examples will thus be taken from across six decades of Cohen's oeuvre. But, as it is not possible in this short volume to discuss all works that raise theodical matters, I apologize to readers who find that a work dear to them is not explored here. Cohen's theodical investigations were lifelong, and many songs present themselves as illustrations. Inevitably, some selection and triage were necessary.

This introduction ends with a brief sketch of Cohen's life. The chapters follow with a look at traditional and contemporary theodicies (Chapter 1) and a discussion of covenant in the Judaic tradition (Chapter 2). All quotations from biblical sources are from the New International Version (NIV). The questions that arise from our breach of covenant are traced through Cohen's verse (Chapter 3). Chapter 4 explores some of the poetic techniques Cohen employed, notably (i) the interweaving of images, some of which evoke bond with God and others, bond among persons, and (ii) entwined images that evoke both bonds at once. Chapter 5 looks at Cohen's use of Jewish and Christian imagery to express both his commitment to covenant and his failure to keep it—notably with the women he loved, the subject of Chapter 6. Chapter 7 explores how, in Cohen's view, betrayal of God, betrayal of persons, and our political betrayals are of a piece, the Cohen trinity. The conclusion looks at his last song collection, *You Want It Darker* (2016), and the posthumous collection produced by his son Adam, *Thanks for the Dance* (2019). All lyrics cited were written by Cohen except where otherwise specified.

—

Leonard Cohen:
A Biographical Sketch

Leonard Norman Cohen was born to the Lithuanian emigrée Marsha Klonitsky and Nathan Bernard Cohen, a middle-class Orthodox Jewish family, on September 21, 1934, in Westmount, Quebec, Canada. Cohen's great uncle, Tzvi Hirsch Cohen, served as chief rabbi of Montréal. Leonard's maternal grandfather, Rabbi Solomon Klonitsky-Kline, wrote commentaries on the Talmud. His paternal grandfather, Lyon Cohen, was the founding president of the Canadian Jewish Congress and cofounded the *Canadian Jewish Times*, the first English language Jewish newspaper in Canada. Cohen's father, who owned the Freedman Company clothing firm, died from a lung disease when Leonard was nine years old. The day of the funeral, Cohen recounts, he took one of his father's prefolded bow ties, cut off one of the wings, and buried the bow tie with a note in the family's backyard (Remnick 2016). Cohen said he didn't know why.

Cohen's first mentor in writing was the poet Irving Layton, who taught at Herzliah high school, a Jewish school that Cohen attended from grades seven through nine. He discovered his first poetic inspiration, Federico Garcia Lorca, later at the (traditionally

Christian/secular) Westmount High, where he also taught himself to play acoustic guitar and started a country-folk band called the Buckskin Boys. Yet his affinity for music had begun earlier with his mother, who sang to him and later with him when he went out with high school friends to play guitar at local cafes. "She would sing with us," Cohen said in a 1988 interview, "when I took my guitar to a restaurant with some friends; my mother would come, and we'd often sing all night" (Cohen 1988). Cohen also went around town without his mother, often to the Main Deli Steak House to "watch the gangsters, pimps, and wrestlers dance around the night" (Sax, cited in Castelfranco 2016).

In 1951, Cohen enrolled in McGill University; read Tolstoy, Pound, Eliot, and Proust; and listened to jazz and French cabaretists Edit Piaf and Jacques Brel. This musical terrain gave him, a man with no vocal range to speak of, a landscape on which to have a "singing" career. Cohen could barely carry a tune, but these torch singers lived not by vocal prowess but by strung-out vulnerability. They were a precedent Cohen could follow.

Still in college, Cohen hung out with Layton's poetry circle. "I taught him how to dress," Cohen said of Layton, "he taught me how to live forever" ("Acclaimed poet Irving Layton dies at 93" 2006). In 1956, Cohen published his first book of poetry, *Let Us Compare Mythologies*, for which he won the McGill Literary Award. Critic Robert Weaver called Cohen "the best young poet in English Canada" (Castelfranco 2016). Renowned literary critic Northrop Frye offered "restrained praise" (Nadel 1996).

With a three-thousand-dollar grant from the Canada Council for the Arts, Cohen went to London to write, hated the dreariness, and reportedly bought a plane ticket to Greece when a bank teller told him he'd gotten his tan there (Remnick 2016). He stopped on Hydra, an island of hills, whitewashed houses, and intermittent electricity, and he stayed there, eventually buying a small house and living between writerly discipline and drug-and-sex reveling. He met the Norwegian Marianne Ihlen, her flaxen hair glittering in the sun just like the novels said things should be. They set up house with her small son, her husband having gone off with the latest infidelity. Ihlen became Cohen's muse. The unraveling of their relationship in the late 1960s, as Cohen was getting into New York's celebrity scene, inspired the songs "Hey, That's No Way to Say Goodbye" and "So Long, Marianne" (*Songs of Leonard Cohen*, 1967).

Working from Hydra and Montreal, Cohen published three more poetry collections, *The Spice Box of Earth* (1961), *Flowers for Hitler* (1964), *and the tepidly received Parasites of Heaven* ([1966] 2018a). Two novels were also published, *The Favourite Game* (1963) and *Beautiful Losers* (1966). With romantic-rebel curiosity, Cohen went to Cuba during the 1961 Bay of Pigs invasion. In 1967, he went to New York, hoping to remake his literary career into a more remunerative singer-songwriter one. Much has been written about the drugs, booze, and beddings of the 1960s arts scene, through which Cohen, newly arrived from cobblestoned Hydra, floundered. He later described the Chelsea Hotel, where he lived for a while amid the glitterati, as "a place where you never leave the elevator alone" (Simmons 2012: 238). His reflections on those days are captured in "Chelsea Hotel #2" (*New Skin for the Old Ceremony*, 1974). But the scene was not the best mix with his depression, from which he had suffered since adolescence. "When I speak of depression," he later told Dorian Lynskey, "I speak of a clinical depression that is the background of your entire life, a background of anguish and anxiety, a sense that nothing goes well, that pleasure is unavailable and all your strategies collapse" (2012).

In 1967, singer Judy Collins heard Cohen perform and helped get producer John Simon interested in him. Cohen told Collins that he could neither sing nor play guitar and didn't think "Suzanne" was "even a song" (O'Kane, Medley and Wheeler 2016). Yet John Hammond, a producer who selected his performers on intuition (and helped launch the careers of Benny Goodman, Aretha Franklin, and Billie Holiday), heard Cohen and decided to produce his first album, *Songs of Leonard Cohen* (1967). The "non-song" "Suzanne" became a hit. The album spent over a year on the British charts and sent singers such as Collins and James Taylor looking to Cohen for song material. The following year, Cohen published the poetry collection *Selected Poems 1956–1968*. In spite of Cohen's growing renown—or perhaps because of it—the publisher and modernist poet Louis Dudek, who had published Cohen's 1956 *Let Us Compare Mythologies*, now somewhat dismissively referred to Cohen as "a temperamental romantic, affiliated with the young generation of feelings and flowers" (Dudek 1969: 114).

Cohen released *Songs from a Room* in 1969 and, in 1970, gave a stuff-of-legends performance at the Isle of Wight Festival. At about 4 a.m. he cast magic over five or six hundred thousand tired, angry people who had been sitting in the mud for five days and had booed off the stage such popular performers as Kris Kristofferson. Some had also burned down the concession stand. Cohen told a story about his father, asked everyone to light a match with which to dot the dark, and slowly sang "Bird on a Wire." "A lone sorrowful voice," Kristofferson told Cohen biographer Ira Nadel, "did what some of the best rockers in the world had tried to do for three days and failed" (1996: 26).

Though Cohen was nearly forty, considered ancient for a singer-songwriter, he was beginning to build a career. *Songs of Love and Hate* was released in 1971, and three songs from his 1967 album ("The Stranger Song," "Winter Lady," and "Sisters of Mercy") played on the soundtrack of the film *McCabe & Mrs. Miller*, directed by the renowned Robert Altman, starring Julie Christie and Warren Beatty. Each of Cohen's songs took months or years to complete. But he later told Lynskey (2012), "We're in a world where there's famine and hunger and people are dodging bullets and having their nails pulled out in dungeons so it's very hard for me to place any high value on the work that I do to write a song. Yeah, I work hard but compared to what?" Cohen's 1972 tour was the subject of Tony Palmer's documentary, *Bird on a Wire* (1974). He published another volume of poetry, *Death of a Lady's Man* (1978), and released three more albums *New Skin for the Old Ceremony* (1974), *Death of a Ladies' Man* (1977), and *Recent Songs* (1979).

Yet as the decade progressed, Cohen's new career came to hurdles especially after the album *Death of a Ladies' Man* was bungled by controversial producer Phil Spector. His "big sound" approach overwhelmed Cohen's music. In one recording session, he pulled a gun on Cohen (Simmons 2012: 303). On one hand, Cohen was popular in Europe and acquired a cult following in the United States. The folk music magazine *Sing Out!* wrote, "No comparison can be drawn between Leonard Cohen and any other phenomenon" (Lynskey 2012). Yet Cohen never broke into the top ranks or earned a platinum album or hit single (outside Canada and, curiously, Norway). What's more, the soul-searching and politics of the 1960s were fading into the styles of the 1970s and 1980s, for which Cohen's work—"like prayers or spells" (Schudel 2016)—was unsuited. Not much came of singer-songwriter Jennifer Warnes's efforts to persuade the studios to do another Cohen album because, Warnes explained, "Americans in general—not the Europeans—like to 'keep your sunny side up,' put on a smile, and come out swinging no matter how ruined you've been. And Leonard will say, look at the shreds of my heart" (https://www.youtube.com/watch?v=TOvz0Ozf4G8).

In 1984, the midyear of Cohen's career, the magisterial poetry collection *Book of Mercy* was published, and the companion album *Various Positions* was released. They did not improve sales. *Various Positions* includes the famous "Dance Me to the End of Love," "If It Be Your Will," and "Hallelujah," which has been recorded in over 300 versions and has become one of the most "oft-performed songs in American musical history" (Maslin 2012). Alan Light wrote a book about it, *The Holy or the Broken: Leonard Cohen, Jeff Buckley, and the Unlikely Ascent of Hallelujah* (2012). It comprises nearly half of Babette Babich's masterful *The Hallelujah Effect* (2013). Yet in 1984, it made little impression. The album *Various Positions* was not released in the United States.

It wasn't until Warnes's *Famous Blue Raincoat*, her 1986 album-homage to Cohen, and Cohen's own taunting *I'm Your Man* (1988) that audiences were again drawn to his work as they had been twenty years earlier. Cohen was in his fifties. "If It Be Your Will" (*Various Positions*, 1984) and "Everybody Knows" (with Sharon Robinson, *I'm Your Man*, 1988) were picked up and used in the 1990 film *Pump up the Volume*, which introduced Cohen to the children of his earlier followers. Three songs from his 1992 album *The Future* became part of the soundtrack for Oliver Stone's hit film *Natural Born Killers*, starring Woody Harrelson, Juliette Lewis, Robert Downey Jr., and Tommy Lee Jones.

Cohen was now working again, less isolated but not less riddled by demons. In 1994, he published *Stranger Music*, a compilation of his writings, prodded by a sense of achievement or panic. "I was drinking at least three bottles of Château Latour before performances," he said that year at nearly sixty (Remnick 2016).

On August 9, 1995, Cohen entered the Mount Baldy Zen monastery near Los Angeles after studying with the Zen master Kyozan Joshu Sasaki Roshi on and off since 1969. Cohen was ordained a Rinzai Zen Buddhist monk, was given the names "Solitary Cliff" and *Jikan*, meaning something like "ordinary silence," and then silenced his song-making for five years, serving as Roshi's personal assistant. He shoveled snow, lit fires, got up at 3 a.m., meditated, froze, and cleaned toilets. In 2012, Roshi faced a series of sexual abuse charges from students and Buddhist nuns dating back to the 1970s. An independent Buddhist panel found the charges credible even as others could not square them with the

Zen master they knew (Vitello 2014). Cohen, who had left Mount Baldy in 1999, told David Remnick somewhat cryptically, "Roshi was a very naughty guy" (2016). Sylvie Simmons, whose biography *I'm Your Man* came out in 2012, blogged that "whatever Leonard might have thought about this in private, it's hard imagining him having anything to say publicly on a man he loved. His forty-five-year relationship with Roshi was one of the most durable and devoted of Leonard's life" (Simmons 2014). Though Cohen's life and art were littered with failed relationships, this was a bond that would not be broken.

Within a week of leaving Mount Baldy, Cohen flew to Mumbai to study Advaita Vedanta with Ramesh Balsekar, spiritual leader and former president of the Bank of India. Advaita Vedanta holds to something like a covenant that cannot be breached because the individual soul is one with ultimate reality. As there is no separate "you," "I," or reality "out there," one cannot abandon or be abandoned, perhaps a comfort to Cohen in his struggle with failed commitment. He stayed in India for several months and, returning to the United States, began to rebuild his career with the 2001 *Ten New Songs* (with Sharon Robinson). The album, no less "dark" than his earlier works, again captured European and Canadian audiences, earning Cohen four 2002 Canadian Juno Awards and the 2003 Companion of the Order of Canada, Canada's highest civilian honor. *Dear Heather* (2004) was less despairing, perhaps the result of Cohen's depression at last lifting. Or perhaps because he, at age seventy, was for the first time comfortable with his relationship with composer/singer Anjani Thomas, twenty-five years his junior. Thomas sang the lyrics on the cowritten 2006 album *Blue Alert*, sounding, critic Brian Johnson wrote, "like Cohen reincarnated as woman ... though Cohen doesn't sing a note on the album, his voice permeates it like smoke" (Johnson 2005: 48).

In 2005, Cohen's daughter Lorca—named after Cohen's boyhood idol Garcia Lorca—was tipped off to improprieties in her father's financial accounts. Cohen discovered that his friend, manager, and briefly lover, Kelly Lynch, had stolen much of his savings, $8.4 million worth. Since 1996, she had been selling rights to his work, placing the proceeds into a trust over which she had 99.5 percent control. Cohen sued Lynch for $5 million, was countersued by the investment banker handling his accounts, and won his case in 2006. Lynch failed to respond to the court judgments, and it was unclear even in 2016, the year of Cohen's death, whether he would recover the stolen funds (Glaister 2005; Macklem, Gillis and Johnson 2005; "Leonard Cohen awarded $9 million in civil suit" 2006; "Leonard Cohen 'unlikely' to recover stolen millions" 2006).

The financial loss sent Cohen on the road for a series of world tours, 387 performances between 2008 and 2013. Though in his seventies, or perhaps because of it, he was at last met with unquestioned critical and popular acclaim. Even before the tours began, a cinematic tribute to his work, *Leonard Cohen I'm Your Man*, was released in 2006. Philip Glass composed music for Cohen's 2006 poetry collection, *Book of Longing*, which Glass and Cohen performed live. The CD of the collaboration, *Book of Longing. A Song Cycle Based on the Poetry and Artwork of Leonard Cohen*, was released in 2007.

The tours began in 2008 with less of the old booze and drugs. *New York Times* writer Larry Rohter wrote, "Cohen appears to see performance and prayer as aspects of the same larger divine enterprise." His songs are like "collaborations between Jacques Brel and [monk and scholar] Thomas Merton" (Rohter 2009). Cohen performed throughout North America, Europe, Russia, New Zealand, Australia, Turkey, and Israel, where he dedicated his concert to "reconciliation, tolerance, and peace" between Israelis and Palestinians. He stunned audiences by closing his concert there with *birkhat ha'kohanim*, the Jewish priestly blessing over the people. He tried to perform in the West Bank, but his would-be Palestinian hosts found it politically unfeasible. Proceeds from the Tel Aviv event were donated to a charitable fund for Israeli and Palestinian peace groups ("Leonard Cohen's Tel Aviv Concert Sells Out" 2009). Theologian and professor Donald Grayston described the concerts this way: "he evinces in his singing and stage presence what I would characterize as *delight*, evidence that he has, in [Thomas] Merton's phrase, recovered Paradise—that he is speaking to us from Eden regained ... He has become in his eighth decade a spiritual teacher" (Grayston 2009).

Cohen's 2009 performances earned $9.2 million, placing Cohen among Billboard's "highest money makers" (Waddell et al. 2010). Live recordings of the 2008 and 2009 tours were released in 2010 as the CD/DVD, *Songs from the Road*. Cohen's poetry was again collected, this time by the popular Everyman's Library Pocket Poets, as *Poems and Songs* (Faggen 2011).

The title of Cohen's twelfth studio album *Old Ideas* (2012) signals "old" imagery long recognizable in Cohen's work but also "old" in being about aging, memories, and final years. The album reached the highest positions on the music charts of any in his career. After Cohen's final tour in 2012–13, he released *Popular Problems* (2014, with Anjani Thomas and Patrick Leonard) and, in 2016, the growling genius of *You Want It Darker*. The collection was produced on Cohen's dining room table by Cohen's son Adam and was released three weeks before Cohen's death on November 7. He had leukemia and fell and died that night in his sleep.

The tributes began. That week, Hillary Clinton was defeated by Donald Trump. *Saturday Night Live* featured actress Kate McKinnon as Clinton, reflecting on the state of democracy by singing "Hallelujah." Montreal's tribute followed in December, itself followed by the commission of two staggering city murals in Cohen's honor. The one-year anniversary tribute featured performances by k.d. lang, Elvis Costello, Adam Cohen, Patrick Watson, Sting, Damien Rice, and Courtney Love, among others. On February 23, 2017, Adam Cohen and Sammy Slabbinck, who had worked on the 2016 album, created a posthumous video tribute with heretofore unseen footage. The title track was awarded a Grammy for Best Rock Performance in January 2018, also the year of the posthumous collection of poems, drawings, and other writings, *The Flame* (Cohen 2018b). The Montreal Contemporary Art Museum curated an exhibit dedicated to Cohen's work, *Leonard Cohen: A Crack in Everything*, which broke attendance records. It went on to an international tour.

In November 2019, Adam Cohen released *Thanks for the Dance*, a collection of songs recorded at the same time as *You Want It Darker* but not included in the 2016 release. Also contributing to the new album were Daniel Lanois, Beck, Jennifer Warnes, Damien Rice, Leslie Feist, among others. *Rolling Stone* called it "a magnificent parting shot that's also that exceptionally rare thing—a posthumous work as alive, challenging, and essential as anything issued in the artist's lifetime" (Hermes 2019).

1

Theodicy:
Arguments with God about Evil, Suffering, and God Himself

First Remarks

As this book traces Cohen's theodicy through his poetic work, we might begin by looking into the sorts of questions that theodicy poses and attempts to answer. While not a detailed introduction to theodicy—several books offer such a course, including Peckham (2018) and Scott (2015)—this chapter aims modestly at providing some general background to the theodical aspects of Cohen's work. It seeks to highlight a few theodical questions and approaches to addressing them. The chapter is organized by theodical approach rather than chronologically as many key theodicies have been explored over time, and the central ideas within each approach gain clarity when discussed together. Cohen took up some of the theodical questions outlined here throughout his life, others, less so. In this general background chapter, I'll briefly note the ones of significant import to Cohen. Exploring them as expressed in his work is the task of the rest of the book.

The most important question for theodicy is why suffering and devastation occur when an omnipotent and good God could prevent them. In considering both evil (harmful events, intended or not) and intentional evil or sin, we may ask: why do the wicked succeed in their treachery or at least get away with it (Jer. 12:1; Pss. 10:4-5, 94:3-7)? Why does God allow these things (Jer. 5:19; Pss. 10:1, 11)? "It seems that there is no God," Thomas Aquinas wrote as he contemplated the atheist retort to evil's prevalence, "by the word 'God' we understand a certain infinite good. So, if God existed, nobody would ever encounter evil. But we do encounter evil in the world. So, God does not exist" (*Summa Theologiae*: Ia, q.2, a.3, ob 1, cited in Davies and Leftow 2006: 24). In the eighteenth century, the philosopher David Hume put the problem this way: "Is he [God] willing to prevent evil, but not able? Then he is impotent. Is he able, but not willing? Then he is malevolent. Is he both able and willing? Whence then is evil (*unde malum*)?" ([1779] 1990: 108–9).

Over the last century, investigations of why God allows evil often begin by arguing that evil *could* logically emerge even given a loving, omnipotent God. That is, there is some reason why evil might logically occur. Thus, in light of this reason, the presence of evil does not mean that there is no loving, omnipotent God as both could exist at once (van Inwagen 2006: 7, 65). A second part of the theodical effort is to demonstrate not only that God could exist along with the world's evil but that, as God is both good and the ground for all existing things, evil (one existing thing) must be part of some greater good. Peter Van Inwagen, in line with much Christian and Jewish theodicy, notes, "A theodicy is not simply an attempt to meet the charge that God's ways are unjust: it is an attempt to exhibit the justice of his ways" (2006: 6). Importantly, theodicy today as in the past remains an open debate where solutions to the puzzle of evil are proposed but never final or completely satisfying.

This is certainly how Cohen saw it. The aim of theodical questions, on his view, is not to come to an ultimate understanding of God and evil but to better understand our distress-filled world and how to live somewhat better in it. As we'll see throughout the following chapters, Cohen's questions, frustrations, and anger at God aim not at a final judgment about him. Rather, they emerge from the recognition that there is much humanity cannot grasp about God but that part of the human task is to try to understand what we can so that we may live better with him and with those he loves, other persons (see Chapters 2 and 3).

A Loving God and Natural Disaster

Theodicies address suffering caused by unintended human error, intended human harm/sin, and natural forces. Starting with natural occurrences—metaphorically unruly forces, watery unformedness (Gen. 1:1), "sea monsters," and the "leviathan" (Ps. 74:14)—a key theodical question is: why did God, who could have created the world in any way, create natural processes that injure and kill innocents? Why does he not shut the doors to them (Job 38:8)? Voltaire famously confronted these questions in his poem "On the Lisbon Earthquake," written in response to the palliative explanations given for the 1755 earthquake that, as Voltaire wrote, killed infants at their mother's breast.

Voltaire challenged Gottfried Wilhelm Leibniz's claim that, as a perfect God created the cosmos, it must be "the best of all possible worlds." Voltaire's vivid descriptions of nature's brutality make a case that it is not. He further attacked the idea, popular at the time, that as this is the best possible worlds, all aspects of nature are just as they should be. Thus, no part of nature—including the tectonic geophysics that caused Lisbon's earthquake—could be changed without disturbing the "chain" of natural laws that God created for this "best" world. In retort Voltaire asked, can't God make the chain of natural laws operate with less brutality? He further rebutted Alexander Pope's dictum that "what is, is right"; what exists, is correct. It is unlikely, Voltaire replied, that every Lisbon baby had committed a wrong so grievous as to warrant being crushed under Lisbon's rubble—thus making the earthquake "right." He sardonically noted that "what is, is right" includes murder, rape, and so on, which cannot be "right."

Voltaire's questions led him to agnosticism. Cohen—perhaps because of the importance of covenant and relationship in Jewish thought (Chapter 2)—doubted neither God's existence nor his bond with humanity. Indeed, Cohen's theodical frustration emerged from *within* his bond with God. But Cohen did raise a query related to Voltaire's: if all the world's phenomena are created by God, is God not ultimately responsible? If some things are not "right," is not God, who made all things, foundationally accountable? More specifically for Cohen, if it's "right" in God's vision for each person to act covenantally with God and other persons, when we do not do this "right" thing, is not God ultimately to blame?

A Loving God, Human Evil, and Free Will

Moving from natural disaster to intended human evil/sin, many theodicies find explanation in our free will. As this is among the most important theodical traditions, I'll discuss it here first. Free will is generally understood as (i) living in circumstances that allow one to take or not take an action or (ii) the absence of external factors forcing one's hand (e.g., wanting to buy grapes, one cannot go to a shoemaker, but as no external factor is forcing one's trip to the greengrocer, that choice is freely taken). The first premise of free will theodicies is that free will indeed allows persons to make immoral decisions that cause suffering. But lacking this option, we would be not moral actors but rather machines preprogrammed to always do good. The consequence of being a creature capable of moral choice is the possibility of immoral choice.

The notion that humanity's free will is the source of worldly evil and suffering is among the first ideas of the Bible, in which the special tree in Eden (Gen. 3) brings not immortality, as in the Gilgamesh epic of neighboring Mesopotamian culture, but rather wisdom. And the wisdom it brings is that humanity has the capacity, the free will, to follow or flout God's ordering of the natural world (Sarna 1966: 26; Hayes 2012: 40). Adam and Eve may refrain from eating from the tree, following God's wish, or they may eat from it, flouting God. The decision is theirs and it is of a moral nature: with the freedom to make choices comes responsibility.

On this understanding, evil emerges not from the actions of capricious gods whom one might influence by magic, as in the pantheons of societies surrounding ancient Israel, but "is a product of human behavior, not a principle inherent in the cosmos. Man's disobedience is the cause of the human predicament" (Sarna 1966: 27). With this knowledge, humanity (Adam and Eve) must leave Eden, their paradisical home of childlike living without responsibility, and enter the adult world of work, childbearing, family, and moral consequences. As the Bible continues, with its stories of righteousness on one hand and idolatry and abuse of the needy on the other, "Humans and humans alone are responsible for the reign of wickedness and death or the reign of righteousness and life in their society" (Hayes 2012: 158).

Understanding evil as emerging from humanity's free will was also Augustine's approach in *Free Choice of the Will*, which set much of the ground for future Christian free will theodicies. An agent lacking the choice to do wrong cannot be a *moral* agent who *decides* to do right. "Their unusual power of self-determination," Kathryn Tanner writes, "means humans can become anything along the continuum of ontological ranks, from the top to the bottom"

(2010: 134). The free will to determine one's actions allows persons to do good, ill, and the range in between.

If God does not control humanity's free will, does this free will limit God as we do what God wishes us not to do? Free will theodicies hold that it does not. Rather, in the cosmos God created, God can do all that is possible but not what is impossible within his created world (Lewis 2001b: 18). God, in his created world, cannot make a triangle have four sides. In an example that connects us to Cohen's work on covenant, Michael Horton writes, God "is bound to us (better, has bound himself to us) by a free decision to enter into covenant with us and the whole creation. God is not free to act contrary to such covenantal guarantees" (2005: 33). Covenant is a moral commitment of each party to the other. Thus, humanity must have the free will to accept or reject it. Otherwise, it would not be covenant but pre-set obedience. God, seeking covenant with humanity (and not blind obedience), cannot strip humanity of the free will needed to make this choice. One might say that God gave humanity free will so that we can, among other things, make the moral decision to commit to covenant.

John Peckham (2018) calls the arena of human free will "the rules of engagement" between God and humanity. God, he writes, "'does whatever he pleases' (Ps. 115:3; cf. 135:6), but he is not always pleased by what occurs because part of what pleases him is to respect, for the sake of love, the free decisions of creatures, which often displease him" (2018: 50). Peckham notes biblical and modern arguments for a "cosmic battle" between God and evil forces that seek to distance humanity from God. He notes also that God neither preempts evil forces from trying to entrap humanity nor does God stop humanity from succumbing to them. For such interference would remove human choice and the potential for moral action (Peckham 2018: 103–4, 107, 113).

Among the most important contemporary advocates of the free will argument is Alvin Plantinga, who distinguishes between a free will theodicy, which explains the necessity of evil, and his free will defense, which more modestly suggests that the presence of evil does not obviate the existence of God or his love for humanity. While God could end evil, the option to do wrong is unavoidable if persons are to act freely as moral beings. As this is a *logically* sufficient reason for God to allow the possibility of evil, the presence of evil is not proof that God is malevolent or does not exist. As the potential to do wrong is a necessary condition of moral agency, this human capacity is also *morally* sufficient. It compromises neither God's goodness (he seeks our moral adulthood) nor his omnipotence (1974a, 1974b). Summarizing his argument, Plantinga writes,

> A world containing creatures who are significantly free (and freely perform more good than evil actions) is more valuable, all else being equal, than a world containing no free creatures at all ... The fact that free creatures sometimes go wrong, however, counts neither against God's omnipotence nor against His goodness; for He could have forestalled the occurrence of moral evil only by removing the possibility of moral good. (1974a: 29, 30)

Why is the capacity for moral choice important? To some, not being a machine is desirable in itself, but for theists like Cohen, being a moral agent has two other important features. It is one way we are in God's image (*b'tselem Elohim*). As God acts freely, humanity, in his image, has some analogous (limited, imperfect) ability to act freely and make choices. Moreover, the reciprocity of covenant—God commits to humanity, and humanity to God—presupposes that persons are free to make that commitment. They are free to exercise *yetzer ha'tov* (the will to good) but also *yetzer ha'ra* (will to evil) and reject covenant. Without this freedom, there is no covenantal *agreement*, only social engineering. In Lenn Goodman's words, "The covenant itself ... rests on (and thus cannot create) the freedom of the covenantors" (1991: 41–2). In a broad summation of free will arguments, C. S. Lewis notes, "Free will, though it makes evil possible, is also the only thing that makes possible any love or goodness or joy worth having" (2001a: 48; see also Rice 2014: 47).

The free will argument has been both persuasive and beset by challenges, one being the question of the source of evil: if it was not created by God, God is not the creator of all existence. If it was created by God, why and how is it consistent with God's goodness? Second, how did people, created good in an evil-less world, come to the idea of evil in the first place? Rabbinic sources note that the biblical Cain had no idea how to kill his brother, "did not know from where the soul departs," stumbling on it only by clumsy trial and error (*b. Sanhedrin* 37b, in English at https://www.sefaria.org/Sanhedrin.37b?lang=bi section 10). Third, while Aquinas held that God in the end turns evil to good ends (Thomas Aquinas [1265–73] *Summa Theologiae*: Ia, q.2, a.3, ad 1; see Davies and Leftow 2006: 26), this leaves us with an uncomfortable cost–benefit analysis. Does the final good (moral agency) justify the staggering suffering we perpetrate on each other (Meister 2012: 33)? Does a good for humanity overall justify the brutality perpetrated against a particular person? Humanity, John Roth writes, drawing on G. W. F. Hegel, has "more power and more freedom than is good for us" and as a result, our "history is largely a slaughter-bench" (2001: 10,7; Hegel [1837] 2004: 21).

Fourth, even if free moral agency is of supreme importance, could God not preserve it within a narrower scope of human action? This may be called the compatibilist position, where free will is compatible with some shaping of events by God. Persons would still choose from a variety of actions and thus be moral agents, but the worst evils would not be among the possible choices. In fact, human conduct may already be circumscribed: evils more heinous than we can imagine may be beyond our ken. Why could God not further limit the human range while preserving free will between (somewhat narrowed) alternatives?

Fifth and more provocatively, could God have created humanity to always make the moral choice? That is, not to choose among a narrower range of evils but to make the moral choice from whatever range of options is available. In this challenge to free will theodicies, people would still struggle with alternatives, and human experience would be that of a moral agent. Only God would know that the outcome of any human deliberation would be the moral one. As long as one recognizes God as having knowledge we cannot have (that we will choose the moral option), this challenge to free will theodicies stands. David Griffin among others finds this unacceptable as true freedom: "If this being [God] knows infallibly that next year I will do A, instead of B or C, then it is necessary that I will do A. It may seem to me then as if I make a real choice among genuine alternatives, but this will be illusory" ([1976] 2004: 61). Yet J. L. Mackie counters that, "if God has made men such that in their free choices they sometimes prefer what is good and sometimes what is evil, why could he not have made men such that they always freely choose the good?" (1992: 97).

Last, Richard Rice (2014) holds that the free will argument addresses the possibility of evil but not its execution (*contra* those who hold it addresses both). On Rice's view, an omniscient God *ab initio* knows that humanity will perpetrate grave wrongdoings. Why has he allowed them to actually occur—given that we could remain moral within a narrower range of action or, as Mackie proposes, with no wrongdoing at all? Is the historical record of brutality not the responsibility of God, who created humanity as it is? This question was central to Cohen and will appear and reappear in the coming chapters.

Evil as the Absence of the Good

In addition to his free will theodicy, Augustine makes another argument in *Free Choice of the Will* and elsewhere in his work. Evil, he holds, does not obviate the existence of God, who creates all things good, because evil is not a "thing." It is an absence. Therefore, no contradiction pertains between the phenomenon of evil and the idea that all "things" are created good by a good and loving God.

Augustine begins, following the neoplatonist philosopher Plotinus, by holding that all existing things are expressions of their ideal forms, which are perfect and good. "Matter," Augustine writes, "participates in something of the ideal world [ideal forms], otherwise it would not be matter ... [A]ll existence as such is good" (Augustine [390] 1953: 11.21). Evil, as it is not an expression of the ideal or good, cannot be an existing thing: "For evil has no nature of its own. Rather, it is the absence of good which has received the name 'evil'" (Augustine [426] 1998: *City of God*, XI.9, 461; see also Evans 1982). To understand evil, one must look to the human will: "Perverted will, then, is the cause of all evil" (Augustine [388–95] 1955: III.17.48). Such perversion must have occurred after God's creation of the world as he creates only what is good (Gen. 1). Since humanity was good at creation, humanity's corporeal nature cannot itself be evil (Smith 2000: 141). The source of evil, then, is not human corporeality but human will and freedom, which renders us moral agents by allowing us to make choices, including bad ones.

Furthering the argument, Aquinas in *On Evil* holds that sin, intentional human evil, is the absence of humanity's created good nature. He begins by theologizing Aristotle, who somewhat like the neoplatonists held that each thing has its internal, built-in way of being (form). In Aquinas' iteration, God gives this internal, primary direction to all existing things, and all things then follow this internal direction as they act in the world. This means that all things have some causative capacity of their own. Aquinas called this "secondary causality." God acts not only directly in world but also in or through the capacities of each created thing. "Divine providence works through intermediaries ... not through any impotence on [God's] part, but from the abundance of goodness imparting to creatures also the dignity of causing" ([1265–73] 1948 *Summa Theologica*: 1.22.3). God created the cosmos and acts both directly and *coincidently* in it through the causative capacities of created things ([1265–73] 1948 *Summa Theologica*: 1, 103, 5).

On Aquinas' view, the human will too has divinely given inner direction: "to be moved voluntarily is to be moved of one's own accord, i.e., from a resource within. That inner resource, however, may derive from some other, outward source. In this sense there is no contradiction between being moved of one's own accord and being moved by another," that is, by God ([1265–73] 1948 *Summa Theologica*: 1.105.4.2). Following one's divinely given inner direction leads to good. But humanity, with divinely given freedom, may abandon that good on the mistaken idea that something else is better. Evil is thus the "deprivation" or absence of the good that is our inner direction or "ordering" ([1265–73] 1948: *Summa Theologica*: I, 19, 9).

A century earlier, Maimonides (1135–1204), perhaps the greatest of medieval Jewish philosophers and a source for Aquinas, had argued similar free will and evil-as-absence theodicies. Maimonides, whom Aquinas called "Rabbi Moses," begins (like Augustine and Aquinas) with creation as good: "the true work of God is all good" ([1190] 2008: III.10). He reiterates the free will presupposed by covenant: it is a reciprocal commitment by parties free to make such a bond (*Mishneh Torah*, chapter five). He confirms this freedom in *Guide to the Perplexed*: "man should have the ability to do whatever he wills or chooses among the things concerning which he has the ability to act" ([1190] 1956: III.17). Evil, then, emerges from the distorted will or choice—for instance, the pursuit of foolish aims like excessive wealth and pleasure (Halbertal 2014). And this results from an absence of human wisdom. In the case of natural disaster, evil is the absence of optimally running natural forces. "All evils," Maimonides concludes, "are negations" ([1190] 2008: III.8 and III.10).

Maimonides rejects the idea that suffering is punishment for sin or that innocent sufferers will be rewarded in the afterlife. Summing up his evil-as-negation (or as absence) theodicy, Maimonides writes, "All the great evils which men cause to each other because of certain intentions, desires, opinions, or religious principles, are likewise due to non-existence, because they originate in ignorance, which is absence of wisdom" ([1190] 2008: III.11).

While holding to his analysis of evil as absence, Maimonides differs from Augustine and Aquinas in finding that evil is only secondarily a matter of our fallen *will*. Primarily, it is a matter of the inadequate development of wisdom. It is not so much sinful will as ignorant mind. Maimonides thus precludes the challenge to free will theodicies which asks how humanity, created good by a perfect God, came to use will wrongly. As evil is not a matter of evil will, we need not ask why we use our wills for evil ends. Avoiding this problem, Maimonides turns to the human mind, which, by dint of its finitude and boundedness in nature, is limited. Evil thus emerges from the absence or underdevelopment of wisdom. Eschewing evil is a matter of filling the absence of wisdom with the development of one's reasoning and mind (Hartman 1976: 135). This development entails studying philosophy and God's word. Thus, wrong choices may be averted. (The idea of developing and maturing the mind emerges again in more contemporary theodicies, such as that of John Hick, discussed below.)

Such intellectual efforts, on Maimonides' view, are moments of divine-human sharedness. They are "the bond between us and Him, that intellect which overflows from Him" to guide us in life. Maimonides continues: "Those who have obtained this overflow … can never be afflicted with evil of any kind, for they are with God and God with them" ([1190] 1956: 3.51). The suffering of righteous, wise persons occurs as they become distracted from the wisdom of God ([1190] 2008: III.51), while "those who approach Him are best protected" ([1190] 2008: III.18). So committed was Maimonides to philosophical study that he considered the "intellectual love of God" to be a *mitzvah* or divine commandment. He concluded, with humanist universalism *avant la lettre*, that access to God is not limited to those in the Israelite covenant but open to all (Hartman 1976: 210, 212–13). On Maimonides' understanding, we will always have God's words of wisdom to study as we can never achieve full understanding of them or of God himself. Neither positive descriptions of God (the *shelosh-esreh middot* or thirteen attributes of divine mercy) nor statements of what God is not (the *via negativa*) can fully capture the divine "mind" ([1190] 2008: I.58).

The medieval commentator Moses ibn Tibbon (1195–1274) was careful to note that, on Maimonides' account, God does not intervene in the actions of the wise to protect them, as that would obviate free will. Rather, wisdom guides better choices, moving us from physical pleasures to spiritual ones. A century later, Aquinas elaborated on the Christian iteration of this idea: identifying with Jesus' suffering teaches us "to consider temporal goods or evils as nothing, lest a disordered love for them impede [humanity] from being dedicated to spiritual things" (1264 *De Rationibus Fidei*: 7). For both Maimonides and Aquinas, embracing the spiritual over the material is the path to the good.

In their emphasis on philosophical and theological study, Maimonides' works reflect a long-standing Jewish emphasis on learning from which Cohen also drew—in his case to study Judaism, Buddhism, Christianity, Advaita Vedanta, and Sufism. But Maimonides also leaves us—and Cohen—with the question of why God, who wants humanity to freely choose covenant and the good, made it so difficult for us to develop the wisdom to do so. We may recall Cohen's remark cited in the introduction, which now sounds like a direct address to Maimonides: "The religious promise is very cruel that if you get enlightened you can live without suffering ... because no one can live without suffering ... It doesn't matter how advanced or fulfilled or enlightened an individual is" (Hesthamar 2005). Maimonides proposed that nearing God through study and "enlightenment" best protects us from evil and suffering. In Cohen's experience, it doesn't. In the way God made us, we never arrive at the wisdom sufficient to shield us from inflicting pain and suffering it.

Evil-as-absence theodicy remains influential in contemporary theology, for instance, in the work of the Swiss theologian Karl Barth (see, for instance, Rodin 1997). Barth located the idea of evil-as-absence amid existentialist, post-Heideggerian discussions of existence and nothingness. Barth described evil as "Das Nichtige," or nothingness, that which is not and which God rejects (1960: 289, 353). "Nothingness is that from which God separates himself and in face of which He asserts Himself and exerts His positive will ... God elects, and therefore rejects what he does not elect. God wills, and therefore opposes what He does not will. He says Yes, and therefore says No to that which He has not said Yes" (1960: 351).

In positing evil as the rejected no-thing, without ontological or existential status, Barth not only echoes Augustine but he also comes to the difficulty inherent in all evil-as-absence theodicies, which may serve as a summing up of this section. If God created the world good, how did the absence of good begin? If it began with the human will choosing wrongly, how did this possibility occur to persons created good by a perfect God? When wrongdoing occurs, is this not the responsibility of God, who created the human will as it is? In upcoming chapters, we'll see how this last question dogged Cohen through much of his work.

Punishment Theodicies

Punishment theodicies agree with the freewill argument that evil and suffering do not obviate the existence and goodness of God, yet the two approaches differ in their areas of focus. The freewill argument holds that the possibility of choosing evil is unavoidable if human choices are to be those of moral agents and not pre-set dolls. Punishment theodicies focus on the usefulness of punishment in making us moral—in making us reconsider past wrongdoings and future temptations. It serves as rehabilitation and penance for sin, both consistent with a good and moral divine. The medieval Jewish philosophers Saadia and Yehudah Halevi took this position in holding that suffering is punishment for (intentional) wrongdoing. The heartbreaking eleventh-century poem "Eileh ezkera" (These I Will Remember) grapples with the slaughter of Jews during the first crusade through a punishment narrative set in antiquity. The poem explains the torture and execution of rabbis in the Roman period as punishment for a sin committed more than a millennium earlier when Joseph's brothers sold him into slavery (Gen. 37:12-28). The rabbis of the Roman era were punished for the earlier sins of Joseph's brothers, and by analogy, the sufferings of the crusade were understood also as punishment for past sins.

One must appreciate this elaborate effort to grapple with the brutality of the crusades, but it also highlights the difficulties of punishment theodicies. Why are rabbis of the Roman period to suffer for a wrong committed more than a millennium earlier, and how can one be sure it was this specific wrong that caused their torment? If suffering is to work as deterrent, punishment, or rehabilitation, the link between wrongdoing and suffering/punishment must be clear. "Man must know," Aquinas wrote, "the cause of his punishment, either to correct himself or to endure the trials with more patience" (1989, *The Literal Exposition on Job*: 10.1). Yet in punishment theodicies, there may be little discernible link between wrongdoing and punishment, or the proposal of such a link may be untenable as with the suffering of children. The logic of punishment theodicy holds only if all humanity including children is continually sinning and in need of perpetual punishment and rehabilitation. Suffering that may occur at any time even to those who appear righteous makes sense only if we, constant sinners, are ever in need of chastening punishment.

Ideas drawn from punishment theodicies appear on occasion in Cohen's work, but far more frequent are two other ideas. First, God has set us in a paradox by our very nature: we are created for commitment to God and other persons but cannot sustain it. Second, we have much to learn about suffering from the crucifixion, which appears as a trope throughout Cohen's writing. Cruciform theodicies may thus be helpful in understanding his intent, and it is to these we now turn.

Cruciform Theodicies

Cruciform theodicies distinguish between two understandings of God: one, as a transcendent whose perfection and goodness do not change, and another, as a transcendent who feels and suffers along with humanity. On the first view, God engages with humanity without being altered by the experience. His immanence in world does not affect his transcendence and radical otherness (Weinandy 2000: 145). His actions toward us are motivated by his goodness and perfect nature, not by emotion. In contrast to this concept of divine impassibility is a theology developed substantially in the twentieth century, in response to two world wars and the Nazi Holocaust. On this theology, God suffers alongside humanity. To be sure, it is with an anguish radically different from human anguish but it is anguish nonetheless. He is motivated as a concerned parent is (Hos. 11:1) or, when we break our commitment to him, as a husband betrayed by his wife (Hos. 2). God grieves when we fall away. As Cohen wrote in divine voice, "it was you [humanity] who covered up my face" (Lover Lover Lover, *New Skin for the Old Ceremony*, 1974).

In developing the notion of the suffering God, the postwar German theologian Jürgen Moltmann argues that divine suffering is not restricted to Jesus, as proposed in the *communicatio idiomatum* (the "communication" or distribution of attributes among Trinitarian persons, with Jesus, the Son, being the sufferer; Moltmann 1993a). Moltmann holds that if God's engagement with humanity (the "economic Trinity") is one with God himself (the "immanent Trinity"), Jesus' suffering as a fully human person must extend throughout the immanent Trinity, to the Father and the Holy Spirit. As God and Jesus are of the same substance or *homoousios*, God suffers both Jesus' physical pains of the crucifixion and the Father's pain of losing a son (1993a: 244). "What happens on Golgotha reaches into the innermost depths of the Godhead, putting its impress on the Trinitarian life in eternity" (Moltmann 1993b: 81). God suffers, Moltmann concludes, *from* human brutality, *with* those who suffer, and *for* humanity in toto (1993b: 60).

From Jesus' human-divine suffering, we learn what to do with our own worldly hardship: turn it into love and giving, as Jesus loved and gave. This was the kind of love and covenantal commitment that Cohen understood—and understood that he failed. Babette Babich insightfully writes, "As a Jew, Cohen reminds us to feel for Christ, not to be a Christian necessarily but to get the point about Christ" (2014: Kindle Location 2407). Cohen got "the point about Christ"—to love the other and give for her sake—but he could not sustain it. He ran through commitments like water, "rinse and repeat, again and again" (Babich 2013: 50). While Moltmann and cruciform theologians like Marilyn McCord Adams (1992: 169–87) believe we can find positive purpose in suffering, Cohen asks where responsibility lies when we don't. Surely it is a human failing, but is it not also our Creator's who made us able to fail as we do?

Soul-Making Theodicy

Somewhat akin to cruciform theodicies, which seek to turn suffering into love, soul-making theodicies see hardship also as preparation for a better future, as training of sorts for moral development and action. John Hick begins with the Augustinian idea of original sin, in which all humanity after Adam and Eve carry their sin of rebelling against God in Eden and eating from the forbidden Tree of Knowledge. Throughout Christian thought, this sin has ranged in meaning from a tendency to sin, on the less damning end of the spectrum, to the idea of sweeping distortion and depravity of human nature. Hick finds original sin incompatible with a loving God (2007). It also doesn't explain, he notes, how evil came to the minds of prelapsarian human beings who knew only good. This "is to postulate the self-creation of evil *ex nihilo*!" from nothing!

(Hick 2007: 250). Hick posits instead that humanity was created not fully formed but with the potential for relationship with God. Persons are able to mature into God's "likeness" by acting morally and striving toward this relationship. Hick bases his theodicy on at least two sources, one being the second-century church father Irenaeus and the other, modern "romantic" theologies.

Irenaeus is understood as having a "maturational" anthropology consistent with the Eastern church's doctrine of *theosis*, humanity's potential to become more godlike. Humanity may mature from being in the "image" of God into moral conduct, the "likeness" of God. The process of maturation is *ascesis*, the discipline of ridding oneself of immorality in partnership with God and his grace. (For opposing views of Irenaeus, see, for instance, Scott 2015: 100, 114.) From the markedly different perch of modern "progress," late-nineteenth-century "romantic" theologies too carry with them a sense of moral improvement. They emphasize not human wrongdoing but the forgiveness of the loving Father. On this view, humanity is not ever hobbled by sin but moves toward salvation by God's love and grace. Both Irenaeus's "maturational" anthropology and the "romantic" sense of moral progress serve as background to Hick's idea of moral development.

On Hick's account, in order for humanity to mature into moral capacity, our experience must provide moral challenges by which to grow and develop. These challenges include the possibility of choosing evil and wrestling with that temptation. Hick's "soul-making" theodicy is somewhat like the free will argument with the addition that the option to do evil not only makes us moral agents but also provides training for moral agency. "The reality," Hick writes, "is not a perfect creation that has gone tragically wrong, but a still continuing creative process whose completion lies in the eschaton" (2001: 41). The "soul-making" effort moves humanity from a self-centered way of living to a spiritual, other-centered life (2007: 257). The mistakes and suffering along the way teach us empathy, fairness, and giving of the self. A world without wrongdoing "would be a world without need for the virtues of self-sacrifice, care for others, devotion to the public good, courage, perseverance, skill, or honesty" (2007: 325)—in short, a world in which we would remain protected children who need never learn to take account of others.

On one hand, Hick's "soul-making" theodicy addresses the question of how humanity, created good, comes to the idea of evil.

We were not created good but rather immature with the potential for good; committing evil is inherent in our immaturity. On the other, D. Z. Phillips notes, this theodicy reprises the cost–benefit problem we found in freewill theodicies. Does our "maturation" justify human suffering and the cruelties of history? Phillips thinks not: "I repeat: suffering is not for anything. This assumption seduces theodicy" (2001: 158; see also Swinton 2007). On Phillips's view, suffering is incomprehensible, and theodical ideas about its benefits, maturational or otherwise, can neither fully explain nor justify it. Moreover, suffering often hardens people, causing them to come not to compassion but to bitterness and anger (Meister 2012: 37).

Sarah Pinnock and others press Phillips's argument in light of the Nazi Holocaust. She wonders if theodicies rationalize brutality as being part of a divine plan for our maturation or some other worldly good. And she objects: "After Auschwitz, theodicy is exposed as perpetrating amoral justifications of evil" (2002: xi). On her view, theodicy may not be used to justify evil and suffering whatever their ostensible long-term payoffs.

Cohen too found neither the Holocaust nor more quotidian brutalities justifiable by a divine scheme for our improvement (Chapter 7). He was unpersuaded by any payoff plan and struggled with the paradox of God creating us at once so needful of each other and yet so adept at cruelty.

Process Theodicy

With echoes of "soul-making" theodicy, process theodicy also emphasizes the world's and humanity's incompleteness and perpetual development. Grounded in Alfred North Whitehead's "Philosophy of Organism" ([1929] 1978: xi), it understands all entities—cells, persons—as "societies" of interactions and moments of experience. Larger entities, like persons, are integrations of smaller societies such that reality is a landscape not of substance and permanence but of dynamism and interdependence. The emergence of a "subject" such as a person occurs with the "concrescence" of previous experience and interactions, which can then be transmitted to other "subjects" or future moments of experience (see Griffin [1976] 2004: 277). John Cobb and David Griffin suggest the analogy of a wave or film to explain a "subject" that is identifiable in itself but exists only for a time as constituted by its component "societies" and environment (1976: 14).

God, in process theology, is "dipolar." He is at once the "primordial" source of all creative possibilities, that which gives shape and primary direction to all things—not unlike Aquinas' notion of divine inner direction for each entity in creation. But God is also "consequent," God's self-expression in particular things, which emerges as particular things themselves develop. Thus, God too is in process and development: "In this aspect, he is not before all creation, but with all creation" (Whitehead [1929] 1978: 343). With this, the idea of God "above," "beyond," or transcendent to nature is abandoned. "It is as true to say," Whitehead wrote, "that God creates the World, as that the World creates God" ([1929] 1978: 348). Both human creativity and human evil may occur as God does not control us—not only because he granted us free will but also because he is in perpetual reciprocity and emergence with us. The future is open, and the end of the world, undetermined.

On this view, natural disasters occur from the workings of the laws of nature, which God shapes with primary direction but does not determine or control. Natural disaster is thus metaphysically a possibility inherent in an ever-developing cosmos. Moral evil emerges from humanity's free will, which God similarly directs toward the good but does not determine. It is the nature of God not to compel but to be a kenotic love that self-empties into the cosmos in ever interaction with it (Oord 2015).

Like the maturational "soul-making" theodicy and the cruciform emphasis on learning from the cross, process theodicy avoids the question of how evil began in a world created good. Creation is not so much good as emergent. It also avoids the question of why God created evil forces because he didn't. As he gives grounding direction to all but is not the omnipotent determiner, *moral* responsibility for evil cannot be laid on his account as he is not in a controlling position. "God," Griffin notes, "has no monopoly on power. God's power is the creative power to evoke or persuade; it is not the unilateral power to stop, to constrain, to destroy" (Griffin 1991: 24). Process theodicy does, however, hold God *metaphysically* responsible for evil as the cosmos emerges from his primordial being, from his self-expression, and, importantly, from the primary direction he gives each entity. While God does not determine the development and consequences of his creation, he does determine its foundational nature and direction. Here is where God's responsibility lies.

Cohen learned much from traditions that, like process theology, find spiritual ground in something other than an omnipotent God. But in looking at humanity's sins, Cohen nonetheless found God accountable—however much sin may come from our free will, "maturation," or the cosmos's unfolding processes. He found God not only metaphysically responsible, as process theology does, but morally so. Whether God cares about or is indifferent to human suffering, as Paul Draper argues (2001: 181–2, 198), he is answerable for its occurrence as he is answerable for all existence.

Cohen understood our particular existence as relational and covenantal. We are created for and need reciprocal bond with God and others. Thus, Cohen's theodical problem is thus: is not God responsible for our propensity to breach covenant? The next step in looking at Cohen's theodicy is to explore the meaning and nature of covenant.

2

Covenantal Theology and Its Place in Cohen's Work

Distinction-amid-Relation as the Structure of Existence

Cohen's theodicy centers on the question of why God made humanity for covenantal commitment yet ever ready to breach it and thus suffer abandonment and loss. Cohen had high expectations for covenant—what it offers and obliges each of us. As we are created with covenant as our *modus vivendi*, failing it harms living itself. And this left Cohen with frustration, anguish, and ire at himself, the fail-er, and at God, the creator of our capacity to fail. What, then, is the nature of covenant? To explore its meanings, I draw on Jewish tradition, philosophy, and Christian and Muslim sources where they illuminate this core precept.

To explore covenant with God, we might begin with an idea about God himself. In the Abrahamic traditions Cohen plumbed, notions about God evolved over the centuries of writing and redacting the biblical books. But in the Hebrew Bible we now have, likely pulled together in the immediate post-exilic period (fifth century BCE), God may be thought of as the source of all there is, the ground for the possibility that things exist at all. There could be nothing, but there's something. The source of all "something"—items, thoughts, language, laws of physics—is what some people call God. In the biblical creation story, for instance, God is already present as an immaterial, infinite, all-guiding force—unlike in the neighboring Mesopotamian creation stories, which tell not of the eternal presence of God but of the birth of the gods into an already-existing world in which they war with each other for control. Moreover, because the gods and humanity are born into the same world, the boundaries between them are fluid and include sexual and other relations. The powers of the gods are not their own but emerge from their access to already-existing primordial stuff, and the human world they affect is not guided by moral concerns but by their often childish caprices. Fortunately, the gods are close enough to humanity to fall under human influence through magic. Yet, in the Hebrew Bible, God does not engage in skirmishes with other gods to create the world. God is wholly other to world and humanity, infinite and immaterial, the creative "power" or "force" of existence, with no possibility of boundary-blurring and with a vision not of a capricious but of a moral universe. While magical events occur in the Bible, they do not affect God but rather human persons and accomplish their ends only by the act and will of the divine.

To be sure, many narrative elements of Mesopotamian myths reappear in the Bible. The biblical God YHVH shares features with the Canaanite gods El and Baal and even the Babylonian god Marduk. The daily lives of many Israelites and Judeans living through the millennium of the Hebrew Bible's writing, redaction, and the Second Temple period (1000 BCE–70 CE) included pagan and monolatrist beliefs and cult practices. Yet, Christine Hayes notes, "The biblical writer transforms the story so that it becomes a vehicle for the expression of different values and views." In that biblical view, "the pagan picture of an amoral universe of competing good and evil powers is replaced by the picture of a moral cosmos. The highest law is the will of the deity, who imposes not merely an order but a morality upon the universe" (Hayes 2012: 4–5, 23). In the Gilgamesh flood story, for instance, the gods are victims much as humanity is of natural disaster brought on by their caprice while in the biblical flood narrative (Genesis 6–9), God is the source and controller of the flood to end human immorality. Nahum Sarna writes, "The message of the flood story seems to be that when humans destroy the moral basis of society, they endanger the very existence of that society, of all civilization" (Sarna 1966: 52).

By the time of the Hebrew Bible's redaction, the idea of a transcendent God over a world and history of moral concerns was in play and place. Ian Barbour describes this God as a "structuring cause" or "designer of a self-organizing process" (2000: 164). After the kabbalist thinker Ein Sof and philosopher F. W. J. Schelling, the source of existence is not so much what precedes effects— not cause before effect—but what is realized *as* it yields effects. To capture the idea, Aquinas wrote, "God himself is properly the cause of universal being which is innermost in all things," adding somewhat poetically, "in all things God works intimately" ([1265–73] 1948: Ia, q. 105, art. 5). Two centuries later, Nicholas of Cusa, vicar general in the papal states, wrote of God unfolding into all existing things, *explicatio*, while all is enfolded in God, *complicatio* (*De ludo globi* 1463: II). Kabbalist thought reprises the idea with the image of God's inhaled breath that opens space for all existence and the exhaled breath as the space where all creation exists. In the words of Gen. 2:7, God breathed *nishmat cha'im*, the spirit of existence, into humankind.

On one hand, each particular thing is radically different from the source of existence—differences in materiality/immateriality and finitude/infinitude. Yet, on the other, each particular partakes of this source to exist at all. We participate in or partake of the source of existence in order to be. We do so, however, not identically or proportionally (we are not like God only smaller). We partake of God/structuring cause analogically, as an analogy expresses its referent: with different surface features but with an undergirding of-a-kindness. A figure that illustrates this well is the *imago*, the idea that we are made in God's image, *b'tselem Elohim*. God in the Jewish tradition is infinite, incorporeal, and imageless. Thus, humanity cannot be in his image as there is none. There are no divine features, no physiognomy, that we share with God. *B'tselem Elohim* must be understood not literally but analogically: we partake analogically of an undergirding of-a-kindness, of God's imageless "image," though there are no surface features to be shared. The Christian Orthodox tradition suggests a related doctrine of *theosis*, the potential to become more godlike. The church father Gregory of Nyssa held that becoming more godlike is possible precisely because we partake of God/structuring cause. Owing to this undergirding of-a-kindness, we may move toward him in the eternal process of *epektasis*, the striving toward the spirituality of the divine.

The radical difference from God yet intimate partaking/relation with him is the way anything comes to be. *The structure of existence is difference-amid-relation.* Martin Buber's words echo Aquinas' "intimate" God: "Of course God is the 'wholly Other'," Buber writes, "but He is also the wholly Same ... He is also the mystery of the self-evident, nearer to me than my 'I'" ([1923] 1958: 79). God, at once radically other, is yet more intimate than we are to ourselves.

Cohen described it this way in the shimmering "Love Itself" (*Ten New Songs*, 2001, with Sharon Robinson):

> In streams of light I clearly saw
> The dust you seldom see
> Out of which the nameless makes
> A name for one like me.

In the kabbalist tradition of Isaac Luria (1534–72), sacred vessels that originally contained God's light shattered under God's brilliant power. In the stream of divine luminescence, the song's narrator sees the dust we seldom see, the dust from which God makes us in an act more intimate than any other: creation (Gen. 2:7). Cohen then plays with "name" and "nameless." The Name is a reference to God in the Judaic tradition (*hashem*). But God's name, the tetragrammaton YHVH, is also unknowable and "nameless" as it is unpronounceable and unutterable. It reflects the apophatic (or *via negativa*) strain in Jewish thought wherein God himself is unknowable. In this lyric, the infinite, incorporeal nameless Name that is God forges from dust, in that most intimate act of creation, a finite, material person, one with an identifiable name. The radically different divine is yet radically intimate within us.

Distinction-amid-Relation: With God, among Persons

What does this mean for relations among persons? As difference-amid-relation is the way all things exist, not only are persons distinct from God yet in intimate relation with him, *we are distinct from each other yet in necessary relation*. There is no other way to be.

Aquinas' explanation may be helpful. We partake of God to exist though we are distinct from him and from each other. Indeed, our distinction from God and each other is implicit in our relations as relation presupposes two entities. As Hans Meyer correctly notes, "a subject is required from which the relation proceeds, and another subject really distinct from the first to which the relations extends" (1954: 115). Moreover, each one of us individually, within ourselves, is also a composite of different, distinct features or essences. Thus, there is a double difference: within persons and between each person and another. But the monotheistic God, of whom we partake, is not a composite. He is neither a group of persons nor an aggregate of different essences. He is the only One where relation (for instance, within the Trinity) is not between different subjects, not a move outward, but a procession within one unified existence (Thomas Aquinas [1265–73] 1948: Pt. 1, Q. 27, art. 1). So how is it that we, composites within individual persons and distinct from other persons, analogically partake of something unified, simple, without "components"?

On Aquinas' account, we are composites but at the same time also expressions of the unity that is God. "Thus," Mary Hirschfeld writes,

> there must also be a unity to creation if creation is to give witness to the fact that God is one. God communicates this unity by ordering created beings to one another and all things to him [Thomas Aquinas, *Summa Theologica*: I 47.3] ... These two features—the *heterogeneity of created beings and their ordering to one another (and ultimately to God)*—need to be respected. (Hirschfeld 2018: 92; emphasis mine)

In the Jewish tradition, Emmanuel Levinas's works elaborate the idea of distinct persons ordered to each other as we are to God. "My very uniqueness," he wrote, "lies in the responsibility for the other man" (1994b: 142). In the Greek Orthodox tradition, John Zizioulas echoes, "The person cannot be conceived in itself as a static entity, but only as it *relates to* ... [it is] in communion that this being is *itself* and thus *is at all*" (1975: 409). Or in Elisabeth Moltmann-Wendel's words, "Life begins as life together" (1995: 43). Kirk Wegter-McNelly, building on the German theologian Wolfhart Pannenberg, summarizes: cosmos is "a place in which entangled independence-through-relationship is the fundamental characteristic of being" (2011: 136). On one hand, even identical twins differ in character and approaches to life, as the Mishnah explains: "the supreme king of kings ... fashioned each man in the mold of the first man, yet not one of them resembles another" (*m. Sanhedrin* 4:5). Yet, on the other hand, "the individual," Martin

Buber writes, "is a fact of existence insofar as he steps into a living relation with other individuals" ([1947] 1993: 203).

Importantly, distinction-amid-relation is not a binary with distinction on one side and relation on the other. It is rather reciprocal constitution: each becomes the distinct person she is *through* layers and networks of relations. No individual occurs "outside" relations. Neither is distinction-amid-relation a "third way." It does not posit a first way (a distinct person) and second way (a relational one), which undergo dialectical transformation to yield a "third way." Rather, the nature of existence is reciprocally constituted distinction-*amid*-relation.

This understanding of God and humanity—this radical difference amid necessary intimacy—stands in contrast to post-Cartesian notions of the distinct, completed individual who is herself first and then comes into contact with world and others—what Susan Grove Eastman insightfully calls the first-person understanding of the self (2017). "In our private silos," Eastman notes, "we cannot understand another's actions as reaching across time and space to transform us, even if that other is God. If we are essentially isolated, lonely individuals ... how can we be touched by others and reconstituted in new relationships?" (2017: 164). The biblical view, she holds, is second-person: each becomes who she is through a nexus of relations with others, environment, and transcendent source.

We become ourselves through relations nearby: no infant develops alone, and children lacking physical and emotional contact suffer cognitive and emotional impairment (IJzendoorn et al. 2011; Nelson et al. 2014). Adults who become isolated suffer from increased risk of suicide, higher mortality rates (Pantell et al. 2013), and morbidity, including depression and other emotional difficulties (Cacioppo and Cacioppo 2014; Laugesen et al. 2018; Leigh-Hunt et al. 2017). The nearby relations that form us are in turn informed by relations that extend out through our paths of global connectedness. Our educational, social, and economic opportunities; nutrition and health care; and the tensions our families, workplaces, and communities are under are determined by those who are not necessarily physically close by.

If the nature of existence is distinction-amid-relation, how should we act? What does being singular yet in networks of necessary relations entail? Aristotle argued that we can know what we should do or aim at—our *telos* or end—from the way we are, from our nature or ontology: "The nature of a thing," he writes in Book 1 of *Politics*, "is its end." The nature of a thing, what sort of being it is, determines its fullest thriving and thus what it should aim for. Conversely, a thing's best flourishing tells us what sort of being it is.

Extending the argument, Aquinas held that nature/ontology and flourishing/*telos* are reciprocally constituted. The two are always already present in each other. One does not precede the other nor are they separate characteristics that must be kept in "balance." Rather, an understanding of human nature/ontology is presupposed in the discussion of aims and development while our aims/*telos* reflect back on our nature/ontology. The alternative—setting aims without their constitution in the nature of a thing—would yield such misguided goals as fish having universal access to bicycles. The nature of a thing and what it should aim for, its best thriving, are of a piece.

Neurobiologist Darcia Narvaez calls this our "baseline." "To approach eudaimonia or human flourishing" she writes, "one must have a concept of human nature, a realization of what constitutes a normal baseline, and an understanding of where humans are—embedded in a cooperating natural world" (2014: 429, 436). Narvaez's argument is twofold. Like Aristotle and Aquinas, she holds that we know what makes us flourish from our nature, our normal baseline. Second, as it is our nature to be embedded in and dependent on cooperating structures, our flourishing requires that we *see and see to* the cooperating structures that make us who we are. Thriving means to at/tend to the well-being of the persons and networks that form us.

For Cohen, it sounds like this:

> I brushed up against the man in front of me.
> I felt a cardboard placard on his back ...
> it said "Please don't pass me by—
> I am blind, but you can see—
> I've been blinded totally—
> Please don't pass me by." ("Please Don't Pass Me By,"
> *Live Songs*, 1973)

Passing others by precludes seeing and seeing to them. It forecloses at/tending to our connection with them, however close or attenuated. And no flourishing can come of that.

Distinction-amid-Relation
as Covenant with God
and among Persons

One name for this "seeing and seeing to" is covenant. Attending to others in covenantal commitment is the *modus vivendi* and aim emerging from our nature as distinct persons amid relation. Covenantal attention is the way we flourish given our relational nature with persons and God. In cosmogonic myth, gods are mythopoetic and unchanging. It "describes a sequence of sacred events," Henri Frankfort writes, "which one can either accept or reject" (Frankfort and Frankfort 1959: 251). In the biblical covenant, by contrast, God and Israel are in relationship together: God forms relationship with Israel, and Israel returns relationship by fulfilling God's vision for the world. The freedom of persons to accept or refuse covenant is foundational to covenant as a reciprocal relationship. Without this freedom, there is no covenant but only compulsion. "Covenant religion," Stephen Geller notes, "is the locus of an implicit doctrine of free will, because Israel is always confronted with the choice to obey or not obey" (2014: 1990).

In Christine Hayes's words, "In the covenant relationship, Yahweh and Israel meet in a reciprocal sanctification. This is the language, logic, and meaning of Lev 22:31–32" (2012: 162).

It is also the logic of biblical law, which not only secures societal peace and civil benefits but also ensures the covenantal relationship, to which both parties agree. Law is "naturally placed within a narrative of covenant making; the laws attain their authority not only because of the divine voice that utters them, but through the Israelites' consent" (Halberstam 2017: 29). Not only God but each person is responsible in this agreement: "A distinguishing formal feature of Israelite law is the addition of a rationale or motive clause for certain laws, particularly the humanitarian laws. One of the most common rationales appeals to Israel's experience in Egypt and addresses the Israelites as persons of intelligence and compassion, capable of moral reasoning" (Hayes 2012: 139). Robert Bellah provides a useful sum: covenant is "a charter for a new kind of people, a people under God, not under a king ... a people ruled by divine law, not the arbitrary rule of the state, and of a people composed of *responsible individuals*" (Bellah 2011: Kindle

Locations 4700–1, 4864, emphasis mine; see also Walzer 1985). This kind of individual is capable of and responsible for covenantal commitment and the "moral correspondence" (*dmuth Elohim*) to be God's cocreators in furthering God's covenant in the world. Unlike the political suzerainty treaties of the nations surrounding ancient Israel, which enshrine class distinctions and codify unequal obligations among political unequals, covenant establishes *reciprocal* commitment between unequals, between humanity and God and between persons of different status (see, for instance, Shepherd 2014: 116–17). The legal codes of Eshnunna and Hammurabi and of the Hittites and Assyrians, for instance, provide different punishments for persons of different social status while biblical codes apply law equally and include extensive requirements for aid to the needy and stranger. The *lex talionis* (an eye for an eye) establishes two principles: proportionality of sanction to crime (an eye for an eye, paid in financial compensation, not more or less) and the same sanction for all. The reciprocity of relationship even among unequals is symbolized at the harvest. As God's gift to humanity is life and sustenance, we acknowledge reciprocal commitment by symbolically giving tokens of that sustenance, fruits of the harvest, at God's temple. The symbolic gift to God is recognition of mutual responsibility. In turn, covenant among persons is also drawn within the framework of covenantal bond with God and is also reciprocal. The "ritual of cutting a covenant in the context of the sharing of material resources in a sacrificial and celebrative rite invokes the presence or witness of God. It is enacted within a framework of duties and rights that form a system of justice" (Lee 2011: 78).

While covenant is reciprocal, it is not contingent on contractual fulfillment of terms. It has been God's offer to humanity *ab initio* in spite of humanity's repeated breaches. In covenant, stipulative features might appear (as a parent might stipulate that a child clean her room). The Mosaic code guided the Hebrews in realizing righteousness with God and neighbor. Yet covenant is not stipulative in motive or *telos* (one doesn't have children *so that* they clean their rooms). Said another way, God does not covenant with humanity so that we bring fruits of the harvest. Covenant from God is an irrevocable offer of commitment.

With whom is God in relation? With humanity, symbolically through Adam, Eve, and Noah, and with the Israelite people for their sakes and for "the blessing of all humanity" (Gen. 12:3, 26:4,

28:14; Pally 2016: 196–202). The rabbinic *Mikhilta de-Shimon* (bar Yochai), commenting on Exod. 19:2, further notes that the Torah was given not in any country but in the open desert to ensure that it belongs to all because its principles are for all. "The Torah," the Talmud explains, "speaks the language of human beings" (*b. Nedarim 3a. Berachot 31b*). Emmanuel Levinas called this understanding of covenant "universalist singularity," the "primordial event in Hebraic spirituality" (1994c: 144). "To be with the nations," he wrote, "is also to be for the nations." The "paradox of Israel is that of an exceptional message" nonetheless "addressed to all" (1994a: 199).

Cohen understood covenant as such "universalist singularity." In a 1994 interview, he explained, "A confident people is not exclusive. A great religion affirms other religions. A great culture affirms other cultures. A great nation affirms other nations. A great individual affirms other individuals, validates the beingness of others" (Burger 2014: 388). Grounded in our ontology or "baseline" of difference-amid-relation, covenant does not assimilate others but rather commits to them in their different ways of flourishing.

Distinction-amid-Relation: The Moebius Strip Covenant— Beyond Dyad to Community

As *all* things are distinct beings amid relation, we are not only distinct from God yet in necessary intimacy with him. We are also distinct from each other yet in necessary relation. Covenant is a relationship of reciprocal at/tending between a covenant-seeking God and humanity *and* among persons created in the image of a covenantal God and so bestowed with a covenantal "baseline." The idea here is twofold: first, that the covenants between person and God *and* among persons are of a piece. In the requirements for atonement of wrongdoing, for instance, appealing to God is not sufficient. One must seek forgiveness from the persons one has wronged: "it is only just action toward other people, and loyalty to YHWH, that can resolve the dispute" (Halberstam 2017: 37). Or as the philosopher Franz Rosenzweig wrote in *The Star of Redemption*, "Love for God must be externalized in love for the neighbor" ([1921] 2005: 230). Love of God is "the highest of the commandments" and love of the neighbor is "the embodiment of all the commandments" ([1921] 2005: 190, 221). Second, human covenants are not only person-to-person but among networks of persons and among corporate bodies or communities.

Unlike contract, which protects interests, covenant protects relationships. "Contracts," Jean Lee writes, "form the basis of the market while covenants form the basis of community" (2010: 59). Lee continues, covenant is the "promise with one or more counterparty under common pursuit of shared values for long term cooperation and well-being of the community." It is the promise, shared values, and *telos* of long-term communal well-being that are key and distinguish covenant from other human transactions. Eric Mount summarizes: "Covenant is a distinctively, though not exclusively, Hebraic metaphor and model that locates the relational self in a community of identity, promise, and obligation with God and neighbor" (1999: 1). Or as Stephen Geller succinctly put it, the Hebrew Bible God is not so much a concept, an "ism," as a relation (Geller 2000: 295–6).

While covenant begins bilaterally—between God/Adam, God/ Noah, God/patriarchs—it extends out, into networks of persons. Persons give to God by giving to third parties, those in need. In Hebrew, such aid is called *hekhdesh*, made holy. Help to persons is holy to God and symbol of bond with him (Kochen 2008: 137). Max Stackhouse explains covenant among persons as "an ethical outworking of the divine-human relationship" (1997: 142). In something of a Moebius Strip, covenantal concern for others builds covenant with God, and—in the imperceptible fold of the Moebius band—covenant with God sustains persons in giving covenantally to persons (Pally 2016: 192–6). Reciprocal giving thus moves from the dyadic me-and-you to a giving network, where gift from God to person (life, sustenance) generates gift from person to neighbor and on to the next person through the networks of giving, thus sustaining them (see Mauss [1923] 1990; Godbout and Caillé 1998; Hyde 1983).

Cohen gets at the Moebius Strip or entwined covenant this way:

The Heart beneath is teaching
To the broken Heart above ...
Come healing of the Altar
Come healing of the Name. ("Come Healing" *Old Ideas*, 2012, with Patrick Leonard)

The heart "beneath" in the covenantal relations of the world "teaches" covenantal love to God's broken heart above, much as in *hekhdesh*, giving to persons makes bond with God. Covenant is bottom-up as well as top-down. As noted above, "Name" is one way to reference God. Thus, Cohen notes the exchange of healing that comes of the human altar-ritual as it reaches "up" to God and the healing that comes of the Name, God, as it reaches "down" to world (see Nicolet 2014).

In the Jewish and Christian traditions, the Moebius Strip of covenantal giving is found in the Ten Commandments: the first three pertain to relations between person and God and the rest, seamlessly, to relations among persons in community. In the First Testament, Lev. 6:2-3 further states: "If anyone sins and is unfaithful to the Lord by deceiving a neighbor," that is, deceiving the *neighbor* breaks faithfulness with *God*. Num. 5:6 echoes: "Any man or woman who wrongs another in any way and so is unfaithful to the Lord is guilty." And it is reprised in the frequent biblical formulation, "behave righteously to others; I am the Lord." Rather than a non-sequitur, this two-part commandment reflects the entwined covenants: righteousness to other persons is inseparable from bond with the Lord.

As we move through the Bible, the Moebius Strip or entwined bond grounds the laws governing the needy, stranger, and enemy. Enemies are protected by "just war" criteria (Pss. 7:4-5) and, importantly, by the requirement that a suit for peace be brought prior to any move of aggression (Deut. 20:10). Captives must be properly cared for (2 Kgs 6:22-23); enemy nations may not be oppressed even during war (2 Chron. 28:8-15), and truces and peace agreements must be honored even if the enemy breaches them (Josh. 9), especially at 9:18). Moving from enemy to stranger, requirements for their aid were extensive (Exod. 22:21; Lev. 19:34) and follow the familiar entwined-covenant pattern: "Leave them [the field corners] for the poor and for the foreigner residing among you ... I am the Lord your God" (Lev. 23:22). Moving again from stranger to the domestic needy, Judaism's poor laws were so substantial that they prodded the emperor Julian to say, "it is disgraceful that, when no Jew ever has to beg ... all men see that our people lack aid from us" (Stern 1980: 549–50, no. 482). A sampling of biblical poor laws includes: *shmitah* and Jubilee debt cancellation (Lev. 25:4-6, 8-13; Deut. 15:1-2); distribution of food to the poor (Deut. 24:19-22); tithing obligations for all others (Deut. 14:22); prohibitions against the return of runaway servants (Deut. 23:15-16) and against the taking of interest from the poor (Exod. 22:25). Manumission of servants is required after six years of work, when they must be not only freed but outfitted with livestock, grain, and wine (Exod. 21:2; Deut. 15:12-14).

Failing these commitments gets you the prophets' ire. Amos notes the importance of compassion over religious rites: "I [God] hate, I despise your religious festivals; your assemblies are a stench to me ... But let justice roll on like a river, righteousness like a never-failing stream" (Amos 5:21-24). Hos. 6:6 reiterates: "For I desire mercy not [animal] sacrifice," as do Ps. 51:17, Mic. 7:2-7, and Prov. 21:3: "To do what is right and just is more acceptable to the Lord than sacrifice" (see also Brueggemann 2010: 42).

Finally, the entwined covenant makes sense of biblical narratives where covenant with God is broken and violence among persons follows—or where covenant among persons is breached and the natural world erupts in disaster. As the entwined covenants with God and among persons are the very structure of the cosmos, where covenant with God is violated, the covenantal fabric of society and the natural world may be rent as well. The Noah and Golden Calf narratives are two examples. In the Noah narrative (Gen. 6-8), humanity's (sexual) wrongdoings so overflow the world that nature responds in a gush of its own fluid. The flood is not punishment from on high but, as covenant among persons is rent, the natural order of the cosmos is undermined. In the Golden Calf narrative (Exod. 32), the breach of covenant with God sunders the fabric of human society and mayhem ensues. The bonds of human relations are undone because bond with God has been gashed. But even so, in all such cases, covenant remains for humanity to reembrace because reciprocal commitment is the structure of a distinction-amid-relation world.

I will close this section by briefly looking at some of the ways covenant has been understood in contemporary Jewish thought. The early-twentieth-century German-Jewish philosopher Franz Rosenzweig argued for the entwinedness of bond with God, among persons, and with world. God, world, and humanity, he wrote in *The Star of Redemption* ([1921] 1971), are brought together by creation, revelation, and redemption, the six forming the Star of David. Revelation, for instance, (i) brings God to humanity, (ii) brings humanity to God (as we understand something of him through his self-revelation), and (iii) brings humanity to the world (as we grasp something of God's creation). Rosenzweig held that humanity, *created* by God and guided by *revelation*, may "anticipate" and "drive toward" *redemption* through its conduct in world. This active anticipation is humanity's ethical and existential (created) task. Rosenzweig makes a double point we have seen before: first, that action in this world among persons is part of what "drives toward" God—the Moebius Strip covenant. Second, humanity has the capacity, the moral correspondence (*dmuth Elohim*), to take such covenantal action.

Abraham Joshua Heschel (1997) worked with similar interdependent concepts: God's revelation is meant to move into human feelings, experience, and, importantly, conduct toward others. "A Jew is asked to take a *leap of action* rather than a *leap of thought*" (1997: 183). Our covenantal commitments toward others are essential to covenant with God, who reveals himself to us for the flourishing of both relationships. We can see the twinedness of these relationships also in Heschel's idea that human "righteousness is not just a value; it is God's part of human life" (Heschel 2001: 255). Righteousness among persons is the part of human life that is of God. It is God's presence in our midst and our bond to him.

Emanuel Levinas's work may be considered an elegy on distinction-amid-relation and the covenantal obligations it entails. It is foundational for him that (i) each person is unique, (ii) one's uniqueness is formed by covenantal commitment to the "face" of the other: "My very uniqueness lies in the responsibility for the other man" (1994d: 142), and that (iii) nearing God happens through such responsibility (1979: 78): "To follow the Most-High is also to know that nothing is greater than to approach one's neighbour" (1994a: 142). For Levinas, this is no "figure of speech" but a description of God, "who approaches precisely through this relay to the neighbor—binding men among one another with obligation, each one answering for the lives of all the others." This "relay to the neighbor" is "the highest possible theological knowledge one can have" (1994c: 171).

Obligation to the other, on Levinas's account, is realized by fulfilling not an abstract set of moral rules but one's specific responsibilities *in situ*. Personal responsibility is what makes one a person. Our responsibilities are determined by the particular needs of the others whom we face. Human beings are able to recognize these particularities—the "distinction" of distinct-amid-relation—and to respond to specific circumstances because we live in time. Levinas recognizes that knowing another person potentially makes her an object onto which we can project our own concerns. While space does not allow two people to occupy it in the same moment, time allows two persons to exist at once. As the other, different from us, exists at the same moment in time as we do, we have the opportunity to see her as her distinct self, not as the object of our projections. Time, he wrote, "in its diachrony, would signify a relationship that does not compromise the other's alterity" (1987: 30–1).

Levinas's well-known critique of Martin Heidegger's *Being and Time* centers on Heidegger's focus on being over relation. Levinas found the separation of being and relation self-defeating. Being, on his view, is a matter of relation. Moreover, since relation with others is where nearing God happens, Heidegger's schema thins engagement with the divine (1996: 137). Relationship with God, Levinas writes, "can be traced back to the love of one's neighbor ... the responsibility for one's neighbor and taking upon oneself the other's destiny, or fraternity. The relation with the other person is placed at the beginning" (1994d: 146–7).

As Martin Buber's theology of the I–Thou encounter is well known ([1927] 2010), I'll highlight only two points relevant to distinction, relation, and covenant. First, though transactional "I–It" encounters among persons are part of daily living, I–Thou relationship—reciprocal recognition and commitment—is the only sort of encounter possible with God. Thus, it is the ground or model for the I–Thou encounter among persons. However, owing to the entwined nature of covenant, moments of I–Thou encounter with persons are also how we come to I–Thou with God. On one hand, Buber holds that "the individual is a fact of existence insofar as he steps into a living relation with other individuals" ([1947] 1993: 203). At the same time, "God appears when people truly meet others" (Breslauer 2006). Persons stepping into relation with others is how God appears in world.

The second aspect of Buber's work I wish to highlight extends the argument: persons must not only step into relation with God and other individuals but also build the sorts of communities where I–Thou covenantal relationship is fostered. "Society," he writes, "is naturally composed not of disparate individuals but of associative units and associations between them" (cited in Alperowitz 1990: 15).

Communities that foster I–Thou encounters among persons guide us to I–Thou relation with God.

The work of Eugene Borowitz brings together much in the preceding discussion (1990, 1991). He begins with an exploration of distinction under conditions of relation and social responsibility: "I too equate all human dignity with self-determination, but only within the context of a covenant with God that gives us our personal significance and makes all God's covenant-partners an essential element of our selfhood" (Borowitz 1991: 221–2). That is, God's covenant-partners, other persons, are essential in constituting selfhood, who we are. Reprising distinction-amid-relation, Borowitz holds that we come to "personal significance," our singular selves, through covenant with God and in relation with all persons, who too are in covenant with God.

On the same pages, Borowitz repudiates "the self as a monad. God makes us individuals but also an inseparable part of humanity. Our finitude also makes each of us necessarily dependent upon others." Thus,

> the self gains its inestimable worth neither by the self-evident nature of its quality nor our willing it, but by being covenanted to God. It cannot then demand a Kantian or Sartrean radical autonomy or self-legislation. ... We employ our will rightfully when God serves as its limiting condition, better, as co-partner in decision making. (Borowitz 1991: 221–2)

Our existence emerges from relation with God and with all created beings as they are also in unavoidable relation with God. Thus, we must see to these necessary relations. Radical autonomy in living (Sartre) or in setting oneself one's own moral code (Kant) is not consistent with the relational nature of humanity. Striving toward such autonomy is misguided or pointless as it is not how human beings live. Rather, it is the bonds with God and persons that are the "limiting condition," the precondition for all actions we take. These bonds set the limits of the possible. Action that violates these conditions, that fails to at/tend to these relations, runs against the grain of our distinction-amid-relation nature. Little good can come of that. Borowitz's conclusion to this passage may serve as the conclusion here as well: "We therefore stand under a religio-moral charge to live in communities and to exercise our personal autonomy with social concern."

Covenant: Leaving the Body for God or with the Body toward God?

The covenantal principles explored thus far center on the entwined or Moebius Strip commitments with God and among persons as the ground for existence and human flourishing. I'll explore Cohen's expression of these ideas by first investigating four alternate proposals about his spiritual project. I'll then look at covenantal commitment as it takes shape in his work.

In the first of four alternate proposals, Thomas Haslam uses text mining technology to note patterns of words and themes across Cohen's oeuvre. He finds "a small core of terms" that "is continuous across all fourteen studio albums, with 'love' as the dominant" (Haslam 2017: 9). Love for Cohen is always twofold, for persons and God, and sometimes, entwinedly, persons through God and God, through persons. Haslam thus disagrees with the famous claim that the 1980s change in Cohen's compositional style was prodded by his switch from the guitar to the Casio keyboard (Simmons 2012: 335). Haslam holds instead that, while the keyboard had certain effects, the more important prod to the style shift was the change in Cohen's relationships: the birth of Cohen's children, the collapse of his relationship with their mother, and the death of his own mother, all in the 1970s. These, Haslam holds, sent Cohen to a "re-engagement with Judaism" (2017: 6). This does not mean, Haslam notes, that Cohen had earlier left Judaism but that "the mysteries of intimacy and the challenges of maintaining a relationship" (2017: 4) became more pressing.

Haslam's proposal is thus not so much an alternate to the covenantal perspective as a specific case of it, where the family relations of the 1970s underscored for Cohen the centrality of commitment and the difficulties of sustaining it. It bears noting, however, that while the events of the 1970s had significant impact, Cohen recognized and wrote about these matters from the 1950s onward, in his two novels and early poetry and songs. Though Cohen's writings about relations with women—a failed covenant that dogged him throughout life—are notably bitter in the late 1970s, the bitterness may be not so much "reengagement" with covenant but expression of a continuing, despairing undertow in his life and work.

In the second alternate approach to Cohen's oeuvre, Jiri Měsíc (2018) suggests that Cohen's spiritual project follows Sufism in its emphasis on purification *from* the body to reach the spiritual. That is, Cohen, on Měsíc's view, does not envision an entwined, Moebius Strip bond with God and persons but seeks to leave the body and worldly relations for the incorporeal soul in contact with God. Desmond Pacey notes a similar *telos* in Cohen's second novel, the pornographic-apocalyptic *Beautiful Losers* (1966). Pacey finds it anchored in the search for a "voluntary loss of self for some higher cause" (1976: 88). Stephen Scobie presses the point further, holding that for Cohen, "The self is not sacrificed to some higher cause; the sacrifice of self is the higher cause" (1978: 10). In all three readings, bodily desires are given up for spiritual salvation.

Yet Cohen was more Jew and Buddhist than Sufi. His project was not a sequential one of body, renunciation, and then spirit but rather finding the spiritual *in* the quotidian and carnal. "I think people recognize," Cohen said when he released *Various Positions* (1984), "that the spirit is a component of love ... it's not all desire, there's something else" ("Leonard Cohen interviewed" 2015). Pacey's reading of *Beautiful Losers* seems to "miss the ironic tone of the novel," Linda Hutcheon notes "and neglects the message of failure" (1974: 48). Indeed in the novel, attempts to surpass the body lead to nothing. As each of the book's characters isolates him- or herself through self-absorbed obsessions that cut off bodily relations, nothing comes of their endeavors. They neither reach their obsessive goals nor love each other.

There is no glorious loss of self or achievement of something "higher." "Each character," Hutcheon continues, "lives an isolated existence that ends in some form of destruction" (1974: 48). As a central male character declares, "Please make me empty, if I'm empty then I can receive, if I can receive it means it comes from somewhere outside of me, if it comes from outside of me I'm not alone! I cannot bear this loneliness. Above all it is loneliness" (Cohen [1966] 1993: 40). While one of the obsessions of *Beautiful Losers* is the seventeenth-century Catherine Tekakwitha (patron saint of Montreal), who in *imitatio dei* tortured and starved herself to death, Cohen's interest is not in bodily erasure but to note that when we cannot attain/sustain the foundational bonds we need with God and others, we flail against ourselves in mad frustration.

Beautiful Losers is a killing field of broken bonds. As the idea of an entwined covenant would predict, nothing spiritual can thus be gained. Whatever Cohen's spiritual quest, it was not to leave the material and relational but rather *in* them. Biographer Sylvie Simmons put it more succinctly: for spiritual ends, Cohen was willing to give up eating meat but not sex (2012: 104). In *Book of Longing* ([2006] 2007), at age seventy-two, he was still quipping about desire:

Dear Roshi
I'm sorry that I cannot
help you now, because
I met this woman.
Please forgive my
Selfishness. (Cohen [2006] 2007: 22–3)

In a poem from the same volume, aptly titled "Disturbed This Morning," he winks again, "I was doing so fine, / I was above it all / ... And now I want you again" ([2006] 2007: 39). More sardonic is "Sorrows of the Elderly," also from *Book of Longing*:

The old are kind
The young are hot.
Love may be blind.
Desire is not. ([2006] 2007: 171)

The third alternate proposal regarding Cohen's project is Aubrey Glazer's impressive *Tangle of Matter and Ghost* (2017). Glazer sees Cohen as a mystic for the postsecular age, one who gives us religious resources in a quasi-secular form that is acceptable to our disenchanted modern living. Cohen, on Glazer's reading, lives with us in Babylon, symbol of exile from the Holy Land, and in modern life, from intimacy with God and each other. But Cohen shows us that, through exile, we may crawl to redemption. "Cohen seeks to discover the imaginal crown of Jerusalem 'by the rivers dark' in Babylon—that is, in exile as homecoming. Precisely in that dialectic lies the key to redemption" (Glazer 2017: Kindle Locations 863–4).

"Exile as homecoming," on Glazer's account, is Cohen's path through our strewn lives and the wry hope he offers. Glazer continues, "The most enriching pathway to a redemption song for Cohen is in confronting the reality of living a fallen life whose very descent is its ascent" (2017: Kindle Locations 2798–9). For Glazer, "the brokenness that is incurred is meant to be a teacher," a guide to relation and redemption (2017: Kindle Locations 2659–60)—somewhat as cruciform theodicies understand suffering. In Glazer's work, we hear echoes also of John Hick's soul-making theodicy, where humanity matures into moral living through the suffering we cause and endure, through the brokenness that teaches us empathy and giving of the self.

Glazer's rich, persuasive work illuminates the theme of exile-as-homecoming in Cohen's writing. To this we may add the covenantal theme, in which suffering is not so readily accepted as a guide to redemption. Rather, Cohen confronts God on theodical charges: is human suffering worth its ostensible goal? Does my maturation or redemption justify another person's suffering? Could God not have created a path with less brutality—with less, in Glazer's terms, exile?

In this covenant-breach aspect of Cohen's work, the issue is not so much that redemption comes through exile but that there is no *sustainable* redemption. We commit to covenant and then bolt. Cohen's songs keen at our human condition. Exile from relation is where we live by our own doing. We don't get "home" to Jerusalem, God, or others through exile. We long for home and lodge ourselves abroad. In an image that runs through Cohen's (and Glazer's) work, we do not sojourn in exile as the Hebrews sojourned in Egypt. We live in Babylon.

Moving from Glazer, we come to his mentor, Eliot Wolfson, who sees Cohen as drawing from the *via negativa* or apophatic school of theology (2014, 2006a). Apophasis in the Jewish and Christian traditions holds that, as we cannot fully apprehend God, he cannot be described using human tools such as language or art. Prayers, blessings, psalms are equally vacant. Whereas *kataphatic* theologies hold that humanity may know something of God from the world he created, apophasis maintains that there is no gleaning God from nature. Humanity may apprehend him only from a place beyond intellect and sense impression, a place of fleeting contact with love itself.

In support of Wolfson's argument, Cohen's "The Window" (*Recent Songs*, 1979) describes God (or what can be apprehended of him) as coming to us from "the cloud of unknowing." The reference is to the fourteenth-century book, *Cloud of the Unknowing*, an exploration of apophasis in mysticism (see also Wills 2014). "All rational beings, angels and men," the author of *Cloud* writes, "possess two faculties, the power of knowing and the power of loving. To the first, to the intellect, God who made them is forever unknowable." Yet "to the second, to love, he is completely knowable, and that by each separate individual" (*Cloud* 2001: 63). Apophasis concludes that, as we cannot know God but only sense his love, we cannot employ human tools (language, images) to describe what is available to us only pre—or perhaps post—cognitively.

Insofar as Cohen believed that we never fully apprehend God, one might say he draws from apophasis. But his complaint about relationship with God is not its inexpressibility but its unsustainability. Cohen had too many words to settle for nonexpression. Even when Theodor Adorno and others insisted that there could be no poetry or art after the Holocaust (1955: vol. 10a, 30), Cohen wrote many words about the Holocaust—indeed, an entire book, *Flowers for Hitler*, in addition to continuing references throughout his work. He walked less in the apophatic tradition as in the steps of Holocaust survivor and poet Paul Celan, who held that our words and images *must* be used to tell of the Nazi barbarism. It is our means of testimony. Celan's 1948 "Todesfuge" ("Death Fugue") was among the works that inaugurated postwar Holocaust writing (Celan [1952] 1993: 37–8). In turn, Cohen's yearning for covenant and despair at our breaches were expressed in six decades of lyrics and poems, cascades of words seeking, as Augustine had it, the embrace that will not leave however much we abandon it. Then, we would not suffer loss or face the mystery of a God who made abandoning so easy for us.

Rather than relying on the Sufi and apophatic trajectories of leaving the body and bodily expression, Cohen drew often from the sixteenth-century kabbalist Isaac Luria, as Wolfson notes in his important article, "New Jerusalem Glowing: Songs and Poems of Leonard Cohen in a Kabbalistic Key" (2006a). Luria held to a key role for bodies in nearing God. He described the sacred vessels which originally contained God's light but which shattered under the light's brilliant force. According to Luria, the sexual union of male and female may repair the broken vessels and right the world. This is not bodily erasure for the spiritual but spirit *in* the corporeal, and so the world heals. It is "a conceit," Michael Posner writes, "deeply embedded in Cohen's work … it is not impossible to read much of his canon as a de facto exercise in *tikkun olam*, a reparation of the world" (Posner 2017: 513).

Cohen put *tikkun olam*, the righting of the world, this way in one of his most forlorn/hopeful lines: "There is a crack in everything, that's how the light gets in" ("Anthem," *The Future*, 1992). He called this "as close to a credo as I've come" (Burger 2014: 366). Cohen's lyric is a reference to Ps. 51: "My sacrifice, O God, is a broken spirit; / a broken and contrite heart / you, God, will not despise." And it is a Lurianic vision wherein the world's cracked-ness is the portal to repair by God's light. If we dare to come to God in our cracked brokenness, so begins the possibility of receiving God's love.

For Cohen, it was not so much bodily *renunciation* that nears us to God but bodily *reunion*. He did not pursue a life of "celibate piety" (Wolfson 2006a: 109). Instead, women are the site, and sex is the act, through which union with the divine may be reached. "In Cohen's work," David Boucher writes, "women are so often the medium through which some sort of fulfillment is attained, whether sexual gratification or religion salvation, or both simultaneously" (2004: 201). Or as Měsíc puts it, "Cohen describes himself as a god in need to use the goddess's body" (2016: 141). For the cover of *New Skin for the Old Ceremony* (1974) and the 1978 poetry volume *Death of a Lady's Man*, Cohen chose an engraving from the 1550 Frankfurt *Rosarium Philosophorum* depicting a heavenly king in sexual union with his queen. That's how you get to God and redeem world.

Covenant in Family, Faith, and Poetry

Cohen grew up in a community where covenant with God and among persons was expressed in religious ritual and community ethics. His family observed Jewish customs, symbolizing bond with God. His maternal grandfather Rabbi Solomon Klonitsky-Kline, commentarist on the Talmud, spent evenings reading Isaiah with Cohen. The family was, Cohen recalls, "very involved in the community, in establishing hospitals and synagogues, a free loan association" (Burger 2014: 237). In "The Hebrew Free Loan Society," he told Arthur Kurzweil, "people could borrow money free! That's a translation of a Jewish idea into action. I saw this all the time, all around me" (Burger 2014: 377). His paternal grandfather Lyon Cohen helped to found many institutions of the Canadian Jewish community. Cohen recalls, "He spoke with great pride that the Jewish community of Montreal had absorbed its refugees from [the] Kishinev [pogrom, 1903, 1905] without ever asking the municipality or the government for a single cent" (Burger 2014: 370–1).

In a foundational sense, Cohen knew that relationship is what one does: "I never rebelled against my parents, even when I was taking acid and living in the Chelsea Hotel … I always thought my family [religious] practice was great, and I've tried to keep it up—in my half-ass way" (Burger 2014: 381). In the "half-assed" years, Cohen lit the Sabbath candles even while on tour and celebrated Jewish holidays with his children. In the years of greater engagement, Cohen studied Talmud, prayed daily, and donned the ritual *tefillin* (phylacteries), symbol of God's covenant and Jewish acceptance of its commitments. Cohen was, he told Stina Lundberg Dabrowski in 1997, "never looking for a new religion. I have a very good religion, which is called Judaism … when I began to study with Roshi [Cohen's mentor in Buddhism], it wasn't because I wanted a new religion. I was always happy with the religion I was born into and it satisfied all the religious questions" (Burger 2014: 414, 453).

Buddhism too was a central practice in Cohen's life as a discipline of the mind and time—of all those minutes in all the years of thoughts and desire flailing about, attaching to this or that rhyme, drug, or bed. Buddhism was a means to center and focus. But Cohen's theistic beliefs were Jewish. He explained to Kirsty Lang in 2007:

> My friend Brian Johnson said of me that I'd never met a religion I didn't like. … That's why I've tried to correct that impression because I very much feel part of that [Jewish] tradition and I practice that and my children practice it, so that was never in question. The investigations that I've done into other spiritual systems have certainly illuminated and enriched my understanding of my own tradition. (Lang and Robey 2016)

Christianity was also among the "spiritual systems" that Cohen plumbed in life and in poetry. "I like the character of Jesus," Cohen told Jean-Luc Esse in 1997, "and I like his role as well but the Old Testament is really the Testament of the victory of experience—it's history, it's men, dealing with the Absolute and who have to deal with other men as well" (Esse 1997).

The First Testament is not an idealistic book or blueprint for living. One doesn't mimic its characters to find the moral life. It is rather a *problem set* of treachery, betrayal, killing, rape, theft, and war. Through the dilemmas posed, humanity is to develop a moral code (Pally 2014: 230). We never quite, or we do but ignore it. Yet Cohen loved this bulky practice-book. In *Book of Longing*, he rather emphatically added, "Anyone who says I'm not a Jew is not a Jew. I'm very sorry but this is final" ([2006] 2007: 158).

With Judaism as his theistic ground, Cohen understood relationship with God as foundational to human living. "I think there really is a power to tune in on. It's easy for me to call that power God … So that I can say 'to become close to Him is to feel His grace' because I have felt it" (Gnarowski 1976: 53). He echoes the idea in footage from the 2019 documentary film *Marianne & Leonard: Words of Love* by Nick Broomfield, "When I get up in the morning my real concern is whether or not I'm in a state of grace." His friend and fellow songwriter Jennifer Warnes said of Cohen, "If he has one great love, it's his love for God" (Todd 2010). And near the end of his life, Cohen reprised, "The older I get, the surer I am that I'm not running the show" (Rohter 2009).

In 1984, the midpoint of his career, Cohen wrote *Book of Mercy* and released the album *Various Positions*, both plunges into covenant. *Mercy* is a psalter throughout, an ode to bond with God. The book's first title was "The Name," a reference to God in Jewish tradition (*hashem*). "I just wanted to sing and dance before the Lord," Cohen told *The Gazette* in 1983 (King 1983). More than two millennia earlier, the ancient psalmist also strove to come before God: "All my longings lie open before you, Lord; my sighing is not hidden from you" (Ps. 38:9).

Psalms 42:2 continues, "My soul thirsts for God, for the living God. When can I go and meet with God?" Cohen's *Book of Mercy* poem six reprises this quest for "meeting" God in a diary of covenantal intimacy: "Tonight, I come to you again, soiled by strategies and trapped in the loneliness of my tiny domain. Establish your law in this walled place … Blessed be the name of the glory of the kingdom forever and forever" ("Sit Down, Master," *Book of Mercy*, in Cohen 1994: 316). Though Cohen knows he is "soiled" by the strategies of worldly pursuits, trapped by separation, and "walled" in loneliness, he, like the ancient psalmist, comes still to God, to follow his law and praise him.

Cohen's commitment to God repeats as an incantation in *Book of Mercy* poem eight: "Blessed are you, clasp of the falling … blessed are you, shield of the falling … Blessed are you, embrace of the falling, foundation of the light, master of the human accident" ("In the Eyes of Men," *Book of Mercy*, in Cohen 1994: 317). In poem forty-five, the "human accident" continues to press his case: "Not knowing where to go, I go to you. Not knowing where to turn, I turn to you. Not knowing how to speak, I speak to you. Not knowing what to hold, I bind myself to you" ("Not Knowing Where to Go," *Book of Mercy*, in Cohen 1994: 332). As with the ancient psalmist who declares he is benumbed and crushed, Cohen—after twenty years of broken relationships and numbing drugs—binds himself to God.

Doron Cohen calls *Book of Mercy* and *Various Positions* "two halves of a diptych" (2016: 2). Haslam calls the album unapologetic "public songful prayer." "This is pop music as liturgy, as a service of the heart" (2017: 6). The album's closing track and summation, "If It Be Your Will," is drawn from a passage in the Atonement Day or Yom Kippur service where the praying ask for forgiveness. May it be God's will to grant it. The song echoes the longing for God that pours out of the Psalms, *Book of Mercy*, and from the soiled, trapped, walled-in man. In "If It Be Your Will" Cohen prays: "From this broken hill / I will sing to you" near you, bind myself to you, "if it be your will / to let me sing."

Cohen's "broken hill" evokes Sinai, where Moses is shattered by the Israelites' idolatry to the Golden Calf. It suggests Jesus broken at Golgotha and humanity broken by banal isolation. From this desolate place, Cohen seeks God and, as the song continues, asks him to

> draw us near
> And bind us tight
> All your children here
> In their rags of light
> In our rags of light
> All dressed to kill
> And end this night
> If it be your will.

"Rags of light" alludes to a rabbinic commentary (*midrash*) on Adam and Eve in the Garden of Eden. The biblical passage describes the pair as dressed in "animal skins" (*ore*). In Hebrew, the word "ore" is a homonym for the word for "light." On this *midrash*, all God's children since Adam are dressed not in literal animal skins but, in a word play, in the splayed rays of God's light. In Cohen's verse, the pronoun switches from "their rags of light" to "our." These luminous children are us. God, the narrator asks, draw *us* in from our godlessness and bind us tight. End these nights where we, vain and self-absorbed, are fashionably dressed to kill and literally kill each other with our self-absorption and aggression. And yet, it is us—creatures who dress over, cover up, God's light with vanity and violence—who nonetheless seek a return to God and to sing. If it be God's will.

Cohen does not use the traditional form, "May it be your will," but the conditional "if." "If" asks if our singing, psalm, and prayer are indeed wanted. It is the unsure, insecure query of every lover: is this what you want? Am I welcome here? Am I doing the right thing? Will you love me? Spurn me? It echoes the query of Ps. 42:2: "When can I go and meet with God?" Does God want my visit, my song? "If"—God, do I understand your will?—also calls up Jesus' prayer at Gethsemane as he awaits arrest and death: "Father, *if* you are willing, take this cup from me. Yet not my will but yours be done" (Lk. 22:42). God, I am not sure of your will; is this what's wanted? Here in *Various Positions* as in *Book of Mercy*, Cohen asks for God's will—is this the right thing?—and commits to it before knowing what it is. "If." This is faith.

The doxa and yearning in these writings are not a moment in 1984 when *Various Positions* was released but a Cohen ostinato found in works written both earlier and later. I will look at one example from 1969 and one from 2014.

In the 1969 "You Know Who I Am" (*Songs from a Room*), Cohen wrote,

> You know who I am
> You've stared at the sun
> Well I am the one who loves
> Changing from nothing to one.

The narrator, like the ancient psalmist, envisions himself in conversation with God, who addresses him as "you." God begins with nothingness but in creation changes absence into one cosmos and the one God of monotheism—"changing from nothing to one." In this image, Cohen draws on the kabbalist idea that God does not precede effects, cause-before-effect, but is realized as he *self-expresses* into creation. In this lyric, God himself changes to become the one God, knowable to humanity. The last stanza concludes:

If you should ever track me down
I will surrender there
And I will leave with you one broken man
Whom I will teach you to repair.
You know who I am.

Like the ancient psalmist hoping to approach God and like the modern psalmist of *Book of Mercy*, the song's narrator writes that if humanity "tracks down" God and sustains bond with him, God will "surrender" and allow himself to be neared. But God will leave one man "broken," perhaps Jesus on the cross, perhaps the biblical Jacob, wounded from wrestling with God's messenger in a fight that binds Jacob in covenant to God (Gen. 32:22-31). This broken man will be repaired by us, humanity, because God will teach us to repair the broken among us. As we do—*if* we do—we near God.

This is the entwined, Moebius Strip covenant. We approach God in healing each other. Forty-five years after "You Know Who I Am," Cohen in "Born in Chains" (*Popular Problems*, 2014) again writes as the wounded and crushed psalmist in search of God. The lines of the song review the failures of his life, the broken relationships, drugs, and booze—the years collecting wounds in the "Egypt" of his life, site of biblical exile and enslavement. But Cohen ends the song by reaching for God, again referred to as the "Name." In the 1984 *Book of Mercy*, Cohen had written, "Not knowing where to go, I go to you" (in Cohen 1994: 332). Here in the 2014 "Born in Chains," he reprises: "I was bound to a burden, but the burden it was raised / ... Blessed is the name, the name be praised."

3

From Covenantal Theology to Theodicy: Failing Covenant with God and Persons

And yet, we fail God. What a sentence! It is the first step in Cohen's theodicy: we are created for covenant with God and persons but do not sustain them. And so we smash the relational foundation of the cosmos, for all the pain that it causes. In "Steer Your Way" (*You Want It Darker*, 2016), Cohen writes,

> Steer your path through the pain
> That is far more real than you
> That smashed the cosmic model
> That blinded every view

What gets in the way of keeping covenant? Everything human. We follow the call of Babylon and Boogie Street, two running themes in Cohen's work. "I'm what I am," Cohen wrote in 2001, "and what I am, / Is back on Boogie Street" (*Ten New Songs*, with Sharon Robinson). A few years later, he explained to Terry Gross, "Boogie Street is a way to describe our lives. We go up a mountain or into a hole [to his Mount Baldy monastery or other retreats] but most of the time we're hustling on Boogie Street" (2006). The song "By the Rivers Dark," also from *Ten New Songs*, uses not Boogie Street but the image of the Babylonian exile from Jerusalem to describe our lives:

By the rivers dark
I wandered on
I lived my life in Babylon ...
Be the truth unsaid
And the blessing gone
If I forget
My Babylon.

Psalm 137:5 promises never to forget Jerusalem, site of the ancient temple, symbol of covenant with God. Cohen by contrast pledges never to forget Babylon, destroyer of the temple, exiler of the people, symbol of whoring, idolatry, and loss. *This* is where we live, and we may not forget it.

More painful than life in Boogie Street and Babylon is that we go there of our own accord—the second step of Cohen's theodicy. The "master of misery" (Wolfson 2006a: 153) knew that we make our immiseration as we break the bonds we need. Simmons describes two of Cohen's "favorite things" as "no strings" and "an escape clause" from commitment (2012: 481). The trouble with Augustine's solution for suffering—to love what cannot be taken away, God and love itself—is that we find even this beyond our ken. The authors of the Talmud knew the difficulty well. The passage on the wiliness of wrongdoing is tragi-comic (Genesis Rabbah 22:6). We know we are created for reciprocal bond and responsibility and we even intend to act so but under all manner of self-delusion, we don't. The reason why is shrouded in mystery and self-deception. "But the mist is surrounded by a mist," Cohen wrote, "and the veil is hidden behind a veil; and the distance continually draws away from the distance" ("You Are Right, Sahara," *Book of Longing*, [2006] 2007: 44). We are made for covenant, but it eludes us in the distance that we are careful to keep, and the mists of the human condition remain.

This human condition was a source of Cohen's anguish and many lines of writing. "Thus the writing process springs out of emergency," Alexandra Pleshoyano writes. "Cohen feels that this emergency is a process that seems to last forever bringing him most of the time to a chaotic and unbearable state of mind" (2013: 22). She cites Cohen's comment to Alan Hustak: "The emergency never ends. At times a peaceful self is born, but it never lasts, it never lasts" (2016b).

The emergency burns without resolution through his last works, *You Want It Darker* and the posthumous *Thanks for the Dance*

(2016 and 2019, respectively), much as it did in the 1967 "Teachers" (*Songs of Leonard Cohen*), a monument to inadequate answers about existence. The narrator encounters a woman, a girl, a man, even a hospital—the last, a symbol of all the therapeutic techniques we use to try to heal ourselves. Following its strict therapy regimens, he exhausts himself and "carves himself to the bone" only to come to this *huis clos*, this exit-less frustration:

Is my passion perfect?
No, do it once again …
Did my singing please you?
No, the words you sang were wrong …
are my lessons done?
I cannot do another one
They laughed and laughed and said, Well child
Are your lessons done?

There is no solution to humanity's existential emergency. Or we already know it but we evade and avoid it.

Failing Covenant with God

Needing and breaching covenant with the divine dogged Cohen. His observation, I "can't seem to loosen my grip on the past" (Diamond 2017), marks both humanity's long-standing covenantal nature and his own past record of failing it. He holds onto both, and both keep after him. Breach of covenant as humanity's *Ur* sin appears early, in Cohen's first published novel, *The Favourite Game* (1963). His protagonist, who shares much of Cohen's biography, recruits the Jewish assent to God's covenant for his confession of failing it. "Holy, holy, holy," he begins, "Lord God of Hosts. The earth is full of your glory. If I could only end my hate. If I could believe what they wrote and wrapped in silk and crowned with gold" (1963: 15). The words of covenant may be written on parchment, wrapped, and placed in the gilded ark, but for Cohen's protagonist/alter ego, hate and skepticism crowd God out.

Cohen spoke again of covenant and our failure to keep it in a 1964 talk at Montreal's Jewish Library titled "Loneliness and History." He began by criticizing his teacher and poet A. M. Klein, who had emigrated to Canada and, lacking funds, stopped writing poetry, became a speechwriter for Samuel Bronfman (owner of the Seagram Distillery), fell into depression, and attempted suicide. Klein's sin, in Cohen's lambaste, lay in having become "too much the theorist of the Jewish party line." Klein "became their clown. He spoke to men who despised the activity he loved most. He raised money. He chose to be a priest and protect the dead ritual. And now we have his silence." Cohen had earlier criticized his own family for attending too much to the material upkeep of the community rather than to engagement with God. His protagonist/alter ego of *The Favourite Game* unsurprisingly does the same (1963: 140).

Cohen later explained that he, as a more mature person, understood the importance of community structures as the setting in which covenant is taught: "Community is a lot more fragile than I understood then," he explained to Winfried Siemerling, "and a lot more valuable, and to undertake the defence of a community is a high call ... But I was a young man then" (Siemerling 1994b: 157). Though Cohen matured out of his young Turk rebellion to re/cognize the importance of community, what that young man sought remained Cohen's grail. It was what his community had taught him to seek: "an impossible longing, an absolute and ruthless longing for the presence of the divine, for the evidence of holiness." Sometimes, the young Cohen said, he still saw this in Klein. "Then he is alone and I believe him" (Leibovitz 2014b).

Need for God's presence gets Cohen's attention. This is what it's all about. But if we sometimes pursue it, we quickly slip away into the busyness of Boogie Street. We may have "an absolute and ruthless longing," as Cohen told Liel Leibovitz, but we always have fifty ways to leave this lover. "We have lost our genius for the vertical," Cohen continued in the Montreal library. "Jewish novelists are sociologists, horizontalists, and the residue of energy left from that great vertical seizure we had 4000 years ago [at Sinai]—that we turned toward ourselves ... This is the confession without which we cannot begin to raise our eyes: the absence of God in our midst." We have turned the Sinaitic "seizure" into the immanence of "horizontality," an occupation with the here-and-now.

Twenty years later in the 1984 *Malahat Review*, Cohen's critique of our stuck-ness in immanence had not improved: "We sense that there is a will that is behind all things, and we're also aware of our own will ... It's the space between those two wills that creates our predicament" (Burger 2014: 166). The estrangement between the two wills is the source of our brokenness and Cohen's lifelong investigation. On Doron Cohen's counting "brokenness" appears in over 10 percent of Cohen's recorded lyrics (2016: 4–5) in such songs as "Suzanne," "Hallelujah," "The Guests," and "The Window." It is not that we are unequipped for covenant and love; it's that we were created for it and break it, nonetheless.

Among the boldest declarations of Cohen's despair at covenant breaches comes from this mid-career period in a jeremiad titled "Israel" (*Book of Mercy*, in Cohen 1994: 323). It is a quest for God and Cohen's struggle with our abandoning it:

> Israel, and you who call yourself Israel, the Church that calls itself Israel, and the revolt that calls itself Israel and every nation chosen to be a nation … To every people the land is given on condition. Perceived or not, there is a Covenant, beyond the constitution, beyond sovereign guarantee, beyond the nation's sweetest dreams of itself. The Covenant is broken, the condition is dishonoured, have you not noticed that the world has been taken away? You have no place, you will wander through yourselves from generation to generation without a thread … Because you do not wrestle with your angel. Because you dare to live without G-d. Because your cowardice has led you to believe that the victor does not limp.

The covenant is for "every people," and every people has broken it. So we wander "through yourselves," through a world filled with other wanderers, disconnected from them and the transcendent. We no longer struggle to live with God, as Jacob struggled with God's messenger and was wounded (Gen. 32:25-31). We think we've won a modern, "sovereign" independence from the transcendent and no longer tolerate the marks of boundedness. We think that we, modern victors of history, do not limp as Jacob limped.

Failing Covenant with Persons

Turning from covenant with God to commitment among persons, Medrie Purdham writes that *Beautiful Losers*, published two years after the Montreal Library speech, is a deep plunge—the sort the proctologist makes—into the modern motives for covenant breaches: autonomy, freedom, and control (Purdham 2012). If these are our *telos*, covenant cannot be. So the novel says in every set of failed relationships. In her essay, "Beautiful Losers: All the Polarities," Linda Hutcheon adds to Purdham, setting out the novel's binaries. Between the poles of each pair there is only the failure of each party to see the other: French/Canadian Indian; Canadian English/Quebecois; US economy and culture/Canadian economy and culture; men/women; everyone/the Jews. "Each generation," one character says, "must thank its Jews and its Indians for making progress possible by their victimization ... the English did to us [Canadians] what we did to the Indians, and the Americans did to the English what the English did to us" (cited in Hutcheon 1974: 45, 47). When we seek control over others rather than seeing and seeing to them, there is little to stop us from abuse.

The novel's male characters seek control by imposing an "ordered system" on the world. They deform a relational cosmos into a mechanical one though they know "there is something arrogant and warlike in the notion of a man setting the universe in order." Even bodies are seen as machines, and expectably, sex doesn't work (cited in Hutcheon 1974: 49, 50, 53). The obsessive aim of one male character is to unleash a totalizing revolutionary politics on the world, one that will "change everything" for Quebec. Another seeks to write a totalizing history that orders the world from an all-knowing distance. Stephen Scobie, with Purdham, notes that Cohen's frequent linking of history and drugs suggests the addictive lure of discourses of control, as Foucault among others illustrated well (Scobie 1978: 52).

Both efforts at control yield nothing as control misses the relational nature of the cosmos. The ostensibly revolutionary bombing has no political effect and brings the bomber not heroism but a ludicrous blown-up thumb. Both efforts are also entirely self-absorbed: our revolutionary finds that "I care more about my red watery throbbing thumb than your whole foul universe of orphans. I salute my monsterhood" (cited in Hutcheon 1974: 48). Our historian in turn has no difficulty occupying himself with his sexual fantasies about a seventeenth-century saint who flogged, burned, and starved herself to death. "I've come after you, Catherine Tekakwitha," he rather revoltingly writes, "I want to know what goes on under that rosy blanket" (Cohen [1966] 1993: 3). By contrast, the female characters seek a sense of control through self-abnegation, self-mutilation, and suicide.

Yet all their flailing efforts, male and female, are but the mad frustration of encompassing immanence, as Cohen said in his 1964 Montreal library speech. The novel's characters are bound to their obsessions because they cannot bond with each other or God. They use each other but are "circumscribed by loneliness" (Purdham 2012: 87). On the night that the female protagonist, Edith, commits suicide, her historian husband dines on a feast of chicken.

The year after *Beautiful Losers* was published, Cohen wrote his despair at our disconnection into "The Stranger Song" (*Songs of Leonard Cohen*, 1967). It is an anthem to the exit.

> And then leaning on your window sill
> He'll say one day you caused his will
> To weaken with your love and warmth and shelter
> And then taking from his wallet
> An old schedule of trains, he'll say
> I told you when I came I was a stranger.

Just as he warms to love and shelter—or because he has "weakened" to them—he's off. For this fellow, lovin' and leavin' is strength and much preferred to commitment or sticking around.

A dozen years later, Cohen's diagnosis of our self-imposed exile from commitment is more mature and precise: relationships don't survive the charnel of broken promises. In "Humbled in Love" (*Recent Songs*, 1979), ripped and dirtied vows, so mangled that "not even revenge can undo them," dissolve the passion that once was. The narrator can still say: "You will never see a man this naked / I will never hold a woman this close." But nothing really remains of togetherness. He is left with this question, "Forced to kneel in the mud next to me / Ah but why so bitterly turn from the one / Who kneels there as deeply as thee?" The image of kneeling calls up the wedding vows, yet the desire to kneel together through the sacramental ceremony or through the messy mud of life has died. Repeated breach of our vows kills love, and then it cannot be revived.

Cohen reprised his bolt-from-shelter sentiments of "Stranger Song" forty years later in "Feels So Good," performed on his 2009 world tour. "You broke me," he writes, "doing all the little things I really like" (2009 World Tour). Strength lies in being untouched, autonomous; kindness, shattering autonomy, *breaks* a man. And the sentiments appear again in "The Night of Santiago" (*Thanks for the Dance*, 2019):

> I didn't fall in love, of course
> It's never up to you

But she was walking back and forth
And I was passing through.

Walking back and forth, she was staying. He, passing through, is gone tomorrow. Though by his own description, the narrator reveled in the sex of his short stay in Santiago, he like the fellow in "Stranger Song," is moving on, not to be entrapped by the woman whose breasts "opened to me urgently / Like lilies from the dead."

Failing Covenant with God and Persons: God's Response

While the passages above sketch Cohen's despair at breaching commitment with God or persons, much of his writing grieves for both at once. As covenant is a Moebius Strip of entwined bonds, breaching one snaps the other. "Love Itself" (*Ten New Songs*, 2001, with Sharon Robinson) includes these lines:

Love went on and on
Until it reached an open door—
Then Love Itself
Love Itself was gone.

These lines might point to lost love among persons, but the capitalization of "Love Itself" suggests also the prime love from God and of God. The love that began with the ancient Sinaitic "seizure" is out the door because we have lost our genius and will for "the vertical," as Cohen said at the Montreal library. We don't fight for it; we slide away for a sense of autonomy, or for something we think is better, or we simply bolt.

"A Thousand Kisses Deep," also *Ten New Songs*, is a dirge of broken promises and gutted relationships with God and persons— or one relationship implicit in the other.

And quiet is the thought of you
The file on you complete
Except what we forgot to do
A thousand kisses deep.

As in "Humbled in Love" (above, *Recent Songs*, 1979), our failing is in what we forgot to do together—the commitments we forgot to make and keep or that we trounced. "Come Healing" (*Old Ideas*, 2012, with Patrick Leonard) comes again to this "old idea" that's been Cohen's since the 1960s:

> O gather up the brokenness
> And bring it to me now
> The fragrance of those promises
> You never dared to vow.

To whom were those promises never made? God? Persons? Both? It is not-promising, not-vowing, not-committing that is the human failing. Humanity carries the fragrance of those sins.

Love's labor is indeed lost. What is God's response? Grief, but not foreclosure. We may trounce our bonds, but rarely does God close the door. Even the door through which "Love Itself was gone" was an open one. Indeed, that is precisely how love left: the door is open for us to leave or stay. Covenants are kept freely or they are not covenants but coercions. Cohen's "Avalanche" (*Songs of Love and Hate*, 1971) is the story of God's covenantal offer to his (free) children and his sorrow at our forsaking it. In the body of Jesus, God steps into the avalanche of human life. He is not embraced but abandoned. God laments,

> You say you've gone away from me
> But I can feel you when you breathe ...
> It is your turn, beloved
> It is your flesh that I wear.

God, having stepped into human flesh to be with humanity, to love and secure us, hopes still that humanity will step up and return covenant. Hey baby, it's your turn.

God's grief at our bolting and yet his irrevocable presence is reprised in the 1974 "Lover Lover Lover" (*New Skin for the Old Ceremony*). When the narrator asks to escape the mess of his present life—grant me another name, a new face, a becalmed spirit—God replies,

> "I never, never turned aside," he said
> "I never walked away
> It was you who built the temple
> it was you who covered up my face."

Humanity walked away, covering God's face with the fetishism of ornamented temples. This is Amos's prophetic charge in modern voice: "I [God] hate, I despise your religious festivals ... But let justice roll on like a river ..." (Amos 5:21-24). God wants not ornaments but relationship reciprocated. Bond with him and among persons is what grounds the halls of justice. The lyric calls up, as Moshe Halbertal notes in his preface, God's anguish in Isa. 65:1: "I revealed myself to those who did not ask for me ...To a nation that did not call on my name, I said, 'Here am I, here am I.'" God offers himself to a people so busy with their various idolatries (worship of other gods, of material things) that they are no longer asking for his offer. And yet, God holds out hope: Isa. 65:8-9 continue: "I will not destroy them all. I will bring forth descendants from Jacob, and from Judah those who will possess my mountains."

So committed is God to waiting for our covenantal return that he hopes even our estrangement will be a path to our arrival. In *Book of Mercy*, poem thirty-four, Cohen writes, "your rebuke still comforts me, you signify yourself among the dangers. Saying, Use this fear to know me, fix this exile toward my return" (Cohen 1984: 34). Even rebuke can become a bond and thus hope for reconnection. God makes himself visible among worldly dangers and temptations and holds this out as an offer: use even fear of God to return to him. Use exile, as Aubrey Glazer notes, as a path home to relationship (Glazer 2017: Kindle Locations 863–4, 2798–9).

Victim, Victimizer, Prophet, Priest

Jiri Měsíc finds that Cohen, in grappling with covenant and its breaches, oscillates between the role of priest and prophet. A priest stands before God to represent the people, victims of suffering, war, and natural disaster. The prophet stands before the people to represent God, victim of humanity's idolatry, greed, and violence (Měsíc 2015). It is the prophet who demands that we change our ways.

In a 1970 interview for *Rolling Stone* magazine, Cohen admits to the prophetic voice: "the songs are inspired. I don't pretend to be a guide. I do pretend to be an instrument for certain kinds of information at certain moments" (Měsíc 2015: 30). Forty-four years later, "Almost Like the Blues" (*Popular Problems*, 2014, with Patrick Leonard) again holds to the prophetic role: the song's narrator has had an "invitation," as Jeremiah and Jonah also unwillingly received, to speak God's words. It "once and for all confirms that Cohen speaks from the position of a prophet" (Měsíc 2015: 36). Yet "Lines from my Grandfather's Journal" (1961, *The Spice Box of Earth*) reveals Cohen's early attraction also to the priestly position: "All my family were priests, from Aaron [brother of Moses and first priest to the Hebrews] to my father / ... To observe this ritual in the absence of arks, altars, a listening sky: this is a rich discipline" (*The Spice-Box of Earth*, 1961: 63). More than thirty years later, Cohen held to his priestly position, telling Arthur Kurzweil in 1993, "When they told me I was a Kohayn [priest] ... I believed it. I didn't think this was some auxiliary information ... So I tried to become that" (2015: 40).

As a young man and as a mature one, Cohen took the liberty of both priestly and prophetic roles. He prophetically railed at humanity for breaching covenant and, in priestly mode, charged God for making us such casual breachers.

Ian Dennis suggests we look at Cohen through a different lens, the victimary (Dennis 2017: 5; Gans 1982). In Christian and Holocaust victimary writing, the victim (the crucified Jesus, the murdered Jew) is exalted, the meek inherit the earth, and the victim is the object of desire and goal of identity. Yet in Cohen's six-decade plunge into (failing) covenant, the victimary is not a separate perspective but of a piece with priest and prophet. The biblical priests were keepers of the covenant and representatives of the victimized people, whose suffering made them doubt God's covenant. The prophets were the alarms of its breach and representatives of the victimized God, who suffers humanity's doubt. Cohen took himself as prophet and priest in both victimized roles: victimized sufferer appealing to God for the people about the cruelties emerging from breached covenant *and* prophet suffering the burden of warning humanity that we are breaching it. "Some moment in time very brief," Cohen said in his 1964 Montreal Library speech, "there must have been, among the ancient Hebrews, men who were both prophet and priest in the same office. I tease my imagination when I try to conceive of the energy of that combination" (Leibovitz 2014b).

Cohen's Godot Theodicy: A Double Bind Is Not a Bond

The tragedy of broken relationship is unavoidable in Cohen's writing. This section turns to why we leave our commitments to

God and persons—why do we so easily bolt? On Cohen's view, humanity is proximately responsible, but God, conclusively.

Beginning with human responsibility, poet Irving Layton is reported to have called Cohen "a narcissist who hates himself" (Hampson 2007), a man riveted by his own failures. Layton was not alone in this assessment. Stephen Scobie in 1978 wrote, "Cohen's vision is so completely self-centered that there is no room in it for any individualized personality, male or female, other than his own" (1978: 11). To be sure, there were limits to Cohen's narcissism. "Large numbers of people," he told journalist Jian Ghomeshi, "are dodging bombs, having their nails pulled out in dungeons, facing starvation, disease … I think that we've really got to be circumspect about how seriously we take our own anxieties today" (cited in Billingham 2017a: 32). But Cohen was also narcissistically gripped by his self-appointed role as covenant fail-er par excellence. In "Please Don't Pass Me By" (*Live Songs*, 1973) he writes, "I can't stand who I am." That was in 1973. Nearly thirty years later in "In My Secret Life" (*Ten New Songs*, 2001, with Sharon Robinson), written after coming to the *Gelassenheit* of his Zen monastery years, Cohen's assessment of himself had not improved. The song ends with Cohen reporting that he's too chilled and icy to make room for anyone. He, in his mid-sixties, struggled still with the temptations of exit over covenant, with being cold and too "crowded" for others. And he mourns the loss that he authors.

But why does he—do we—author it? In Samuel Beckett's play *Waiting for Godot*, we wait for God to come to us, though he never does. In Cohen's theodicy, it is we who never arrive. At least two barriers to relationship stand bold in Cohen's work. One is pride. "When the heart grins at itself," Cohen writes, "the world is destroyed. And I am found alone with the husks and the shells. Then the dangerous moment comes: I am too great to ask for help" ("When I Have Not Rage," *Book of Mercy*, in Cohen 1994: 326). A second barrier, Henry Bean suggests (2018), is that the very intimacy we desire threatens intactness, which we need to be us and simply to be—or so we believe. The intimacy we want threatens existence, or so we feel. It is a terror voiced in "Joan of Arc" (*Songs of Love and Hate*, 1971). Relying on the kabbalist image of God's love as shards of light, Cohen writes, "Myself, I long for love and light / but must it come so cruel, must it be so bright?"

The brightness of our need illuminates—and exposes—our porousness. We are not safely intact in our sealed bodies, tucked into the membrane of control. We are needy of God and persons, and in terror of our necessary dependence, we bolt.

This was Purdham's diagnosis of *Beautiful Losers*: each character in the novel, in pursuit of control, loses all relationship. It is Dennis Lee's reading as well. Capturing the thrust of the 1966 novel, Lee writes, "Radical freedom means a plethora of alienated selves, free-floating I-systems, mocking a self which has been unselved of all but the will to create itself" (1977: 100). Trying so hard to create our singular selves, we lose all others. Twenty or so years after *Beautiful Losers,* Cohen explained in 1988, "The condition that most elevates us is the condition that most annihilates us, that somehow the destruction of the ego is involved with love" (Burger 2014: 219). The 2001 "Boogie Street" is still working this idea: "It is in love that we are made; / In love we disappear" (*Ten New Songs*, with Sharon Robinson).

If love is dissolution, no one would risk it, and certainly not Cohen. "They're selling freedom everywhere," he sang on his 2009 world tour, "it's flying off the shelf / Yeah, they're selling freedom everywhere but love, that's something else" ("Feels So Good," 2009 World Tour). Love is indeed something else. It is the most wanted thing. But in fear of "annihilation," as Cohen put it, we're buying the exit of "freedom."

Wanting yet fearing love is a double bind but it is not a bond. Fear and flight may leave one in thrall (with one's beloved) but not in commitment. Occupied by one's inner fears, one is not occupied by one's lover. Rebekah Howes's insightful essay "Leonard Cohen and the Philosophical Voice of Learning" sums up the paradox of wanting love yet hating the threat to the self that one fears it brings. She writes, "Cohen knows that, like the rest of us, he wears the veil of modern freedom in its various guises: self-certainty, independence, freedom without cost or limit. Equally it is the freedom bent on disowning its violences" (2017: 95). Fearing annihilation in love, we cling to our autonomy, hack off our bonds, and evade the maiming we do to others and ourselves. Quoting from "Closing Time" (*The Future*, 1992), Howes concludes, our predicament "looks like freedom but it feels like death" (2017: 95). That's the "freedom" of "Feels So Good," flying off the shelf to replace love.

We cannot stay with love because we fear it's murder of the self so we choose "freedom," which feels like death. The narrator of "Going home" (*Old Ideas* 2012, with Patrick Leonard) longs for home—with God? a beloved?—"where it's better than before." He longs to go "Without the costume / That I wore," without protective facades. But this narrator has an alter ego "Leonard," whom he calls "a lazy bastard living in a suit." Ah, the debonair suit that became Cohen's hallmark once the dressed-down folk phase loosened its grip on pop music. Of course living in that suit-facade made "Leonard" lazy. The man inside it charms and seduces from behind his sartorial armor. He doesn't have to do the work of sticking around. The narrator of the song may want to go home without protective costume, but his alter ego Leonard inhabits his famous suit and says he "wants to write a love song / An anthem of forgiving." And what is that love song? "A manual for living with defeat." Love and forgiveness are a life of defeat in the battle for autonomy and intactness. Who would choose such defeat? Certainly not Cohen.

Cohen's Unwilling Theodicy

Cohen's final step from covenant to its abandonment to unwilling theodicy—his work is an ode to "say it ain't so"—faces up to this: if the propensity to pride and bolting is human nature, it cannot be only humanity's sin. God is the source of humanity's covenant breaches as he is the source of humanity. Breaking our foundational bonds breaks the relational order of the cosmos. In "Steer Your Way," Cohen writes that the very "blunted mountains weep" for the wreckage we make (*You Want It Darker*, 2016; see also Rosemann 2018: 13–14). But it is not only humanity that wields the wrecking ball. God is the source of our wrecking as he is the source of us. There is good biological evidence against Richard Dawkins's popular theory of the "selfish gene" (Pally 2020; Dawkins 1976). But even if one were to subscribe to it and so chalk up pride and bolting to a biologically determined self-interest, the theodical question remains: why did God create our biology this way? Cohen gnaws at the question of all theodicies: could God not create a human nature, a (free) will, a human mind, and a learning or maturational process that do not allow the cruelties of our repertoire? Not only in the end but throughout our brutality, God is complicit.

This is a shocking query. Not only did the God who made us for covenant make us able to break it but the God we *trust* to sustain us in covenant doesn't. He has left us to fail in our free will. Moshe Halbertal notes that Cohen's flummoxed response falls in the Jewish tradition of the lament and the biblical book of Lamentations, written in grief over the destruction of the Temple in Jerusalem (586 BCE). The genre's central feature is the gasp—the disbelief and outrage at the world upended: it wasn't supposed to be this way. We are supposed to be able to trust God to sustain our bonds. How can our failures happen and rehappen? This rhetorical "how"—not the practical "how do I open this?"—is how the book of Lamentations begins: "*eicha*": how is this devastation possible? The biblical lamenter, Halbertal writes, is in a "stance of bewildered protest, or perhaps bewildered outrage, or perhaps bewildered brokenness." It is more than loss; it is a trauma that shatters "our capacity to read reality as a whole" (2017: 4). It is, Halbertal continues, the wounded incredulity of a child abused by a parent. It is not that the author of Lamentations thought punishment was not warranted for Israel's sins but that the total devastation of the nation broke the foundational covenant between Israel and God, that Israel would live in the promised land. And *this* was not supposed to happen.

The lamenter's protest, in the Jewish tradition, is permissible within the covenantal, almost familial, bond with God. Unlike a reverential, distanced awe before the transcendent, this lament, outrage, and protest are—along with doxa, beseeching, and love—part of the covenantal conversation (Halberal 2020). We adore our loved ones on one hand but also lose our tempers, get fed up, slam doors, and come back ten minutes later to apologize. So too in the Jewish conversation with God.

In Cohen's theodicy, the gasp of the world upended goes something like this: if covenant is the way of creation and yet we are made to easily breach it, how can we understand the coherence of God's creation? How can we trust this God and the covenant he offers? If we cannot trust him and his covenant, how can we trust persons, made in his image? If neither God nor persons are trustworthy, perhaps autonomy and intactness are indeed the means of survival. But then we suffer from loneliness and loss. How—*eicha*—can this be?

The anguish and protest of lament appear in Cohen's work in many forms. Cohen mockingly describes God's complicity in human failings in "Lover Lover Lover" (*New Skin for the Old Ceremony*, 1974): "He [God] said, 'I locked you in this body / I meant it as a kind of trial.'" Here, God admits that he, author of our bodies, is the author of our trials. It is for Cohen an anguished "gotcha" moment: God really is responsible. He made us for committed love yet gave us bodies—wandering desires—that betray it. What kind of rigged "trial" is that? What kind of God? How could this have happened? The lyric echoes Paul in Rom. 11:32: God "bound everyone over to disobedience so that he may have mercy on them all." God makes us disobey his lesson of love just so he can feel magnanimous in granting us mercy for our sins? Is this a trap designed to snare us? It is certainly terrifying.

Even in the reverential *Book of Mercy*, a testament to covenant, Cohen goads God with the difficulties he made for us. How—*eicha*—can his creation work this way? "Blessed are You," Cohen writes, "who have given each man a shield of loneliness so that he cannot forget you" ("Blessed Are You," *Book of Mercy*, in Cohen 1994: 318). God created us to suffer in loneliness and then uses our suffering to force our attention to him. This is not a loving God. "You [God] are the truth of loneliness" Cohen continues, "and only your name addresses it." This is God's truth: our loneliness? *This* self-absorbed deity is the Lord our God? Not nice.

Perhaps the most well-known instance of Cohen rubbing God's nose in humanity's sins is "Hallelujah," from *Various Positions*, released the same year as *Book of Mercy* (1984). He begins with the tools of his musicians' trade, the chord that pleases God and "goes like this, the fourth, the fifth / The minor fall, the major lift." Chords in the major key are played in joy at a sense of oneness with God. But elation ends when that bond is broken and we are adrift, alone with the minor keys of forsakenness. This song, in the companion album to the psalter *Book of Mercy*, echoes Psalms 51, with its description of falling toward God (the major key)—"according to your great compassion / blot out my transgressions"—and away from him (the minor), "Against you, you only, have I sinned / and done what is evil in your sight" (see also London 2012). "Hallelujah"'s chorus falls somewhere between fatalism and irony: God has made the world such that we inevitably fall away from him, yet we long for nearness and praise him nonetheless in hallelujah: "the holy, or the broken Hallelujah! ... with nothing on my lips but Hallelujah!"

In the next verse, bonds are broken both between men and God and between men and women: "She tied you to a kitchen chair / she broke your throne, she cut your hair." The musician-king David is broken by Bathsheba, whose beauty moves David to sin and so to lose bond with God. Samson, defender of the Israelites, is broken by Delilah, who seduces him and, cutting his hair, emasculates him, so preventing him from fulfilling his promise to God to defend the nation.

Yet again Cohen comes to the idea that covenant betrayals cannot be only humanity's sin. As God created us, it is his design and he to blame. As "Hallelujah" continues, Cohen draws on the Jewish belief that humanity cannot know God's name as we can never fully know God. Cohen taunts, "You say I took the name in vain / I don't even know the name / But if I did, well really, what's it to you?" You, God, charge me with breaking covenant (as the sinning David and Samson did) and with taking your name in vain. But you didn't even tell me your name—so how much covenant did you really make with me? And anyway, you created me so that I may violate it. If I, your creation, break it, what do you care? It's your doing.

David Weiss Halivni notes in his memoir on the Holocaust that if we press for explanations of suffering and brutality, of the hacksaws we take to each other, we come first to humanity but ultimately to God. While Halivni concludes that human evil "must remain suspended in mystery" (Halivni 1996: 156), Cohen was not so content. He demands that God answer. Eli Wiesel, also in writings on the Holocaust, is closer to Cohen. Wiesel considers that "the only way to accuse G–d is by praising him" (1978: 38; see also Jacobson 2000)—by reminding him that he is our creator and inaugurator of the covenant that he may not break. God, on Wiesel's account, cannot let humanity go to all possible violent extremes simply because we are "free." Having made us, he is responsible for us in the freedom he created. And has bound himself to our fate.

This has something of "Hallelujah" in it. Cohen is angry with God, who bound us to this double bind—who made covenant a condition of existence, made us poor at sustaining it, and lets us flounder in our free will to ignore it. Yet the way to God and to life in his cosmos is through the "hallelujah," as with Wiesel, through doxa. We must remind God and ourselves of the covenantal bond. In his 1984 version of the song, Cohen concluded with a verse not in later, more popular versions but which captures his theodical intent: "Even though it all went wrong / I'll stand before the lord of song / With nothing on my tongue but hallelujah." To approach God with the praise of "hallelujah"—this is what we have, what each of us is given, as the way to love and serenity in a world that goes wrong and which we don't understand. The ancient psalmist put it this way in Ps. 51:17: "My sacrifice, O God, is a broken spirit; / a broken and contrite heart / you, God, will not despise."

Do We Want This God?

Do we really want this God? On Cohen's account, we have no choice. There is no opting out of the covenantal grammar of world. "There is only one achievement," Cohen said in 1988, "and that's the acceptance of your lot" (Burger 2014: 203). Cohen's struggle with God is struggle-*amid*-covenant. We recall his explanation to Arthur Kurzweil that he never rebelled against Jewish tradition (Burger 2014: 381). Drawing on Judaism's foundational prayer, "Hear, O Israel, the Lord is God, the Lord is One," Cohen understands this God as the only God whom we cannot avoid as he is the source of existence.

Book of Mercy and "Hallelujah" may taunt God but they are nonetheless psalters of dependence and doxa. "You let me sing," Cohen writes in *Book of Mercy*, "you lifted me up, you gave my soul a beam to travel on" (poem six, in Cohen 1984: 19). The sister album *Various Positions* includes not only "Hallelujah" but also "Heart with No Companion," which begins with the lines, "I greet you from the other side / Of sorrow and despair"—from the place of rejection, rejecting others, and being left in despair. The heart indeed has no companion. The image of the "other side" draws from the kabbalist notion of the demonic force, the *sitra ahra* ("other side," place of suffering). Though the narrator finds himself in that place of sorrow, bereft of God, he nonetheless "greets you ... with a love so vast and so shattered / It will reach you everywhere." Following the kabbalist image of God's love as shattered light, our sorrow and despair open a way to this light and vast love.

We have seen this before in "Anthem": "There is a crack in everything, that's how the light gets in" (*The Future*, 1992). In "Anthem," it is through our cracked brokenness that a space for God's light is made. In "Heart with No Companion," it is through the "other side" of sorrow. Cohen continues "No Companion" with this paradox of love: "Tho' your promise count for nothing / You must keep it nonetheless." We never fully grasp God's creation, why God has made us so that our promises and commitments do not "count" toward anything and cannot be counted on by others. Yet there is no choice but to keep them.

Why? For *relation is the condition of our (isolated) being*. We have no choice but to keep reaching for the promise we do not keep, be it to God in hallelujah or to others around us. "Dance Me to the

End of Love," again on *Various Positions*, reprises the idea: "Raise a tent of shelter now / though every thread is torn." Raise the promise of shelter though the tent threads are torn and offer no protection. The broken threads cannot be counted on just as our promises cannot be. Yet we must keep them. There is no avoiding the effort to make shelter or commitment. For we are bound by our nature to build bonds against isolation. Cohen held to this belief into his last years, writing in "Come Healing" (*Old Ideas*, 2012, with Patrick Leonard):

> O solitude of longing
> Where love has been confined
> Come healing of the body
> Come healing of the mind

Love lives confined by the solitude and longing of our own making, but there is no alternative to it. It is our only healing. For relation is the condition of our (isolated) being.

4

Failing Covenant with God and Persons: Doubled Imagery in Cohen's Work

The covenants with God and among persons are not separable in Cohen's cosmology and work, and so too the failures to sustain these bonds are not separable. In the Moebius Strip of covenant, we fail God *as* we fail each other. As Cohen in 1985 put it to the documentary filmmaker Stefan Troller, when in the space called "love," he could not distinguish between speaking to other persons, a lover, or God (cited in Lebold 2018: 10). Indeed, so it seems. In Cohen's writing, grief at our twined miscarriages of covenant is also not separable.

Central to Cohen's images are those that describe rent relationship with both God and persons, often lovers. In "Death of a Ladies' Man," for instance, (on the eponymous 1977 album), Cohen writes,

> The man she wanted all her life
> was hanging by a thread.
> "I never even knew how much
> I wanted you," she said.
> His muscles they were numbered
> and his style was obsolete.
> "O baby, I have come too late."
> She knelt beside his feet.

The description of a woman who was so inattentive that she "never knew" and casually comes "too late" may refer to a human relationship—to the women Cohen felt did not love him as he wanted to be loved, who were not faithful, left him hanging, or, as it emerges in later lines of the song, who were controlling. Or it may point to Christ, abandoned and hanging crucified. The woman is just a bit too late to do anything about the cross. The image of inattention and abandonment works twice, in the human and divine realms.

Two techniques are employed in Cohen's doubling of images: first, the interweaving of separate images (one evoking bond with God, and the other, bond with persons) and second, single images that call up both relationships. The latter technique may also spin a conflation of God and persons to illustrate the Lurianic kabbalist idea of the spiritual *in* the carnal—union with God through erotic union. In the most radical instance, the conflation is expressed in Jesus, the God-man. In several of Cohen's works, Bernard Wills notes, Jesus "is heavily eroticized. As the word made flesh he reveals the beauty and vulnerability of the sexualized body" (2014: Kindle Locations 3885–6). In the spiritual moment of the divine come to us, we may see the beauty and fragility of human flesh come to us in intimate union. Human sexuality and divine incarnation are conflated.

Both techniques, separate interwoven images and entwined/ conflated imagery, may involve a sudden change of narrator or addressee. The "I" or "you" in one line may mean God, in another, the narrator, lover, or listener, and in yet another, all humanity (see also Babich 2014: Kindle Locations 2280–304). Describing Cohen's "you"s and "I"s, Winfried Siemerling notes, "As soon as they are posited, neither of these identities seems to remain in place for long" (1994a: 27).

The Mobile "I" and "You"

"Hallelujah" (*Various Positions*, 1984) is a storm of pronoun instabilities. The narrator first taunts "you," a conflated God/ woman, who doesn't much care for his attempts to sing and please her/him: "But you don't really care for music, do ya?" Then "you" is King David and Samson: "And she broke your [David's] throne and she cut your [Samson's] hair." A bit further on, "you" is again the conflated God/woman: "You know, I used to live alone before I knew ya." "You" then becomes the anyone: "All I've ever learned from love, / is how to shoot somebody who outdrew ya." Finally, it is the listener: "And it's not a cry that you hear at night /. ... It's a cold and it's a broken Hallelujah."

In another illustration from the same album, the less well-known "Coming Back to You" begins:

Maybe I'm still hurting
I can't turn the other cheek
But you know that I still love you
It's just that I can't speak.

These lines seem like an address to God/Jesus, "you," whose advice to turn the other cheek the narrator, "I," can't follow. Yet later in the song, Cohen writes,

But I have to deal with envy
When you choose the precious few
Who've left their pride on the other side of
Coming back to you.

This "you" may too be God, who chooses his elect. But it also may be a plea to a woman whose fidelity Cohen cannot secure.

Ian Dennis calls this the "not fully reliable first-person position" in Cohen's work (2017: 8). Just who is that "I" and, consequently, the "you"? More intriguingly, Siemerling (1994a) finds that the "I"s that "never stay where we expect them to" (Lee 1977) are a technique in pursuit of losing the self. They are an effort to be unburdened of the self-ness of the subject and its worldly commitments—to be free for some ecstatic, extra-worldly something-or-other (Siemerling 1994a). This recalls Jiri Měsíc and Stephen Scobie's idea that Cohen sought a means to leave the body for—well, for some ecstatic something-or-other. But perhaps more importantly, Cohen's mobile "I"s and "you"s recall Judith Butler's lesson that identity is never stable but an evolving process emerging from our practices and the meanings given to them in context (Butler 2011, 2006; Steinskog 2010). Identity is thus always in flux and mutable. In Butler's classic example, we are not "male" or "female" but assemblages of practices and self-presentations that either construct/reinforce the "male" and "female" of our cultures or challenge these conventions.

On this view, understanding Cohen's mobile "I"s and "you"s involves looking at the assemblage of what each does and what identity each presents in any line of Cohen's work. It entails a readiness for multiple possibilities in which an "I" or "you" may represent more than one set of practices and more than one identity as the reader or listener moves through the lines of lines of verse. Rather than pinning down identity or relationship—love of God as distinct from love of person—it suggests a fluidity among them.

Cohen's mobile pronouns may thus be understood not as an "unreliable narrator" or a yearning to be released from the body. They may be Cohen's effort to get at the Moebius Strip nature of covenant and its breaches. That is, the pronoun mobility may strive not for loss of self but for a description of all the selves in play in the predicament of longing for relationship and flight from it. Both God and the human subject (I) may at the same time be the object (you) of someone else's desire or abandonment. One may desire or be desired by one person and, at the same time, rejected by another. There is no fixed identity in this sad game.

Importantly, as our commitments to God and persons are of a piece, dedication to "you"—or Thou, in Martin Buber's words—may well be to God at one moment, to persons/lover at another, or to both at once. And breaches of commitment—to the "face" of the other in Levinas's terms—may too abandon both. Siemerling adds that Cohen's mobile pronouns make the reader complicit in this entwined bond and abandonment. As the mobility of "I" and "you" describes bonds and breaches with God and among persons, it "transposes both the intimacy and aggression of this self-distancing relationship onto the reader" (1994a: 25). It is as if Cohen is saying, "you" too, my reader, make and break commitment. You too self-protectively hedge your bets and keep your longing and desire contained in intact, free-floating "I-systems" (Lee 1977: 100). You too crave yet leave the bonds that make you who you are even as you are also left by others.

In illustration of Cohen's address to loves worldly and divine, the song "Here It Is" (*Ten New Songs*, 2001, with Sharon Robinson) begins with the human "you"—the king, the homeless, the drunkard, the ill. Yet each verse closes with an iteration of "And here is your love / For all of this." This "you" may be the human person: the king who loves "all of this," his crown and jewels, or the drunkard who loves his drink. But it may also be God, who loves humanity in all these predicaments. Mid-song, one finds a clearer shift from the human to the divine "you": "And here is your love / For the woman, the man." This rings with God's love for all humanity. In the penultimate paragraph, the divine "you" emerges decisively:

Here is your cross,
Your nails and your hill
And here is your love,
That lists where it will.

Cohen wanders from the human to the transcendent without, as he told Troller, distinguishing the "you"s in the lines of his song. "Here It Is" ends with this: "Hello, my love, / And my love, Goodbye." The twined "you"s of the previous verses set up this line to evoke human and divine love. It is through the twined "you"s that Cohen gets across his idea: we need and desire "you," hello God, hello lover. But we do not stay with either, goodbye.

Interwoven and Conflated Images

The 1967 "Suzanne" (*Songs of Leonard Cohen*) is among the most famous instances of both interwoven and conflated imagery. Exemplifying the former, Cohen separates the first and third stanzas, about a fragile love with Suzanne, with the second stanza, about a fellow named Jesus, who speaks to us "drowning men" of humanity but is himself broken and forsaken. "Forsakenness" as God's abandonment of humanity appears in Ps. 22:1: "My God, my God, why have you forsaken me" and is repeated by Jesus on the cross (Mt. 27:46). But here Cohen's theodicy focuses on humanity as we forsake God (and are created able to do so). We recall from "Lover Lover Lover" (*New Skin for the Old Ceremony*, 1974) that it is humanity that covers God's face with ornamented temples, distancing itself from intimacy with God. In "Suzanne" verse two, we abandon God while we are busy with our "wisdom" and all we think important and so let him slip from view even as he speaks to us. We also forsake Suzanne, in verse one, telling her that "you have no love to give her." The "you" in this line is the audience, implicating us all, as Siemerling notes, in flight from connection. In these two verses, the entwined, Moebius Strip covenant is breached twice, *in seriatim*, once with Suzanne (first stanza) and once with God (the second).

In the last stanza, Cohen employs his second doubling technique, images that simultaneously evoke or conflate relationship with God and persons—or a Moebius Strip twining of the two. In this verse, the human Suzanne wears "rags" as the God/man Jesus did and she "shows you where to look amid the garbage and the flowers," amid the refuse strewn inattentively over nature, where Jesus too strode. She carries a mirror, symbol of both human lust (as in the biblical story of Susannah and the Elders) and of salvation (as in the fourteenth-century *Speculum Humanae Salvationis, Mirror of Human Salvation*). The Suzanne of the third stanza is thus a conflated image, both a guide to salvation yet corporeal and erotic—much as the image of Jesus also is, as Bernard Wills notes (2014: Kindle Locations 3885–6).

Mary Ann O'Neil (2015: 92–5), locating Cohen's doubled imagery in the tradition of devotional poetry, notes the movement from the erotic Suzanne of stanza one, who lets men "spend the night beside her," to the spiritualized Suzanne of stanza three. The later Suzanne walks beneath "our Lady of the Harbor," statue of the Virgin Mary atop the mariner's church in Montreal. She wears clothes "from Salvation Army counters," a pun highlighting Susanne's salvific role. And she is the one in whom you can place your faith: "And you know that you can trust her / For she's touched your perfect body with her mind," with her spirit.

This melded person of verse three, part salvific, part erotic, is Suzanne as the God/man Jesus, whom humanity abandons. But if she "gets you on her wavelength," you will not forsake her/Jesus. In an ephemeral moment, you might grasp (both understand and hold fast to) a brief connection, a moment of recognition and commitment observed—in the sense of both noticed and performed. In "Suzanne," Cohen confronts us with the almost-automaticity of our withdrawal from others (stanza one: "You have no love to give her") and from God (stanza two: Jesus is "broken" and "forsaken"). We are so fast to bolt. Yet God does not foreclose. The song ends with the possibility of being "touched" by the mind of the rags-wearing Jesus-Suzanne.

Conflated imagery of this type runs through Cohen's writing. The next section looks at a few examples from early and late works. For instance, in both the less well-known "Ballad of the Absent Mare" (*Recent Songs*, 1979) and "A Thousand Kisses Deep" (*Ten New Songs*, 2001, with Sharon Robinson), the images at first appear to reference human relationships but then open into our bonds and breaches with God. Indeed, the imagery throughout "Ballad of the Absent Mare" may be read as a conflation of both relationships. The insertion of "Whither thou goest / I will go"— Ruth's covenantal pledge to Naomi (Book of Ruth 1:16)—alerts us to the dual-referencing. In the song's key lines, Cohen writes,

> And he [the rider] leans on her neck [the mare's]
> And he whispers low
> "Whither thou goest
> I will go" ...
> Now the clasp of this union
> Who fastens it tight?
> Who snaps it asunder
> The very next night
> Some say the rider
> Some say the mare
> Or that love's like the smoke
> Beyond all repair.

Sunk with the inevitability of rupture, Cohen asks, who fastens and who snaps love? Will it be the other who betrays us, or will it be we who fail the other? And who is the other—lover, God, both? The last line turns to the evanescent nature of love. It is as fragile and fleeting as smoke. We must contend with this truth about human nature as God created it. It is how God made us. Elliot Wolfson notes that the last word in these lines should be read not as "repair" but as "re/pair," re-coupling, after the kabbalist notion that the world's *spiritual* brokenness may be righted by *corporeal* union (2006a: 134). But here, the re-coupling is in vain. Bond with lover/ God is broken and beyond repair.

The 2001 "A Thousand Kisses Deep" (*Ten New Songs*) begins with the following lines:

> The ponies run, the girls are young
> The odds are there to beat
> You win a while and then it's done
> Your little winning streak.

The striving for girls and gain runs thin and then out. You recognize your "invincible defeat," as the next line puts it. You are alone, without divine or human embrace—except for fleeting moments when:

sometimes when the night is slow
The wretched and the meek
We gather up our hearts and go
A thousand kisses deep.

Going "a thousand kisses deep" may again be read as a conflated image as it reaches to persons as to the transcendent, Creator of the "masterpiece," as Cohen describes God in this song. The "thousand kisses" may be a plunge into sex, divine embrace, or into God's grace *through* sex—again the Lurianic kabbalist idea of spirit through carnality. As in "Ballad of the Absent Mare," the moment lasts but briefly.

In Cohen's more intricate writings, nearly every trope does double duty, conflating bond with God and lovers. In the poem "Out of the Land of Heaven" (*The Spice Box of Earth*, 1961), Cohen writes,

Out of the land of heaven,
Down comes the warm Sabbath sun
Into the spice-box of earth.
The Queen will make every Jew her lover.

God sends the Sabbath warmth, his gift to humanity, into the spice box of female sexuality to be enjoyed as sexual union is enjoyed. The "queen" in traditional Jewish imagery is one symbol of the Sabbath. Thus here, the Sabbath/Queen is holiness and eroticism together or holiness approached through the erotic.

Indeed, the title of the poetry collection, *The Spice Box of Earth*, is itself a conflated image. It calls up both female sexuality and the ritual spice box used in the Jewish *havadalah* service, marking the division between the holiness of the Sabbath, ending weekly on Saturday night, and the profane days of the week. The spice box is the bridge between the holy and profane much as women are in Cohen's cosmology. Women are the site, and sex is the act, of possible encounter with God. We recall David Boucher's observation: "In Cohen's work, women are so often the medium through which some sort of fulfillment is attained, whether sexual gratification or religion salvation, or both simultaneously" (2004: 201). The deliciously conflated image of the spice box evokes holy and profane joy at once. In "Out of the Land of Heaven" Cohen continues:

Our rabbi dances up the street ...
And who waits for him

DOUBLED IMAGERY IN COHEN'S WORK   89

On a throne at the end of the street
But the Sabbath Queen.
Down go his hands
Into the spice-box of earth.

In this playful image of double-bondedness, the rabbi plunges into the chasm of spiritual relation through female spice. He meets the Sabbath Queen, but his hands grab the *earthly* spice box.

The Lurianic union of spiritual and sexual bond appears twenty-five years later in "Dance Me to the End of Love" (*Various Positions*, 1984), where Cohen writes,

Dance me through the panic till I'm gathered safely in
Lift me like an olive branch and be my homeward dove
Dance me to the end of love.

The word "panic" may mean sexual insecurity or spiritual crisis, and "safely in" may refer to sexual intimacy or return to God. "Lift me like an olive branch" may refer to spiritual uplifting or male sexual arousal, and "homeward dove" the site of sexual intercourse or peace of the soul. The conflation continues in the next stanza: "Let me see your beauty when the witnesses are gone." Is this the desire of a carnal or spiritual seeker? When all those other suitors/worshippers are gone, show yourself to me. I am your serious adorer. The next line, "Let me feel you moving like they do in Babylon," reads as carnal, only to be followed by "Show me slowly what I only know the limits of / Dance me to the end of love." Cohen asks to be shown slowly, so as not to be overcome, a love so grand that he has known only its limits, not its fulfillment. This love is as likely sexual ecstasy as divine grace and more likely both at once.

Book of Mercy poem thirty-five, published the same year as "Dance Me to the End of Love," is another *tour de force* of conflated imagery. It reads:

Open Me, O heart of truth, hollow out the stone, let your Bride fulfill this loneliness. I have no other hope, no other moves. This is my offering of incense. This is what I wish to burn, my darkness with no blemish, my ignorance with no flaw. Bind me to your will, bind me with these threads of sorrow, and gather me out of the afternoon where I have torn my soul on twenty monstrous altars, offering all things but myself. (Cohen 1984: 35)

On one reading, the "stone" marks the sacrificial altar, perhaps of biblical ritual sacrifice or perhaps the one to which Abraham bound his son Isaac as testament to covenant with God (Gen. 22:1-19). "No blemish" and "no flaw" refer also to the purity required of ritual sacrifice, symbol of covenantal reciprocity. The narrator will burn/sacrifice his darkness and ignorance on the stone altar as one burns ritual incense. For he, the covenant fail-er, has only darkness and ignorance, only his faithful incomprehension of God's ways, to offer in his request to near God, to be bound "to your will." One may hear the echo of Ps. 51:17: "My sacrifice, O God, is a broken spirit; / a broken and contrite heart."

But what of the "Bride"? Her presence suggests another reading, in which "stone" points also to the closed human heart that refuses intimacy. The narrator asks that his heart be hollowed out and opened so that loneliness may be filled by the "Bride." He will burn his darkness and ignorance so that he may be bound to this woman, who too is doubled. She evokes the hoped-for constancy of the marriage bed, but in traditional Jewish imagery, bride (like queen) is an image of God's Sabbath, his gift to us of rest and peace. In a conflated image of double desire for human and divine love, the narrator seeks to be bound to the Bride/God. The bindings themselves will be the threads of sorrow and regret at the infidelity/idolatry he committed at "monstrous altars," those of alien gods and beds of strange women. Perhaps his regret at spiritual and sexual whoring has taught him a lesson and will fasten him to his real love and God. But he has a habit of "offering all things but myself," ever evader of commitment. Will he commit this time?

Cohen is nothing if not aware that he retreats from the bonds he seeks.

Bond with God and Persons in Cohen's Graphic Images

Dual imagery evoking the twinedness of covenant with God and among persons is found in Cohen's sketches and graphics as in his writing. This section illustrates with the Star of David that he created for the cover of *Book of Mercy*. This symbol of Judaism—bond with God and commitment among persons—is usually made of one triangle superimposed onto another, one pointing up to

FIGURE 1 *An image of the Star of David.*

FIGURE 2 *The 1984 cover of* Book of Mercy.

the transcendent, the other down to the worldly, making a six-pointed star.

In Cohen's iteration, the star is comprised of two *hearts*, symbolizing love of the divine and love of persons, or following Lurianic kabbalah, love of God *in* worldly love.

While the composite was first used for the cover of the 1984 *Book of Mercy*, it was used again as the graphic for Cohen's 2012 world tour, as an image in the posthumously published book of poems and drawings, *The Flame* (2018b), and for the cover of the 2019 *Let Us Compare Mythologies* (first published in 1956). The 2012/2019 iteration (Figure 3) adds two more images; the first is the hand position of the priest in the traditional Jewish benediction and the second is the Hebrew letter "shin" [שׁ] (the three-pronged figure between the priestly hands), representing one name of God, Shaddai, connoting God's strength.

The 2012/2019 graphic thus brings together two sets of double bonds. First is the original 1984 twining of two hearts, symbolizing humanity's bond with God together with bonds among persons.

FIGURE 3 *The cover of the 2019 reissue of* Let Us Compare Mythologies *(first published in 1956).*

Copyright © 1956, 2006 by Leonard Cohen. Cover image reproduced by permission of Canongate Books Ltd.

Second is God's love for humanity (Shaddai) twined with human love for the divine, expressed in priestly prayer. In 2009, Cohen ended his concert in Israel enveloping his listeners with *birkhat ha'kohanim*, the priestly blessing over the people.

Since his 1964 Montreal Library speech (Chapter 3), Cohen had been riveted by the men who sustain the offices of priest and prophet. It is to the two central figures of his admiration that we now turn.

5

Those Who Did Not Fail Covenant: Moses and Jesus— Cohen's Jewish & Christian Imagery

Cohen grew up in what he called a "Catholic city." His nanny was Catholic and took him to church. For his high school years, he went to a traditionally Christian school (Burger 2014: 58, 381; Simmons 2012: 20). The power of New Testament imagery and its weight in our cultural–emotional repertoire was, in Cohen's view, unavoidable regardless of one's religious beliefs. "From David to Jesus," he said, "the idea of Law, of revelation, of a sacred life, or a messiah. All that poetry was at my fingertips" (Diamond 2017). While he comically ranted when Bob Dylan converted to Christianity, "I just don't get it ... I don't get the Jesus part," he also explained to Robert O'Brien that the "figure of Jesus is extremely attractive. It's difficult not to fall in love with that person" (Burger 2014: 183).

Christian imagery is central in *Beautiful Losers* (1966) and "Suzanne" (*Songs of Leonard Cohen*, 1967) at the beginning of Cohen's career. It runs through six decades of work (Todd 2016), and four songs in Cohen's final collection, *You Want It Darker* (2106), rely on Christian references. Discussion of the image of Jesus, a figure not of Cohen's tradition, runs through both critiques and appreciations of his poetry (Babich 2014; Billingham 2017a; Dabrowski 2001; Field 2017; among others). While Cohen drew also from Buddhist, Sufi, and Muslim imagery as well as philosophical and literary traditions (Měsíc 2018; Wolfson 2006a), this section looks at the Jewish and Christian tropes that he used for his consistent *telos*: to grasp the impediments that keep humanity from its foundational bonds with God and persons.

The critic Northrop Frye observed that in Cohen, "The Christian myth is seen as an extension of the Jewish one, its central hanged god in the tradition of the martyred Jew" (Frye 1971: 250). Jewish and Christian images are thus often back-to-back or conflated in Cohen's writing, not unlike the interwoven and conflated imagery that he used to evoke relationship with the divine and human loves (Chapter 4). "Born in Chains" (*Popular Problems*, 2014), for instance, though built on the Hebrew Bible Exodus narrative, nonetheless includes an image of the crucified Christ: "I was idled with my soul … But then you showed me where you had been wounded / In every atom broken is a name." The "wound" of the song may reference the wound of the biblical Jacob as he wrestled with God's messenger and was so bound in covenant with God (Gen. 32:22-31). Or it may be Christ's wound in the Passion, or both at once. The wounded man, Peter Billingham notes, is a paradigm for Cohen signifying the human condition of being broken off from the bonds we need. Woundedness is the plight of the First Man, Adam (and so all humanity), who "inhabits," Billingham writes, "an internal state of exile from a pre-Fall Paradise" (2017a: 30). Woundedness is the plight, Billingham continues, of the Jesus-man, who restores "the wholeness (holiness) of humankind and creation" (2017a: 30).

"Born in Chains" begins with a lament for Cohen's "idle" days in the "Egypt" of his life—his years of booze, drugs, broken loves, restlessness, and despair—his years of "chains" and "burden." It then marks his return to The Name, God: "Blessed is the name, the name be blessed / Written on my heart in burning letters." As "name" (*hashem*) in the Jewish tradition is one signifier of God, the passage "In every *atom broken* is a name" may be read as two sets of doubled meaning. One set may be parsed this way: in every atom broken / is a name. That is, every atom broken by our distressed world is inscribed with both the name of God and the name of the person who is made up of these broken atoms. On another reading, in every atom / broken is a name. Every atom of the cosmos is inscribed with the *broken name* of both God and person. "Broken" pertains to "atom" in the first reading and to "name" in the second—or in Cohen's oft-used conflation, the two together.

All four readings reflect the distinction-amid-relation nature of cosmos and covenant. The Name, God, so radically other, is yet inscribed intimately (as Aquinas wrote) in every atom that makes up our names and who we are. It is to this God that we go on return from Egypt.

Interwoven in the Exodus narrative of "Born in Chains" is the image of Jesus wounded on the cross. Jacob, wounded by God's messenger, is evoked simultaneously with the beatings at Calvary. The image of Jesus too helps the narrator leave the chains of Egypt for God's blessings. Babette Babich's insight again comes to mind: "As a Jew, Cohen reminds us to feel for Christ, not to be a Christian necessarily but to get the point about Christ" (2014: Kindle Location 2407). What for Cohen was "the point"? "Any guy," he explained, "who says blessed are the poor, blessed are the meek, has got to be a figure of unparalleled generosity and insight and madness. A man who declared himself to stand among the thieves, the prostitutes and the homeless. He was a man of inhuman generosity, a generosity that would overthrow the world if it was embraced" (Hustak 2016a). The "point" is the radical seeing to, at/tending to, the other. In a word, covenantal love.

We don't embrace it for long and so forsake each other and are forsaken. This is also "the point" about Christ, forsaken at Golgotha and repeatedly by the world ever since. Babich continues, "Even Nietzsche, that consummate anti-Christian, gets that too, writing as he does in The Antichrist: 'There was only one Christian, and he died on the cross'" (2014: Kindle Location 2408). Jesus died betrayed by others, and we have continued betraying him and each other. Babich then concludes, "we're at Golgotha again" (2014: Kindle Location 2412). Not only Jesus but each of us is abused and abandoned. In highlighting Golgotha, Babich echoes a 1968 interview in which Cohen explained:

> Our natural vocabulary is Judeo-Christian. That is our bloodmyth. We have to rediscover law from inside our own heritage, and we have to rediscover the crucifixion. The crucifixion will again be understood as a universal symbol ... It will have to be rediscovered because that's where man is at. On the cross. (Cowan 2016)

We are at Golgotha, bludgeoned and abandoned again. For Cohen, the human condition is Jesus' condition as he uttered, "My God, why have you forsaken me." Indeed, why has God left us with forsakenness as our continuing iteration? In an attempt at an answer, Cohen wrote that when the human heart does not make a space for God, we divide ourselves from each other.

> Into the heart of every Christian, Christ comes, and Christ goes. When, by his Grace, the landscape of the heart becomes vast and deep and limitless, then Christ makes His abode in that graceful heart, and His Will prevails. The experience is recognized as Peace. In the absence of this experience much activity arises, divisions of every sort. (cited in D. Cohen 2016)

These divisions are our Egypt, Babylon, Boogie Street, and cross. We divide ourselves, separate from others, and breach commitment. Thus, we sadden the God of Judaism and Jesus, who show us love, which by the nature God gave us we do not sustain. It is the wrench of both the Jewish and Christian traditions and the core of their theodicies.

In Cohen's view, we are still both "on the cross," betrayed and violated by each other, and yet also on the "biblical landscape" of burning bushes (Exod. 3:2). Here on this landscape, Cohen told Arthur Kurzweil in 1993, we have a chance. Here we, like Moses, may meet God and survive as people and, for Jews, as "a people." "That biblical landscape is our urgent invitation, and we have to be there ... Now what is the biblical landscape? It is the victory of experience. That's what the Bible celebrates" (Burger 2014: 386–7). We must use our experience of this world to bring ourselves to God and to each other. Love, Cohen told Kurzweil in the same passage, "is the only engine of survival."

Moses and Jesus

Moses and Jesus: men of love and forbearance. What grabs Cohen about these two is that they—fully human, riddled with the same fears and temptations that filled him, forsaken by their people and at moments seemingly by God—abandon neither God nor people. They persist in commitment. Jesus, Cohen wrote, "was nailed to a human predicament, summoning the heart to comprehend its own suffering by dissolving itself in a radical confession of hospitality" (Cowan 2016: 56–7). Suffering is turned to hospitality. Moses too extends seemingly infinite forbearance to the Hebrews even after the scandalous Golden Calf idolatry. Indeed, he has more patience than God is able to muster (Exod. 32:9-14). Moses extends his patience and care repeatedly through the forty-year trek to Canaan, the subject of four of the five Pentateuch books.

Sustaining love amid betrayal and suffering: that captures Cohen's attention. It suggests one answer to the theodical question of why God allows us to suffer. It brings us to deeper love, as cruciform and soul-making theodicies suggest. In giving himself to suffering and death, Jesus finds the love-that-will-not-leave, a love that is both covenantal and Augustinian. Cohen caught moments of this love in his life, lost it, missed it, and sought it throughout his own suffering. In "Come Healing" (*Old Ideas*, 2012, with Patrick Leonard) he writes of Jesus as the one who restores us:

> The splinters that you carry
> The cross you left behind
> Come healing of the body
> Come healing of the mind.

It is from the splinters of the cross, from the shards of its lesson of suffering-turned-to love, that humanity may be healed.

In Cohen's cosmology, the cross is the suffering companion to Lurianic *kabbalah*. In Isaac Luria's configuration of the divine and human, we may find union with God in bodily ecstasy. In Christianity, it may be found in the suffering of our earthly bodies turned to hospitality and donation. In neither is it the erasure of the corporeal but rather spirit experienced in and through body.

Love and Anger at the Covenant Keepers

In Cohen's writing, Moses and Jesus are not only inspirational figures for theodical laments. They are also objects of his jealousy: would that Cohen himself were so constant, able to turn hardship into donation and to sustain covenantal bonds. But as he can't, Cohen is left with the bitter undertone found in "Take This Longing" (*New Skin for the Old Ceremony*, 1974).

In this song, Cohen uses doubled imagery to evoke relations not of love but of resentment for both Jesus and human lovers. He

taunts God for preferring Jesus to his flawed human son Leonard.
And he taunts women for preferring other men over himself. The
"you" in the following lines is the conflated God/lover we have seen
in other Cohen works:

> You're faithful to the better man
> I'm afraid that he left
> So let me judge your love affair
> In this very room where I have sentenced mine to death
> I'll even wear these old laurel leaves
> That he's shaken from his head.

The "better man," the constant and committed Jesus, gets the girl
and God's incarnate being. The better man has now left us, but
Cohen still has neither girl nor God and he pouts: let me tell you
what *I* think of your love—of those whom you, God/women, loved
better than me. In mockery, he says he'll even dress up in the laurel
leaves that were scattered over Jesus on Palm Sunday. Cohen is
goading: would that make you love me more?

On one hand, Cohen reveres Jesus—the rest of "Take This
Longing" is a love song—and yet, on the other, resents him for
being loyal in love as Cohen could not be. For someone who took
covenantal commitment seriously, having Jesus and Moses at the
front of the class cannot have been easy. So Cohen in frustration
glowers at God for humanity—and his own—coming up short.
This, after all, is how God made us.

Yet still, Cohen's frustration is anger-*amid*-commitment. His
resentment and mockery flail within the unavoidable bond with
God. Five years later, in "The Window" (*Recent Songs*, 1979),
Cohen's devotion to Moses and Jesus is again at the fore. He begins
by addressing Jesus:

> Why do you stand by the window
> Abandoned to beauty and pride
> The thorn of the night in your bosom
> The spear of the age in your side.

Why, Jesus, do you bother to stand at the window to the world,
exposed to all, while humanity in every age abandons you to beauty,
pride, and the crucifixion's spear?

In an imagistic tour de force, Cohen then forges together Moses,
who stutters the word of God (Exod. 4:10), and Jesus, the word

of God become flesh. Cohen had already used the stutter image to evoke talk with God. In "The Old Revolution" (*Songs from a Room*, 1969), an imprisoned soldier addresses a transcendent that is impotent in the face of human violence. He tells God, "Lately you've started to stutter / as though you have nothing to say." God, flummoxed by humanity's mayhem, stutters as Moses did. In the later "The Window," Moses the stutterer and Jesus the crucified transcend the corporeal. Moses rises above his faltering speech; Jesus is resurrected above his bodily life—both to bring humanity to God. Cohen writes,

> Then lay your rose on the fire
> The fire give up to the sun
> The sun give over to splendor
> In the arms of the high holy one
> For the holy one dreams of a letter
> Dreams of a letter's death
> Oh bless thee continuous stutter
> Of the word being made into flesh.

An ascending list of the natural world, from rose to fire to sun, is the splendor of God, the source of all existence. It is an ascent that calls up Dante's *Paradiso*, in which he climbs through the nine concentric circles surrounding earth till he reaches his spiritual home with the divine.

An alternate reading of the passage draws from the Christian tradition wherein the rose symbolizes Jesus' blood on the cross, which is offered in a trial of fire before reaching the "splendor" of the "high holy one" God. The next line—"the holy one dreams of a letter / Dreams of a letter's death"—is one of Cohen's more inscrutable images. Is the "letter" the Word that becomes flesh, God-in-Jesus, whose earthly death was crucifixion? Is it a reference to the Pauline idea that the letter of the law dies with the fulfillment of the law through faith in Christ/God (2 Cor. 3:2-3)? Or is "letter" God's name, the unknowable, unutterable—barely stutterable—tetragrammaton, YHVH? This God in Christian tradition is the God who was crucified and whose earthly body dies. Bernard Wills offers yet another reading, in which "the word made flesh stutters: it can't utter the unknowable, unmanifested core of the divine nature" (2014: Kindle Location 3979). Even Jesus, the word made flesh, cannot speak the awesome nature of God. But we bless the continuous stuttering effort to bring us to him.

Yet this reading of "stutter" overlooks the famous stutterer of Cohen's tradition (see also Wolfson 2006a: 144). Taking account of *this* stutterer, Moses, suggests that in these lines, Cohen turns in thanks and blessing to the stutterer and the crucified: "Oh bless thee continuous stutter / Of the word being made into flesh." Moses and Jesus: their lives were spent in helping us—"spent" in the sense of "occupied by" (I'm spending time thinking) and in the sense of "used up." May we remember to bless them.

Beseeching the Covenant Keepers: "Gentle This Soul"

The devotion that Jesus and Moses showed to humanity returns Cohen to his theodicy: for all they have done, we abandon them and the humanity they loved. Jiri Měsíc writes, "In Cohen's theology ... we see that G-d is present in the heart of the believer and to reach Him involves both self-criticism for one's failures ... and the aspiration to be purified, the ascent of the liberated soul" (Měsíc 2015). Cohen may well believe that God is in our hearts, as Měsíc says. After all, Cohen's frustration is *amid* commitment. Yet Cohen also knows that our hearts don't stand fast. We don't sustain our bond with God, no matter how thorough our self-criticism or search for purity and soulful ascent. After all, Cohen tried both for much of his life, in Jewish and Buddhist practice, with recidivist covenant breaches to show for it. Our lives are a trial of seeking God, leaving God, and suffering the fruits of our aborted search.

In the refrain of "The Window" (*Recent Songs*, 1979), Cohen again seeks his Moses/Jesus, his "chosen" loves who were once human ("matter") and now are grace (holy "ghost"). This time Cohen comes not in blessing, as above, but beseeching: "gentle this soul" from the suffering we cause to ourselves. Cohen writes,

> Oh chosen love, Oh frozen love
> Oh tangle of matter and ghost
> Oh darling of angels, demons and saints
> And the whole broken-hearted host
> Gentle this soul.

The Catholic theologian Karl Rahner held that matter is "frozen" spirit, whose purpose is to enable spirit itself to flourish. "Matter is, as it were, 'frozen' spirit whose only meaning is to render real spirit possible" (Rahner 1969: 177). Rahner does not demean bodies (and bodily love) but rather saw the material world as of a form of spirit, albeit "frozen." As with Isaac Luria, materiality is radically distinct from spirit yet also foundationally bound to it. Cohen had already used the image of frozen love in the 1961 "Brighter Than Our Sun" (*The Spice Box of Earth*, available online at: https://genius.com/Leonard-cohen-brighter-than-our-sun-annotated). There he wrote,

> And what happened to love
> In the gleaming universe?
> It froze in the heart of God,
> Froze on a spear of light.

As if in echo of Rahner, the warming, generative love of God freezes once it is in the gleaming matter of the world. Love is all of the heart of God but frozen in matter among us. Our hearts, with our love frozen and inexpressible, cannot melt enough to sustain bond.

We can now understand the refrain of "The Window" as beseeching Cohen's "chosen" loves, Moses and Jesus, to "gentle his soul" even as his love for them is "frozen." He strives to sustain love but cannot; he can do no better in his chilled, material form. From Moses, stutterer of God's word, and Jesus, God's word become flesh—figures of the Jewish and Christian traditions—Cohen asks for solace from the wounds of betrayal, from the thorn and spear of the first lines of the song.

Moses and Jesus, may they gentle Leonard's soul.

6

The Double Bind
That Is Not a Bond:
Cohen and Women

First Thoughts

Cohen was riveted not only by failure to sustain covenant with God
but also covenant with women. He elliptically called himself "the
poet of the two great intimacies" ("Commentary—My Wife and I,"
in Cohen 1994: 230). Nearly two decades after that modest self-
assessment, in introducing the song "Ain't No Cure for Love" (*I'm
Your Man*, 1988), he told his Seattle audience, "I studied religious
values. I actually bound myself to the mast of non-attachment,
but the storms of desire snapped my bounds like a spoon through
noodles" (Cohen 2012). When Cohen was a teenager, he told Susan
Lumsden in 1970, he started writing notes to the girls he liked.
"'They began to show them around and soon people started calling
it poetry.' When it didn't work with women," Lumsden continues,
"he says, 'I appealed to God'" (Nadel 1996: 3).

Cohen held to the possibility of covenant between men and
women as he held to the possibility between humanity and God. He
wrote in the 2006 poem "Thing,"

I am this thing that needs to sing
I love to sing
to my beloved's other thing
and to my own dear sweet G-d
I love to sing to Him and her. (2007: 112)

Indeed, whatever made him able to write songs, he said, "is rooted in some kind of inspired confusion of womanhood, godliness, beauty, and darkness" (Burger 2014: 204). For Cohen, women and God are beauty but they are also the darkness of not being able to hold onto their beauty or to them. "For Cohen," Ian Dennis observed, "as just about everyone has noticed, the sacred and sexuality are always connected, which is to say that complete sexual fulfillment is as impossible as being God" (Dennis 2017: 12). Cohen did not contemplate being God, but sexual contentment was for him as impossible as sustaining bond with the divine.

As he failed to sustain covenant with God, Cohen foiled human intimacy. In this, he reprises his Godot theodicy (Chapter 3): I am waiting for you, God, woman, but it is I who may never arrive. Such commitment feels too risky, threatens one's sense of an independent self. In the early poem "You Do Not Have to Love Me," Cohen writes, "I prayed that you would love me / and that you would not love me" (*Selected Poems 1956–1968*, in Cohen 1994: 120). The doubled "you" may be God or a woman or, most typically for Cohen, both at once. Jiri Měsíc notes that Cohen, for decades touted as a troubadour, failed the troubadour's most important pledge: faithfulness. He was, Měsíc writes, in constant pursuit of "other conquests" (2016: 141). Cohen's inconstancy was not much changed nearly four decades later. In "By the Rivers Dark" (*Ten New Songs*, 2001, with Sharon Robinson), the narrator is hunted and struck by "him," who is identified this way:

Though I take my song
From a withered limb
Both song and tree
They sing for him.

This "him" is the transcendent, for whom both art and nature sing. "He" reveals the narrator's inner self. And what sins are found there? "And I saw within / My lawless heart / And my wedding ring." The narrator, whose heart has abandoned the wedding vows and law, breaches bond with God, source of law, and woman both.

Cohen not only foiled relations with women but did so in much the way that we foil bond with God: by the distance come of idolization and adornment. We recall the lines in "Lover Lover Lover": it was humanity "who built the temple / it was you who covered up my face" with the gildings of the sacred. This is the point also about women. Set in ornamented temples or on a pedestal as man's "better half," God and women cannot be *encountered* as Martin Buber wrote of the I–Thou bond (2010). Babette Babich notes, "The fantasy that women could constitute the fairer or as Goethe supposed the 'higher' sex, is also a way of dis-imagining their humanity" (2014: Kindle Locations 2382–4). What's left is a dazzling icon. And no relationship can come of that.

If feminine beauty, like God's grace, is too great in its awesome dazzle, one must protect oneself from it lest it subsume one and take control. In short, one must bolt. "There's a sense," Simon Riches rightly observes, "in which Cohen finds his view of female beauty almost overwhelming, even unsustainable" (2014: Kindle Location 2133). Or, as Cohen himself put it, "the destruction of the ego is involved with love" (Burger 2014: 219).

In Cohen's cosmology, women and God can be up there, in revered distance, but they cannot be here with me. I will adore thee on condition that I am free of thee. Sylvie Simmons insightfully quotes Cohen: "'My mother taught me well never to be cruel to women,' Leonard wrote in an unpublished piece from the seventies. But what he also learned from Masha [his mother] was to count on the devotion, support and nurturing of women and, if and when it became too intense, to have permission to leave" (Simmons 2012: 47). While Cohen wanted and had many relationships with women—music critic Thom Juric called him "the elder statesman of the bedroom" (Elliott 2015: 134)—they were shot through with both idolization and his need to bolt.

Bound to the Bind That Isn't a Bond: Idealization and Flight

Cohen is again bound to the double bind that is not a bond: desiring, even idolizing women yet fearing the power (he feels) women have over him. To begin with the idolization, both sexual and spiritual, Pamela Erens writes, "The descriptions of the female body could be written only by someone who adores its every form" (2018: 198). In 1988, Cohen declared the covenant of marriage "the foundation stone of the whole enterprise" and in 1993, reprised, "Monogamous marriage and commitment, all those ferocious ideas, are the highest expression of male possibility" (Raab 2017: 17). In 1992, as if in reply to Erens, Cohen said, "I don't think a man ever gets over that first sight of the naked woman. I think that's Eve standing over him, that's the morning and the dew on the skin. And I think that's the major content of every man's imagination" (Johnson 1992). It was at least for Cohen, who in the last year of his life wrote,

I loved your face, I loved your hair
Your T-shirts and your evening wear
As for the world, the job, the war
I ditched them all to love you more. ("Moving On,"
Thanks for the Dance, 2019)

Perhaps more important than the female body was the "inspired confusion," as Cohen put it, of the female and the divine (Burger 2014: 204). In "Our Lady of Solitude" (*Recent Songs*, 1979) Cohen writes,

And the light came from her body
And the night went through her grace …
Mistress, oh mistress, of us all …
I thank you with my heart
for keeping me so close to thee.

With some echo of Luria's kabbalist vision, women here are the passage from worldly solitude to the holy. This may be simply Cohen's conflation of spiritual uplift with a more carnal sort of elevation but it is among the most important and revelatory of his motifs. The light of God comes from the female form ("the light came from her body"). The night passes—or is passed, is spent—through "grace," female gracefulness, divine mercy, or both. We find a similar idea in "Joan of Arc" (*Songs of Love and Hate*, 1971), "then she clearly understood / if he was fire, oh, then she must be wood." "She" is the means through which fire, spirit/God, blazes, somewhat as "her body" is the means for the light to come through in "Our Lady of Solitude." "Suzanne" too, from the same period, presents eroticism as salvation: Suzanne wears *Salvation* Army rags and holds the mirror that is at once a symbol of eros and redemption (Chapter 4; O'Neil 2015: 94).

That's the way to God, through the female portal. "Cohen does indeed perceive and present his real or imagined mistresses as mediators between the male lover and an absolute bliss attainable only through the experience of female love and beauty" (Lebold 2018: 3).

Confessing Flight as Seduction

Yet, for all Cohen's yearning for the female for its corporeal or spiritual ends, "interest in the other sex," Babich notes, "as with the identification of being a ladies' man traditionally betrays self-interest" (2014: Kindle Location 2377). *Death of a Ladies' Man* is Cohen's cheekily titled 1997 album. Babich then dismantles the defense of Cohen admirers that "Cohen isn't misogynistic because he's really not talking about women ... but just about himself" (see also Babich 2013: 49–50). Tim Footman is one of the admirers who writes, "There is also a deep thread of solipsism in his love-lyrics, in that, instead of focusing on the woman he loves, his attention is on the love itself, the transaction with himself as protagonist. It's all about Leonard" (2009: 184).

Missing in this Cohen-defense is that he was misogynistic in his own talented way *because* he talked only about himself. The feint of Cohen devotees that he wasn't actually talking about women won't acquit him of the charge of not talking about—or seeing or listening to—real women. Idolizing women left Cohen in thrall but not in conversation with them. This is a mode of breaking bond not sustaining it.

Cohen also understood the attention he got for confessing his exit from commitment. The self-hating narcissist (Hampson 2007) bares his soul, always willing to expose his sins for renown. In "The Traitor" (*Recent Songs*, 1979), a testament to fear that women control and "paralyze" the will, Cohen writes, "I'm listed with the enemies of love." Yet Douglas Todd notes how bearing his wayward soul made women and fans love him even more (2010). Near the end of his life, Cohen was confessing still about confession-as-seduction. In these lines, he purrs,

Have mercy on me baby
After all I did confess
Even though you have to hate me
Could you hate me less? ("Anyhow," *Old Ideas*, 2012)

For Cohen, admitting to lovin' and leavin' was a stratagem to lure women and audience alike. He disliked holy men, he told Steve

Sanfield, because "they know how to get at people around them, that's what their gig is." Cohen understood this "because I was able to do it in my own small way" (Simmons 2012: 186). Cohen wanted both to abandon himself to his loves and yet remain the harem puppeteer.

Michael Ondaatje archly noted that Bob Dylan and Cohen were "public artists" who made careers "on their ability to be cynical about their egos or pop sainthood while at the same time continuing to build it up" (cited in Simmons 2012: 205). Cohen fed his "pop sainthood" back into his writing, milking it for art and stardom. "You will only sing again [stay a pop star] if you give up lechery," he writes in the poem "Another Room," a public admission of concupiscence (*Death of a Lady's Man*, in Cohen 1994: 225). "Choose," he continues. "This is a place where you may begin again. But I want her. Let me have her. Throw yourself upon your stiffness and take up your pen." He did take up that pen, not to privately struggle with "lechery" as he called it—that gets you a therapist not an audience—but to write about it for still more fan and female attention.

"There was a need for such a connection between Leonard and his audience" one friend remarked in the documentary *Marianne & Leonard: Words of Love* (Broomfield 2019). "One night, he had so many people up on the stage with him that it was like this big love in right in the middle of our concert ... We were playing in Amsterdam and he invites the entire audience to come home with us to his hotel. And they did."

In the end, the applauding crowds gave Cohen a perfect sort of devotion, one that anoints with love yet left him unencumbered when the stage lights went down. In return, he gave audiences his staggering, self-confessing art.

Idolization and Flight in Life

Cohen's reverence for female flesh and spirit notwithstanding, he bolted into and out of relationships with women. He never married and found even serial monogamy constraining. His successive—and successively broken—long-term intimacies began in the 1960s with Marianne Ihlen, muse and target of "So Long, Marianne" and "Hey, That's No Way to Say Goodbye" (*Songs of Leonard*, Cohen 1967). By the end of the 1960s, ensconced in New York's sex-drugs-and-rock-n-roll scene, Cohen left her and her son, whom he had helped to raise. Later he said, "I wanted many women, many kinds of experiences, many countries, many climates, many love affairs" ("It was a beautiful slow movie" 2019). Ihlen died of leukemia three months before Cohen's death in 2016. His final e-mail to her read, "Dearest Marianne, I'm just a little behind you, close enough to take your hand. ... I've never forgotten your love and your beauty ... Safe travels old friend. See you down the road. Love and gratitude.—*Leonard*" (Dalziell and Genoni 2018). Their relationship is the subject of Nick Broomfield's 2019 documentary film, *Marianne & Leonard: Words of Love*.

Cohen's ruptured passions continued with Joni Mitchell (mid-1960s), who called him a "boudoir poet" (Simmons 2012: 175). She was followed by the artist Suzanne Elrod, whom Cohen never married though they had two children together. (The muse for "Suzanne" was not Elrod but Suzanne Verdal, wife of Cohen's friend, the Canadian sculptor Armand Vaillancourt). Describing Cohen's early days with Elrod, Simmons writes, "Leonard seemed as smitten with this headstrong, sexual young woman as she was with him. But he also appeared to have one eye on the door" (2012: 225). True to form, Cohen described Elrod as a woman who "outwitted me at every turn," which gave interviewer Mikal Gilmore some sense of the war Cohen felt raged between them (Burger 2014: 506). Yet Cohen also said it was his "cowardice" and being "too afraid" that prevented him from marrying (Burger 2014: 463; Lisle 2004). Describing the end of his decade-long relationship with Elrod, Cohen said, "every relationship I had broke down. *Every single relationship broke down*" (Nadel 1996: 218).

Cohen's next love was photographer Dominique Issermann, who made the music videos for "Dance Me to the End of Love" (*Various Positions*, 1984) and "First We Take Manhattan" (*I'm Your Man*, 1988). Her photos were used on the cover of his 1994 book *Stranger Music* and the 1997 compilation album *More Best of Leonard Cohen*. In 2010, Issermann returned as official photographer of Cohen's world tour. The 1990s saw Cohen's relationship with actress Rebecca De Mornay, who coproduced the 1992 album *The Future*. In dedicating the album to her, he refers to the biblical passage in which a girl Rebecca comes to the aid of Eliezer, Abraham's emissary (Gen. 24). Eliezer, Hebrew for "God comes to my aid," is also Cohen's Hebrew name, Eliezer ben Nisan ha'kohen ("Leonard Cohen's Temple of Song" 2016). The modern,

De Mornay Rebecca, it seems, had come to his aid. Cohen said he had a "formal relationship" with her, but whatever that meant wasn't meant for long. In 1994, he left her to spend five years in the ascetic Buddhist monastery on Mt. Baldy, California, a rather emphatic exit. "Finally she saw," Cohen said, "I was a guy who just couldn't come across" (Remnick 2016).

At age sixty-three, Cohen said, "I had wonderful love but I did not give back wonderful love ... I was obsessed with some fictional sense of separation" (Burger 2014: 419). He said much the same in the documentary *Marianne & Leonard: Words of Love*, "A large part of my life was escaping ... so it was a selfish life ... I guess the kids suffered and people close to me suffered because I was always leaving" (Broomfield 2019).

It was only in the opening decade of the twenty-first century that Cohen, in his seventies, seemed to find some contentment with a woman, the composer and singer Anjani Thomas, twenty-five years his junior. Lyrics from this period suggest that her influence did not undo his long-standing anger-amid-need for women. It did, however, give him a glimpse of the female subject, one who is not just the object of his desire and ire. In 2006, he told Christine Langlois, "'I never met a woman until I was 65. Instead, I saw all kinds of miracles in front of me,'" the dazzling, unencounterable icon. Langlois continues, "He says he always loved women, 'always appreciated what they could do for me' but always saw them through his own 'urgent needs and desires. Once that started to dissolve, I began to see the woman standing there'" (Langlois 2006: 15).

Idolization and Flight in Art

Until he came to this septuagenarian wisdom, Cohen's yo-yo of attraction and flight made for persistent panic in his poetry as in life. Babich notes that in Cohen's work "the lover makes a promise to the beloved and seemingly always, nearly immediately breaks his word" (2014: Kindle Location 2307). Even "I'm Your Man," a rosary of all the things he would do for the woman who has left him, is ambiguous (*I'm Your Man*, 1988). Does he mean the words "Here I stand / I'm your man" or "I'd crawl to you baby / and I'd fall at your feet"? Or is he being sarcastic as the stage performances suggest, mocking the demands he feels women make on men. And then comes the line: "The chain's too tight." Love enslaves. Then the

Ur Cohen cop-out: "I've been running through these promises to you / That I made and I could not keep." He promises that "I'll do anything you ask me to," but his broken vows litter the bed he left.

On one hand, Cohen is terrified of women providing too much and so trapping him. On the other, he is angry when they don't provide enough, leaving him needy. Both circumstances grip him with the fear of losing control to them, women. On his first album, he wrote with both longing and sarcasm, "But you stand there so nice in your blizzard of ice / Oh please, let me come into the storm" ("One of Us Can't Be Wrong," *Songs of Leonard Cohen*, 1967). The song continues as a rap sheet of the men who have been lured and destroyed by ice princesses.

The paradox of not-enough and too-much lovin'—both leading Cohen to bolt—runs through the examples below in a rough chronology of his work. To begin, early in Cohen's career, Michael Ondaatje criticized the novels *The Favourite Game* (1963) and *Beautiful Losers* (1966) as portraits of women who are "flesh" that "drowns out all personality" (Ondaatje 1970: 13). Northrop Frye somewhat less charitably wrote, "the erotic poems follow the usual convention of stacking up thighs like a Rockette Chorus Line" (Footman 2009: 25). Women here are little else but Cohen's own "needs and desires," as he told Langlois (2006). He seeks them out yet fears his desire will break his autonomy, like the fellow in "Feels So Good" who says, "you broke me doing all the little things I really like" (2009 World Tour). And so he flees.

Edith, the main female character of *Beautiful Losers* (1966), "is purely a body, an initiator of or receptacle for sex ... Any other women who incidentally appear are also, simply, sexually available bodies" (Erens 2018: 200). The men of the novel want them and then want to move on, a desire Cohen critiques but takes as the way of the world, certainly of his world. Wanting to move on is fear of intimacy too close, but in *Favourite Game* (1963), the protagonist (and Cohen's alter ego) rages also at women who don't stay close enough. Describing a woman who goes with other men, he jeers that her mouth "belongs to everyone, like a park" (cited in Erens 2018: 198). There is a good deal of using women as portals for male pleasure and anger, often indistinguishable. The protagonist "falls into a love affair," Erens writes, "with a woman named Shell, oscillating between a happy thralldom and a panicked desire for flight" (2018: 198). Cohen again fears the love too close. As the name Shell suggests, the protagonist is drawn to her as a luminescent surface without interiority, precisely what Ondaatje and Frye criticized. As the novel closes, the protagonist wants to be able to love his mother, best friend, and lover but knows that he is unable and "unavailable." He writes, "Dearest Shell, if you let me I'd always keep you 400 miles away and write you pretty poems and letters" (cited in Simmons 2012: 368).

I will adore thee if I can be free of thee. Cohen may love the female form, as Erens notes, and the access he believed it grants to the spiritual world. But he did so always with an eye on the exit, willing and perhaps determined to leave the most wanted bonds if (he feared) they constrain him.

In an early text reworked for *Death of a Lady's Man* and collected in *Stranger Music* as "Death to This Book," Cohen was rather more direct in his rage at women and constraint: "fuck this marriage ... Your dead bed night after night and nothing warm but baby talk" (1994: 224). This is both fear of women constraining him and anger at not getting enough from the women he fears constrain him ("your dead bed"). It was a sentiment that did not get cozier with time. A decade later, in "Why Don't You Try" (*New Skin for the Old Ceremony*, 1974), he writes, "You know this life is filled with many sweet companions / Many satisfying one-night stands / Do you want to be the ditch around a tower?" The echo of "bitch" constraining male arousal was unavoidable. On the same album, "Is This What You Wanted" imagines his revenge against female demands: he stays seventeen, he writes, while she becomes aged and wrinkled. In the important "There Is a War," from the same collection still, Cohen admits that his participation in the Israeli army's entertainment detail (during the 1974 Yom Kippur War) was prodded not only by concern for Israel but significantly by wanting to escape domestic life with Elrod. And perhaps most of all, by the fear of being controlled by the women who arouse him. Cohen writes,

A war between the man and the woman ...
Yes, I rise up from her arms, she says "I guess you call this love"
I call it service ...
You cannot stand what I've become,
You much prefer the gentleman I was before.
I was so easy to defeat, I was so easy to control
I didn't even know there was a war.

The plaint of emasculation by love continued through the decade. "Iodine" (*Death of a Ladies' Man*, 1977) begins,

I needed you, I knew I was in danger
Of losing what I used to think was mine ...
And though I failed at love, was this a crime?
You said, Don't worry, don't worry, darling
There are many ways a man can serve his time.

Women, in Cohen's fear-scape, imprison. And what was the sex like? On the same album, Cohen answers, "Quick as dogs and truly dead were we" ("I Left a Woman Waiting"). But more desolate is the song's conclusion: this is "The way it's got to be, lover." The war between men and women makes a charnel house of love but it is the way of the world, surely of Cohen's.

The poetry volume *Death of a Lady's Man*, published the next year, is riddled with fear of obliteration in love. The book, through verse and commentary on verse, tells of the narrator's marriage, fears of marriage, infidelities, artistic career and failures, and spiritual seeking. The wife, the narrator says, withholds and rejects, saying, "Even though the purity of your love is affirmed by the unanimous quiver of every feather in the celestial host, I am not going back to the axe of your love ... I will be never again the cup of your need" ("A Woman's Decision," in Cohen 1994: 244). She refuses sexual access, and worse, in the commentary to "She Has Given Me the Bullet," the narrator moans, "There is the bullet but there is no death ... There is the rotting and the hatred and the ambition but there is no death" (in Cohen 1994: 259). Life with "her" is a living death, and "she" has given him the bullet by which to annihilate himself. The narrator of this poem may be rueful about lost love, but keeping it is "giving in." Later in the poem/novel, Cohen writes in sardonic tones both bitter and resigned, "I am satisfied and I give in. Long live the marriage of men and women. Long live the one heart" ("Commentary—Final Examination," in Cohen 1994: 294). Unsurprisingly, the marriage crashes; the spiritual seeking remains frantic and unfulfilled. In a commentary to the poem "O Wife Unmasked," Cohen blurts: "Claustrophobia! Bullshit! Air! Air! Is there an antidote to this mustard gas of domestic spiritism?" (Cohen 1979: 129).

In *Death of a Lady's Man*—as in *Favourite Game*, "Why Don't You Try," "There Is a War," and "Iodine"—Henry Bean seems to be on-target about Cohen's fear-world (Chapter 3): love threatens the sealed protection that autonomy ostensibly brings. The sneering prominent during his relationship with Elrod ebbed after the 1970s but not the dread that commitment to women, like commitment to God, risks dissolution. Faithfulness is being in "service," unshielded by the membrane of intact. "Desire," Dennis writes of Cohen, "dissolves identity. And sexual desire, proportionate to its strength, most efficiently" (2017: 12). So Cohen bolts.

Like desire itself, neither the fear of entrapment nor the bolting mellowed with age. "Women," Cohen told Gavin Martin at age fifty-eight, "only let you out of the house for two reasons: to make money or to fight a war" (Martin 1991, cited in Simmons 2012, 272). A year later, he wrote,

> She stands before you naked
> You can see it, you can taste it …
> It don't matter how you worship
> As long as you're
> Down on your knees. ("Light as the Breeze,"
> *The Future*, 1992).

For a second, the narrator of the song "was healed and my heart was at ease." But fear of entrapment returns:

> it ain't exactly prison
> But you'll never be forgiven
> For whatever you've done
> With the keys …
> And I'm sick of pretending
> I'm broken from bending
> I've lived too long on my knees.

At seventy-eight, Cohen allowed himself this lambaste: "You were young and it was summer / I just had to take a dive / When I knew was easy, the darkness was the price." In the darkness that is relationship, a snide Cohen continues: he doesn't smoke, drink, or have "much loving," because loving, well, "that's always been your call" ("Darkness" *Old Ideas*, 2012). As with "My Life in Art" and "Why Don't You Try," this is both fear of entrapment and anger at women for not putting out, both leaving him at a loss for control.

Cohen's fear of women calling the shots persists into the 2019 posthumous song collection, *Thanks for the Dance*, produced by Cohen's son, Adam. The collection's opening song, "Happens to the Heart," begins with summer sex, "The rivalry was vicious / The women were in charge," which left an "ugly mark." An ugly mark— that's what you get if women run things. Several verses later, the narrator tells us:

> I studied with this beggar
> He was filthy, he was scarred
> By the claws of many women
> He had failed to disregard.

If you don't "disregard" women, if you let women get to you, they will turn you into a beggar for their love (they won't put out) and scar you with their grasping talons (but if they put out, it ensnares you). The narrator finally tells us this:

> I was handy with a rifle
> My father's .303
> I fought for something final
> Not the right to disagree.

He doesn't want any of this namby-pamby "we'll agree to disagree" that women whine at men. He wants to set the way things go, if need be by force. And he is terrified that failing to do so will end in defeat. As usual, Cohen is nothing if not aware of himself, ready to confess his need for control.

But control, as Cohen knew, cannot bring relationship. If control is our *telos*, covenant cannot be. Cohen's inconsolable anger and flight delivered him to his theodicy much as did inconstancy with God. In the Godot theodicy we've seen, he is waiting for God, but it is Cohen who never arrives—or he arrives and then flees. In his writing about women, Cohen is waiting for her and similarly takes flight. At the end of "There Is a War," Cohen begs the woman to come back into the fray: "Why don't you come on back to the war / can't you hear me speaking?" Yet it was not she who left but he. Cohen, author of these lines, knows he left, knows he wants her back, and knows that were she to return, he would flee. After all, it is to a "war" that he invites her. So he comes to the question ever implicit in his complaint: why is our deepest desire at once a war, a battle unto dissolution? Why is life created so?

Troubadour and Crooner: Inconstancy and Covenant

Christophe Lebold makes the interesting suggestion that Cohen was first troubadour, then soldier at war with women, and then "crooner," who sacralizes romantic love, binding it to a higher, spiritual peace (Lebold 2018). On Lebold's account, the 1960s troubadour, expressed in songs such as "Suzanne," "Sisters of Mercy," "So Long Marianne," and "Winter Lady," is the devoted, chaste lover of women who endures the trial of unfulfilled love as a path to spiritual fulfillment. Yet the troubadour also grasps the risks of such a path: as women lure male desire, they enslave and then abandon these hapless souls. The soldier, Lebold continues, appears in *New Skin for the Old Ceremony* (1974), which includes "There Is a War," and in such songs as "Don't Go Home with Your Hard-On" (*Death of a Ladies' Man*, 1977, with Bob Dylan and Allen Ginsberg as backup vocalists). There Cohen writes, "And the lips that say, Come on, taste us / And when you try to they make you say Please." Gone is the troubadour's goddess, replaced by the ice princess "in a mutual game of humiliation and enslavement" (Lebold 2018: 7). The crooner emerges in the mid-1980s and strikes a peace by uniting sexual love with spiritual fulfillment. Cohen, Lebold writes, "turns songs into spiritual weapons that break open our hearts and converts concerts into spiritual experiments" (2018: 13).

But while Cohen wanted women (troubadour), feared and fled from his desire (soldier), and understood sexual ecstasy as linked to spirit (crooner), Lebold's phases may not be as distinct as he sketches. "So Long Marianne," "Hey, That's No Way to Say Goodbye," "Stranger Song," and "Master Song" are of the early "troubadour" period yet they already sound the soldier's charge against the entrapping female and emasculation in love. Indeed, "One of Us Cannot Be Wrong" appears on Cohen's earliest album (*Songs of Leonard Cohen*, 1967) with the acid remark that "the duty of lovers / Is to tarnish the golden rule." Already here, it is the nature—the duty—of love to hurt. So the "soldier" extends back through the earliest "troubadour" album. Lebold recognizes that "Cohen's early universe is arguably bleaker than the troubadours' ... [lovers] are usually unable to retain each other" (5). Yet this must be the grand understatement of Cohen scholarship. Cohen's early "troubadour" universe is not where lovers tepidly are "unable to retain each other" but where wild adoration is shipwrecked in the "war" between men and women.

Similarly confounding Lebold's phases, the "crooner" is found in the "soldier" phase of the 1970s, as Lebold also recognizes (2018: 8). The cover of the 1974 *New Skin for the Old Ceremony* is already of crooner sensibility, a reproduction of the 1550 *Rosarium Philosophorum,* depicting a heavenly King in sexual union with his queen, melding erotic and spiritual embrace. By contrast, the cover for the 1988 *I'm Your Man,* ostensibly of crooner times, shows Cohen still engaged in his "soldier's" war with the women he desires. He appears in a seductive suit and T-shirt eating a banana, literally a biting comment on the war between the sexes, in which women bring men to devour their phalluses.

The genius of the crooner phase, Lebold writes, is that "Cohen brought to rock music the idea that the function of the heart is to be broken again and again so that it can be healed again and again, the love song being the sacred space where that operation can occur" (2018: 12). But this understanding of broken hearts and healing misses Cohen's unresolved theodical question: why must the heart love and lose? Is our bond-and-bolt inconstancy the way God made us to be, and can we abide this divine? Cohen may have sought to establish "a sacramental space," as Lebold writes, and to "bridge the gap" between ourselves "and our love, and—if we are so inclined—ourselves and God" (2018: 12). But Cohen did not consider bond with God or among persons a matter of "inclination." It is the structure of the cosmos. Sacramental spaces—houses of worship, verses of song—do not resolve our failure to live by it. Cohen's "crooner" years notwithstanding, the theodical anguish remained and dogged him.

The Female Subject, Briefly

It may not have been a resigned, spiritual crooner phase that changed Cohen but age (Billingham 2017a) and Anjani Thomas, Cohen's partner during his eighth decade. Cohen himself seemed aware of this in telling Christine Langlois, "I never met a woman until I was 65" (Langlois 2006: 15). But in his seventies, he indeed met Thomas in a way he had not met women before. There are some remarkable shifts in the work he did with her, even if they did not broadly influence his work or continue into his later writings. "A Street," written with Thomas (*Popular Problems*, 2014), features not only the expectable female "you"—the idolized object to be adored and left in self-protection. It introduces the female subject, "I." Thomas and Cohen write,

> You left me with the dishes
> And a baby in the bath
> You're tight with the militias
> You wear their camouflage
> I guess that makes us equal
> But I want to march with you.

In lines not included in the 2018 compilation *The Flame*, the song continues,

> The party's over
> But I've landed on my feet.

In this song, it is the woman who comes out of relationship "on my feet" after the guy left her with the dishes and baby and ran off to war. She appreciates the relationship for what it was and moves on: "let's drink to when it's over / And let's drink to when we met." After forty years, we come to an answer of sorts to the 1974 "There Is a War" and Cohen's escape into it to evade domestic life with Elrod. In "A Street," the "I" is a woman finally, with herself intact.

The important presence of the female subject, in contrast to the adored but suspect icon, came late to Cohen. In much of his work before his last decade, the female dazzle was as "bright" but also as "cruel" and overwhelming as the kabbalist light of God ("Joan of Arc," *Songs of Love and Hate*, 1971, Chapter 3). How can one take up daily life with a force as compelling and fearful as that? Who can live with desire so awesome/awful—the "miracles" Cohen said women are? Who can escape annihilation? This answerless question is taken up in the section below on the imagery in Cohen's writings on women.

Song of Songs,
Through a Glass, Darkly

In the tradition of Song of Songs, Cohen expresses relationship with God and women in imagery at once erotic and prayerful, pressing further his doubled imagery (Chapter 4). But while the biblical Song of Songs celebrates erotic and spiritual love (and cautions about plunging in inappropriately), Cohen both celebrates it and grieves for our inconstancy. "Take This Longing" (*New Skin for the Old Ceremony*, 1974), for instance, is a hire wire act of the sexual in prayer. The refrain reads:

> Oh, take this longing from my tongue
> Whatever useless things these hands have done
> Let me see your beauty broken down
> Like you would do for one you love.

Lest one think these lines are solely erotic—the lover's desire to see his beloved step out from the façade of beauty and break down under his hands and tongue—a later stanza signals the religious doubling:

> I stand in ruins behind you
> With your winter clothes, your broken sandal straps
> I love to see you naked over there
> Especially from the back.

The narrator stands behind his lover, a position of sexual access, "in ruins," spent. He wants his beloved "over there," not addressing him with her eyes and talk but with only her mute back. At a distance, he is shielded from dissolution; he is intact. Yet we recall that "from the back" is also the way we see God. In the Exodus narrative, Moses wishes to see Adonai, before whom Moses must sever his straps and remove his sandals. Moses, in the ruins of awe, can approach God only at a distance, "over there" and "from the back" (Exod. 33:18-23). The image works at once for God and woman, both desired and at arm's length. The first line, "take this longing from my tongue," is both sexual desire and prayer, or following Lurianic kabbalah, prayer arising from the soaring of sex.

"Hallelujah," written a decade later (*Various Positions*, 1984), is Cohen's most famous paean to relation and rupture in sexual-prayerful doubling. Bob Dylan once asked Cohen how long it had taken him to write the song. Cohen lied, saying two years; it was closer to five with numerous stanzas written and discarded. Of the verses usually performed, there are eight, arranged in various combinations. Cohen asked Dylan how long it took to write "I and I." Dylan said, "Fifteen minutes" (Burger 2014: 251).

"Hallelujah" was ignored on its release in 1984, but in 1991 John Cale did a rougher, more erotic piano version for the Cohen tribute album, *I'm Your Fan*, which got enough notice to come to Jeff Buckley's attention. He did an airy, young man's rendition on his 1994 album *Grace*, which reached a new generation of listeners. Rufus Wainwright's twangy recording for the 2001 blockbuster movie *Shrek* sent the song another leap into renown. But the version that best captures Cohen's paradox of desire and fear torqued with spiritual anguish is k. d. lang's shattering performance at the 2005 Juno awards concert. "If what you want," Babette Babich remarks, "is someone to take the house down with Hallelujah, what you want is k.d. lang" (2013: 30).

The song begins with King David and Samson, men unmanned by sexual passion for Bathsheba and Delilah, respectively (Chapter 3). Cohen is again on the terrain of dissolution by desire.

> She tied you to a kitchen chair
> She broke your throne [David],
> and she cut your hair [Samson]
> And from your lips she drew the hallelujah.

This "hallelujah" may be sexual release, possibly sadomasochistic, or the moan of defeat in the war between the sexes, where ordinary "kitchen" intimacy traps male independence. It is being bound to the kitchen that fells ya'. This does not bode well for commitment.

Yet in stanzas added to the original 1984 release, the song moves to a more layered reckoning with women and God. Cohen knows that love should not be a contest for control: "I've seen your flag on the marble arch / Love is not a victory march." Love is not a matter of victory or defeat. It is "a cold and a broken hallelujah," the exaltation, even one broken by breaches, chill, and doubt, of one lover for another, be it person or God.

The following stanza, not in the k. d. lang version, continues,

> There was a time when you let me know
> What's really going on below

But now you never show it to me, do you?
And remember when I loved in you
The holy dove was moving too
And every breath we drew was Hallelujah.

The first three lines of this verse seem to reveal only a breach with
"you," the twined God/woman. The allusion to "below" may signify
the site of sex but also something like "down here on earth." "Never
show it to me," may mean loss of intimacy with God or woman.
The tag line "do you?" taunts God/woman for being inscrutable, for
no longer showing themselves to the men who haplessly need them.
Yet in the second half of the verse, Cohen returns to unavoidable
covenant. In the mode of Lurianic spiritual elation through sex, the
"holy dove" moves in the rush of sexual ecstasy, creating a moment
with God *in* sexual union. The stanza's final "hallelujah," the one we
say with every breath, is masterfully erotic and a prayer-in-thanks
for our (erratic) moments of erotic-spiritual union.

   "Hallelujah" in all its versions has several endings, at least
two returning to God. The one made famous by Buckley's 1994
recording concludes with the "cold and broken hallelujah." The
failed covenanter, emotionally chilled and shattered, comes to
God nonetheless—until of course he bolts again. Cohen's own
1984 recording reflects the more complex anger-amid-covenant. It
concludes:

even though it all went wrong
I'll stand before the lord of song
With nothing on my tongue but hallelujah.

It went wrong; we fail covenant with others and God. Yet in the
end, standing before him, we have no choice but to commit to
"hallelujah." This commitment is the unavoidable covenant of the
cosmos. It returns us to the psalter *Book of Mercy*, published the
same year. From our inadequate humanness, we seek a God we do
not fully understand, whose embrace is the basis of all embraces,
and from whom we flee. To return in hallelujah.

   "Night Comes On," like "Hallelujah" from *Various Positions*
(1984), contains one of Cohen's most self-aware admissions of his
emotional double-bindedness: "I needed so much to have nothing
to touch / I've always been greedy that way." To be free of needing
to touch—how tempting intactness and independence is. As Henry

Bean suggests (2018), the very intimacy we desire threatens our autonomy and thus existence, or so we believe (Chapter 3). Under the Damoclean Sword of ever-possible annihilation-through-love, self-enclosure becomes self-protection, and we are greedy for it. Cohen knew this to be true of himself at age fifty in "Night Comes On" but also as a young man in 1963, when his protagonist/alter ego in *The Favourite Game* wants to keep the girl Shell "400 miles away" while writing her "pretty poems and letters" (cited in Simmons 2012: 368)—when he wants to be a "hypnotist" of others while remaining untouched, the harem's puppeteer.

Song of Songs before the Female Divine: Darker Still

Also in "Night Comes On" (*Various Positions*, 1984) Cohen further presses his conflated imagery by evoking the divine not as God/ Jesus or God the Father but as the *shekhina*, the Jewish image of the divine as a female presence. Both spiritual and bodily love are now represented by the feminine. Relations with women and God are here fully one—as is rupture of those relationships. To gain or lose one is to gain and lose both. Cohen writes,

> Now I look for her always; I'm lost in this calling;
> I'm tied to the threads of some prayer.
> Saying, "When will she summon me, when will she
> come to me,
> what must I do to prepare?"—
> Then she bends to my longing, like a willow, like a fountain,
> she stands in the luminous air ...
> I want to cross over; I want to go home,
> but she says, "*Go back, go back to the world.*"

The "her" that Cohen is looking for suggests the divine, who bids him to his "calling" (as to the priesthood) and binds him with the "threads of some prayer." Yet it also evokes the woman who bends to his longing and toward whom he wants to "cross over," to be home. This woman may be a lover but also mother. An earlier stanza makes a double allusion to Mother Earth and to Cohen's own

mother, who had died in 1978. Will she, this God/*shekhina*/woman/
mother, summon him or come to him herself? The phrase "I want
to go home" refers triply to the female: the oneness of the mother's
womb, the union of sexual relations ("she bends to my longing"),
and the return to the *shekhina*. But none of these unions lasts; he
cannot go "home." "She"—mother, lover, *shekhina*/God—sends
him back into the quotidian world.

"She" sends him away. Here again Cohen fears rejection—women
won't let him in—as much as he fears control and dissolution by
the women he wants to let him in. He craves the contact, fears he
won't get it, and fears that getting it will entrap him. The double
bind reprises. But it is not a bond, not a *brith* (covenant). Here, it
is doubly not, for the female who sends him away is the *shekhina*.
Bond with God and woman are lost to him at once.

While sex as a portal to spirit is frequent in Cohen's work, the
doubling of God and woman, as with the *shekhina* in "Night Comes
On," is not. But neither is this doubling confined to "Night Comes
On." In the poem "Basket" ([2006] 2007: 51), it is conjured up in a
quite personal way for the artist. Cohen advises the writer of poems
to collect his work and,

> when the basket is full
> someone will appear
> to whom you can present it ...
> and your basket will bounce
> like a speck in the sunlight
> on the immense landscape
> of her lap.

Her lap, indeed. The poet presents his work to the female, whose lap
is not only the site of female sexuality, which receives his body. It is
also the immense landscape of the world, which receives his poems,
wherein lies his soul.

God as Covenant Breaker

Imagining God as a female presence allows for a new indictment in
Cohen's theodicy. The divinity who made us for relation but unable
to sustain it is herself female. Human failure is *her* design. Desire for
the female and anger at her is now projected onto God. And in songs

like "Night Comes On" (*Various Positions*, 1984) she too breaches commitment. She sends us away, back into the world, to Boogie Street and Babylon. Much of Cohen's work asks why God created persons with the capacity to abandon covenant. Foiled relationship is humanity's move even if we are allowed it by God. Here in "Night Comes On," it is *her* move, God's. Cohen ratchets up the charge.

Further indictments follow, again in a rough chronology of Cohen's work. In the music video for "Dance Me to the End of Love," released in 1985, the year after "Night Comes On," a beautiful woman draws a sheet over the face of her dead husband (played by Cohen). She dances away from the body, and when, in a dream-like moment, his hand reaches for hers, she slips out of reach, her wedding ring sliding carelessly into a medical decanter. She moves on to become a stage performer as his soul follows her from afar. In the last frame, she covers her face so he can no longer hold even to her image. In life, it was Cohen who escaped relationship by running to performances and the "many sweet companions / Many satisfying one-night stands" that followed them ("Why Don't You Try," *New Skin for the Old Ceremony*, 1974). Yet in Cohen's fear-scape, it is *she* who is in control and she who leaves.

The video reprises both the fear of the ice princess who won't let him approach ("One of Us Can't Be Wrong") and of the rejecting *shekhina* who pushes him away ("Night Comes On"). *She* holds herself back at a distance, she doesn't put out, and sends him back into the world. The "end of love" in this video is not the romantic "till death do us part" that more sentimental videos accompanying this song portray. It is the bitter plea: not "dance me till the end of love" but dance me till you end our love.

Three years later in "Ain't No Cure for Love" (*I'm Your Man*, 1988) Cohen writes, "And I call to you, I call to you / But I don't call soft enough." However he approaches, it does not seem to be right; she does not come. The ice princess reprises. He longs for her hands, hair, bracelets, and brush and yet is rejected again by *her*. As the song continues, this "her" takes shape as a woman *and* divine spirit. "It don't matter how it all went wrong ... there ain't no cure for love." The first words of the lyric are from the verse in "Hallelujah" where Cohen returns to God: "even though it all went wrong / I'll stand before the lord of song / with nothing on my tongue by hallelujah." In repeating this famous line in "Ain't No Cure for Love," Cohen evokes our longing for God at the same time as he calls to "her" of the bracelets and brush. His longing is doubled for "she," woman and female divine. And it is the conflated God/woman who sends him away.

She breaches *brith*. What an idea: everything Cohen raged about women turns out to be true of God. It is not only humanity that abandons covenant but God. Cohen is no less clear about God's covenant breaches in "Closing Time" (*The Future*, 1992). While the divine here is not figured female, he is as guilty as the *shekhina*/woman of "Night Comes On." He creates us for love, makes sure we can't sustain it, and voids his bond. He sends us away from the (heavenly) gates much as "she" of "Night Comes On" sends us back into the world. Though in "Closing Time," the freedom of severed commitment "looks like freedom but it feels like death," we still cannot stop ourselves from freedom's temptations—from the booze and bar scene of negligent sex—no matter how deadly they feel.

The song conjures up a modern bacchanal:

> And I swear it happened just like this
> A sigh, a cry, a hungry kiss
> The gates of love they budged an inch
> I can't say much has happened since ...
> And the whole damn place goes crazy twice
> And it's once for the devil and once for Christ
> But the boss don't like these dizzy heights ...
> it's partner found, it's partner lost
> And it's hell to pay when the fiddler stops.

"The whole damn place," the whole of humanity, yearns passionately for devilish (sexual) love and love of Christ—or for love of God *in* sexual embrace. The gates of love that budge evoke the gates of heaven. They open an inch. But "the boss," the God who made us for love, doesn't like these heights, be they mystical or material. This is the new charge that we saw in "Night Comes On": *God* disdains the intensity of love even as he creates us for it. So he made us easily able to trounce it. The best we manage is a "partner found, it's partner lost" and the wretched loneliness at the party's end, when "the fiddler stops." God leaves us to this end at Closing Time.

The image of closing time calls up the *Ne'ilah* service, the prayer that closes Yom Kippur, the Jewish Day of Atonement. It is the moment when God determines humanity's fate for the coming year, metaphorically closing the gates of heaven. But, in Cohen's account, God has already turned away and left us to our murderous bacchanal.

The charge of God abandoning his bond with us was written when Cohen was fifty-nine. In 2001, at age sixty-seven, Cohen was railing still, "You kiss my lips, and then it's done: I'm back on Boogie Street" ("Boogie Street," *Ten New Songs*, with Sharon Robinson). "You" may be God, woman, both, or the God/woman of the *shekhina*. Cohen again has but a partner gained or a partner lost and is thrust back into Boogie Street on his own. Two years later, Cohen commented on his sexual encounters in nearly the same words: it "lasted just a few moments, and then it was back to the old horror story ... I'll give you this if you give me that. You know, sealing the deal: what do I get, what do you get. It's a contract" (Hampson 2007). But it is not covenant. While Cohen's resentment may have abated somewhat in his next decade, his years with Anjani Thomas, in these songs, his bond with women remains self-interested contract, not covenant, and he wonders if even God can forge one.

Cohen was still unsure two years before his death when he wrote "Samson in New Orleans" (*Popular Problems*, 2014, with Patrick Leonard): "Was our prayer so damn unworthy / The Son rejected it?" Are we, God's children, so unfit that God has left his own creation? The song is a furious keen for the neglect of the city during hurricane Katrina, a keen as furious as Voltaire's poem for the Lisbon earthquake. Cohen insists on the theodical question posed by David Hume: if God cannot prevent such suffering, he is impotent. If he can and doesn't, he is wretched and has no covenant with us. And would we want one with such a God?

What can be said in summation of Cohen's writings about women and the divine? In the 1967 "Sisters of Mercy" (*Songs of Leonard Cohen*), he wrote that "loneliness says that you've sinned." We leave God and each other. It is our sin though it is by God's design that we are able to commit it. By the 1984 "Night Comes On" and the 1992 "Closing Time," he was charging God with leaving as well.

Cohen spent much of his life making art from his fear of the love he desired: union with God and the female, or God through the female. In their beauty and grace, he found the threat of entrapment and paradoxically of rejection. The ice princess won't let him in, but when she does, he flees in self-protection. In both cases, he is at a loss for control. It's a war. Cohen preferred the less risky intactness of the exit. But then things get worse. In the end, we commit all our bonding and bolting because we were created able to commit it by "the boss," who himself doesn't like passion's dizzying heights ("Closing Time"). What then are we to make of God's covenant, and where does that leave us?

7

Betrayal of God, Betrayal of Persons, Political Betrayals: Cohen's Trinity

Cohen's "political" work was almost always more philosophy than politics. To be sure, it names present iterations of abuse by the rich and powerful. But it more intently seeks to understand the foundations of self-absorption as ground for such abuse. This chapter looks at the role of covenant and its breaches in this self-absorption. "Anthem" (*The Future*, 1992), for instance, describes,

> The holy dove
> She will be caught again
> Bought and sold
> And bought again
> The dove is never free.

We have seen the holy dove in the unavoidable "Hallelujah," signifying Lurianic oneness with God. In "Anthem," the bond with God is violated and traded for gain. Thus, relationship with the very ground for existence is lost to us. Breaking covenant with God—buying and selling the holy dove—is what's going on in the grab for lucre and power.

Cohen introduced the link between politics and covenant in "The Story of Isaac" (*Songs from a Room*, 1969). It begins by retelling Abraham's near-sacrifice of his son (Gen. 22:1-19) and became what critic Mikal Gilmore in 1985 called the best antiwar song of the past thirty years (Boucher 2004: 108). It asks: the biblical narrative ends in forbidding violence, especially disguised as God's command. Covenant with another person, Isaac, cannot be breached. Abraham may not sacrifice him even for the sake of bond with God because the covenants with God and among persons are inseparable. Should Abraham breach one, the other is undone. Now, to all present-day "schemers," as Cohen calls them, what's your excuse for killing children?

In the same period, Cohen joins the crime of rape with betrayal of the covenant of marriage. In *Beautiful Losers* (1966), the main female character Edith is gang-raped in the woods at age thirteen. Her husband, who marries her when she is sixteen, has only this to say in retelling the story: "Follow her young young bum" and "Edith, forgive me, it was the thirteen-year-old victim I always fucked" (Cohen [1966] 1993: 59). Incapable of emotional attachment, the husband ruminates philosophically on the "collective will" that fated Edith's rape: "Who can trace the subtle mechanics of the collective will to which we all contribute?" (Cohen [1966] 1993: 61). From this abstract perch, the self-protective distance of the Cohen repertoire, Edith's husband frees himself from empathy and the covenant of marriage. He is the man who, when Edith commits suicide, feasts on a meal of chicken, slang for young girl.

When Cohen protests our breaches of commitment, he calls for a reckoning. He writes in "Anthem" (*The Future*, 1992),

> I can't run no more
> With that lawless crowd
> While the killers in high places
> Say their prayers out loud
> … And they're going to hear from me.

Beware, you lawless folk, Cohen warns, Cohen will raise his voice against you. The threat is seen again in "Samson in New Orleans," Cohen's enraged eulogy for the city during hurricane Katrina (*Popular Problems*, 2014, with Patrick Leonard):

> So gather up the killers
> Get everyone in town
> Stand me by those pillars
> Let me take this temple down.

From this ire and outrage, one would think Cohen was really going to do something about the lawless and the killers who cloak their crimes in self-righteousness.

But Cohen understood that his moral lapse lay in not making good on his reckoning call. In allowing abuse and injustice, he fails not only law but also covenant. In 1973, he knew that joining the Israeli army's entertainment detail in the Yom Kippur War was a means to escape living with Susan Elrod as much as it was commitment to Israel ("There Is a War," *New Skin for the Old Ceremony*, 1974). In 2001, at age sixty-seven, he wrote with similar self-awareness in "The Land of Plenty" (*Ten New Songs*, with Sharon Robinson),

> Don't really have the courage
> To stand where I must stand.
> Don't really have the temperament
> To lend a helping hand.

This is self-critique on Cohen's part as much as a charge against those who shirk political justice by saying they don't have the temperament for it—the way one might not have the temperament for poker or hockey. The narrator, like many of us, slouches away from the moral and political, or the moral in the political.

After the September 11, 2001 terrorist attacks against the United States, Cohen wrote "On That Day" (*Dear Heather*, 2004). The narrator proclaims, "I'm just holding the fort." Who is this "I" who insists he is just a placeholder with no more responsibility than the man in "Land of Plenty"? The next lines implicate all of us who didn't look at the "sins against g-d" and "crimes in the world"—breached covenant with God and persons—that brought the terrorist attacks to America. Like "Land of Plenty," this is both self-critique and charge against society. Some say, Cohen writes, that the attacks were "what we deserve." Perhaps, he implies, something should be done about those sins and crimes. But "I" is a man of evasion under the guise of "I wouldn't know." Or maybe, as in "Land of Plenty," he just doesn't have the "temperament" to deal with such things as sins and crimes. So they remain unaddressed.

Cohen's dual-covenant theme continues in "Puppets" (*Thanks for the Dance*, 2019) with its inventory of political crimes committed by those who say they're just cogs in the system, just puppets.

> Puppet me and puppet you
> Puppet German
> Puppet Jew
> Puppet Presidents command
> Puppet troops to burn the land.

In "Israel" (*Book of Mercy*, in Cohen 1994: 323), Cohen writes, "To every people the land is given on condition. Perceived or not, there is a Covenant." Here in "Puppets," he accuses: we have broken that bond. As we assure ourselves that we're helpless puppets without responsibility, the land, given by God for our survival, burns. We have left him.

Lyrics as Confessional, Reprised

In his writings about politics, Cohen uses lyrics as his confessional much as he did in confessing lovin'-and-leavin' women (Chapter 6). The *eminence grise* of eliding commitment again bares his soul. *New Skin for the Old Ceremony* is a particularly layered instance. On one hand, Cohen confesses that his political engagement (in the Yom Kippur War) was a self-interested flight from commitment to Suzanne Elrod ("There Is a War"). On the other, in "A Singer Must Die," he also claims sympathy for himself. Love me; I'm the victim. The perps in "A Singer" are those in the political system who have "their knee in your balls and their fist in your face / Yes and long live the state by whoever it's made." The artist, he writes, must die for exposing this:

> Then read me the list of the crimes that are mine ...
> Your vision is right, my vision is wrong
> I'm sorry for smudging the air with my song.

In these two tracks, "There Is a War" and "A Singer Must Die," back to back on the album, Cohen is at once the coward who confesses to leaving woman and child and, because he confesses in *art*, in song, warrants our admiration. He has exposed his sins and so is a martyr to be loved and revered.

The self-presentation as coward and martyr was in 1974. In 2004 in "On That Day" (*Dear Heather*, 2004), with thirty years more skill at the confessional, he executes a double catapult to renown by implicating his audience as well. He wins our adoration when he confesses to his own political covenant betrayals ("I wouldn't know / I'm just holding the fort") *and* when he accuses "you," his audience, of betraying responsibility as well. "But answer me this" he writes, "Did *you* go crazy / Or did *you* report." "Report" is what you do when you sign-in with your commanding officer, when you commit to doing something. Cohen wants to know which one of us stepped up, committed to political action. As we nod gravely that alas, we didn't, we love him for wresting our confession. We are so proud of our self-critique and somber admissions. And we adore him for bringing us to this mature self-recognition.

Cohen's anguish at human cruelty was serious, but he also understood the adulation he got for being cruelty's merciless prosecutor—prosecutor of his own and our sins. Feeling guilty makes us feel like the good guys, and we exalt the prophet who proffers this. As with his confessions about women, it is the perfect form of exaltation. It lathers Cohen with love yet requires no commitment. At the end of the revel, audiences leave—and leave him alone.

The Breach Is Triune in Interwoven and Conflated Imagery

In "On That Day" (*Dear Heather*, 2004), Cohen brings together "sins against g-d," "crimes in the world," and the September 11 political attacks. These are his trinity of covenant breaches: with God, with other persons in the world, and in political crimes—a dark mirror to the Father, the person of Jesus, and the Spirit that is on earth to guide us to the moral life. The following section seeks to make two points: first, that Cohen both conflates and interweaves images of each betrayal among the verses of his songs much as he conflates and interweaves images of the entwined covenant with God and with persons/women. Second, he does so because, on his understanding, we don't betray our commitments sequentially: with God, lovers, and then strangers. It's humanity's great talent to betray them at once, seeing to our self-protection and self-interest in all these arenas. There is little we wouldn't do to others to secure them. After all, a husband is capable of saying about his raped wife, "Follow her young young bum" (Cohen [1966] 1993: 59).

The song "Everybody Knows" (with Sharon Robinson, *I'm Your Man*, 1988) is a template for interwoven images. It begins with politics:

Everybody knows the war is over
Everybody knows the good guys lost
Everybody knows the fight was fixed
The poor stay poor, the rich get rich.

Cohen then slithers into the unfaithfulness of love:

Everybody knows you've been discreet
But there were so many people you just had to meet
Without your clothes
And everybody knows.

The image of the betraying lover then moves to the betrayed God, who was abandoned at Calvary and is discarded again daily:

From the bloody cross on top of Calvary
To the beach of Malibu
Everybody knows it's coming apart
Take one last look at this Sacred Heart
Before it blows
And everybody knows.

We betray God on the cross and on beautiful beaches. With covenant thrice trounced, in politics, love, and faith, the world is ready to blow.

Indeed, what bonds remain to keep it together if covenant is thrice done for? As they are of a piece, breaching one rends the others, and humanity is adept of gashing all three. The interweaving and conflation of images to present this human talent appear in works both before and after "Everybody Knows." I'll look at one example from the 1970s, before "Everybody Knows" was written, and one or two from each decade after.

"Field Commander Cohen" (*Tour of 1979*, 2001) begins as an indictment of both US foreign policy ("Parachuting acid into diplomatic cocktail parties") and quotidian US living, from waiting in line to racial inequities. But the song then turns to a more specific accusation: "But many men are falling, / Where you promised to stand guard." Who is this "you" who fails to protect? It has the feel of the "I" in "On That Day," the evader of responsibility who is "just holding the fort" or of the puppet-people in "Puppets." Cohen may mean political leaders given the public trust, or citizens responsible for their democracy, or God in covenant with the world, or a conflation of all three. None stands guard. Cohen continues, "I heard you cast your lot along with the poor," which suggests he is addressing God. Yet in the next passage, "you" is in hock with the "Yankee dollar" and so is likely a human exploiter. The lines wrap together covenant between person and God and among persons of the body politic. Both bonds, it appears, have collapsed. We are not saving ourselves, and even God is no longer our savior. He is not standing guard.

The final verse adds something else: "Ah, lover come and lie with me, / if my lover is who you are." This seems to be neither the divine nor the political but, as in "Everybody Knows," the appearance of the personal. Cohen completes his trifecta. The covenants with God, in politics, and in personal relations are of a piece and are broken. The song ends with Cohen reporting these lines: "Till love is pierced and love is hung, / And every kind of freedom done, then oh, / Oh my love." "Pierced" and "hung" in the Cohen lexicon are words of the crucifixion. Until Jesus, in his love for humanity, is crucified and understood by us and until political freedom is with us, we do not have love. Till then, what ties are left to bind the world?

Moving forward a decade, on the same album as "Everybody Knows" (with Sharon Robinson, *I'm Your Man*, 1988), Cohen links his trinity of betrayals to our daily commercialism and to the hegemony that the United States casually assumes. In "First We Take Manhattan," he writes, "I don't like your fashion business mister / And I don't like these drugs that keep you thin. / I don't like what happened to my sister...." His response is first a prayer: "I prayed for this, to let my work begin." The work is to take down Manhattan, center of America's financial empire, and Berlin, symbol of US military might during the Cold War, when the song was written. Taking on greed and militarism, paragons of trashed covenant, is the holy work which we pray to begin. Or the work would be holy were we to do it, which, Cohen observes, we don't or don't for long.

The 1992 album *The Future* contains perhaps Cohen's darkest comments on politics, in the title song "The Future" and the song "Democracy," both of which I'll discuss here. "The Future" is Cohen's answer to the book of Revelation, which presages the apocalypse. Cohen's apocalypse, what he thinks the future brings, will make Stalin and the Berlin Wall look like lightweights compared to the destruction we are inviting by the way we live. He writes, "Take the only tree that's left / And stuff it up the hole / In your culture." He looks at the way we abuse sex and drugs, torture each other, and destroy the planet. We owe God penance not only for breaches with him but with each other and the natural world. The trinity of covenant breaches reappears. He concludes, "Things are going to slide, slide in all directions / ... When they said repent /

I wonder what they meant." He doesn't wonder, actually. Cohen knows we don't repent our rent commitments, or that we do until we rend them again.

It is in "The Future" that Cohen famously called himself the "little Jew / Who wrote the Bible." He is the biblical prophet of calamity: "Your servant here, he has been told / To say it clear, to say it cold." The prophet/narrator of the song has seen nations emerge and collapse and concludes, "Love's the only engine of survival." But we're too late. We have gashed and shattered too much.

It's over, it ain't going
Any further
And now the wheels of heaven stop
You feel the devil's riding crop
Get ready for the future
It is murder.

"Democracy," inspired in 1992 by the fall of the Berlin Wall three years earlier, is both more hopeful than "The Future" and a sardonic lambaste. The refrain blares: "Democracy is coming to the USA." This may be hope but it is mostly sarcasm. The song reminds us that the problem from which we run is political but more deeply, lost prayer, grace, and covenant, here expressed as the Sermon on the Mount. Cohen begins with the political:

It's coming through a hole in the air
From those nights in Tiananmen Square ...
From the wars against disorder
From the sirens night and day
From the fires of the homeless
From the ashes of the gay
Democracy is coming to the USA.

From the struggles at Tiananmen Square and with the cops, poverty, homelessness, and prejudice, something of democracy may rise. But a few stanzas on, Cohen comes to the spiritual:

from the staggering account
of the Sermon on the Mount ...
From the wells of disappointment
Where the women kneel to pray

For the grace of God in the desert here
And the desert far away
Democracy is coming to the USA.

The political covenant of democracy will emerge from the covenants preached in Jesus' sermon, remembered in kneeling prayer, and promised in grace—if it comes at all.

Cohen evokes his broken trinity again in *Ten New Songs* (2001, with Sharon Robinson). I'll look at the first and final tracks, "In My Secret Life" and "Land of Plenty." In the first, we find the interweaving of bonds with God, among persons, and in politics—all shattered. It begins with broken love,

I miss you so much
There's no one in sight
And we're still making love
In my secret life.

Interwoven in this personal longing is political abandonment,

Looked through the paper
Makes you wanna cry
Nobody cares if the people
Live or die.

The song closes much as "Everybody Knows" does, by looking at our abandoned commitments and loneliness as we are blocked—or block ourselves—from relation with others and God.

I'm always alone
And my heart is like ice
And it's crowded and cold
In my secret life.

Again as in "Everybody Knows," with covenant thrice trounced, in politics, love, and in our hearts, what remains to bind our world together?

We know Cohen's "cold" and "frozenness" from earlier writing (Chapter 5). In the 1961 "Brighter than Our Sun," for instance, Cohen writes, "And what happened to love / In the gleaming universe? / It froze in the heart of God" (*The Spice Box of Earth*, available online at: https://genius.com/Leonard-cohen-brighter-than-our-sun-annotated). With a chill, the refrain of the 1979 "The Window" echoes: "Oh chosen love, Oh frozen love / Oh tangle of matter and ghost" (*Recent Songs*). In these works, love, ever vibrant in the heart of God, is frozen in our material human condition. In the 2001 "In My Secret Life," the hardness of ice blocks us still. We are alone, our giving to others and receiving from them stymied. In politics, as in love, we retreat into the safe intactness of cold.

In the album's final track "Land of Plenty," Cohen takes up the prophetic voice as he did a decade earlier in the 1992 "The Future," the prophetic voice of apocalyptic calamity. In the first verse of "Plenty" he writes, "Don't really know who sent me / To raise my voice and say." He doesn't know from where the call comes but once given this voice, he argues for the forgotten in politics and in faith—not only the poor and imprisoned but Christ:

> For the millions in a prison,
> That wealth has set apart
> For the Christ who has not risen,
> From the caverns of the heart ...
> For what's left of our religion,
> I lift my voice and pray.

The Cohen catechism is reprised: the abandonments of others and of God are bound.

The prophetic voice is taken up again in "Almost Like the Blues" (*Popular Problems*, 2014, with Patrick Leonard). Cohen writes, "I've had the invitation / That a sinner can't refuse / And it's almost like salvation." Cohen has again been called like the unwilling Jeremiah to expose the litany of our political sins: starvation, murder, rape, burning villages, torture, disappeared children are the sampling in this song. So though the smart set, "the great professor / Of all there is to know," dismisses God, heaven, and the consequences of hell, Cohen, now called, cannot evade the prophet's task. It is daunting. Following the invocation of our abuses, Cohen confesses he is overwhelmed,

> I have to die a little
> Between each murderous thought
> And when I'm finished thinking
> I have to die a lot.

Each reckoning with human brutality kills off another piece of the self. A bit of us dies in the face of our savagery. What's a prophet to do? "So I let my heart get frozen / To keep away the rot." Here again is the image of frozenness. It both keeps him from sustaining love as we saw in "Brighter than Our Sun," "The Window," and "My Secret Life." But it also protects him from the pain of brutality and maimed love. That, after all, is the point about being frozen and intact. It seal us from pain and love, or the pain of love.

Alas, the freeze doesn't really work. The prophets and God feel the pain of the hacksaws we take to each other. That's the "point" of being a prophet as it was the "point" about Jesus (Babich 2014: Kindle Location 2407). The rest of us, by contrast, treat the cruelties that are not happening to us as newsy entertainment. In "Almost Like the Blues," Cohen's recitation of human suffering includes not only torture and disappeared children but the self-mockery of "all my bad reviews." This is both an admission of personal self-absorption by the covenant fail-er par excellence and a public *j'accuse*. In our self-absorbed worlds, the victims of our disregard are invisible to us, blocked by the barriers of class and race. We whine about the narcissistic wounds of bad reviews as if they were the equals of starvation and murder. Cohen's ledger of our cruelties ends sardonically, "It was acid, it was tragic / It was almost like the blues" as if the mayhem we perpetrate has the entertainment value of a good blues set. The persecution of the Jews and gypsies, he continues, was also entertaining, not "boring" at all. So frozen are we—all but the prophets and God—that the world's butchery rolls by like whatever we're watching on the telly.

What's the tally? We break the commitments we need with those we know and those we don't know in the politics of our globally entwined lives. We know it and do it nonetheless. This is the wiliness of *yetzer ha'ra*, the will to evil, in rabbinic thought (Gen. Rabbah 22:6). It is Paul's observation in Rom. 7:19: "For I do not do the good I want to do, but the evil I do not want to do—this I keep on doing." It is the theodical puzzle that hounded Cohen: we are recidivists in triune betrayal. But, Cohen whispers, why is this so? Is this not of God's making—the work of the God who said "I locked you in this body / I meant it as a kind of trial" ("Lover Lover Lover," *New Skin for the Old Ceremony*, 1974)?

The 2012 "Amen" (*Old Ideas*) is among Cohen's most important political works and in some ways a companion piece to the 1988 "Everybody Knows" both in political import and in imagery that interweaves the personal, political, and theological. I will close this section with it.

While in the earlier song, "Everybody knows it's coming apart," in "Amen," we thrice do not want to know. The song begins with the personal refusal to know: you can tell me what's going on in all the groaning places of the world when I'm off drugs and sober. Till then, I'm too out of it to pay attention. Political blindness then moves in: "Tell me again / When the victims are singing / And the laws of remorse are restored." Let me know about the world's brutality when the victims are healed, law is reinstated, and the citizenry, content. In a staggering image, religious complacency then enters: tell me of the world's sins "when the filth of the butcher / Is washed in the blood of the lamb." Tell me about the suffering when our butchery is already redeemed. Cohen continues, tell me "when the rest of the culture / Has passed thru' the Eye of the Camp," when the world has grappled with the Nazi concentration camps of Auschwitz and Dachau. This is as likely, Cohen writes, as an elephant passing through the eye of a needle (*b. Berakhot* 55b) or a camel doing the same (Mt. 19:23-24). Until then, the narrator doesn't want to be bothered.

Bothered with what? The last line of every verse takes a turn. It is not only the world's butcheries that the narrator avoids but love. Cohen writes at the end of each stanza: "tell me that you want me" "love me" "need me *then*," later, after I'm sober, victims are healed, and humanity, redeemed. Tell me at the vanishing horizon of after-all-is-saved, at the messiah's arrival. Don't tell me now. The addressee could be a woman. Perhaps the narrator can't bring himself to talk of love with misery rampant. Or maybe he wants to evade her by making the bar to love impossibly high: don't tell me about love till the messiah is with us.

But these lines are also a theodical indictment. The "you" implicit in "don't' tell me" about love may be understood also as God. To suggest this reading, each verse closes with "Amen." Cohen charges: You, God, don't tell me about your wanting and needing love with humankind while you allow us such barbarism. You can wax grandly covenantal in your Scripture and revelation after you've stopped the mayhem here. Until then, your love is not frozen but hot air.

The Holocaust

In his trinity of covenant breaches, Cohen understands political brutality as rooted in our daily breaches of covenant with God and among persons. This understanding undergirds Cohen's work also on the Holocaust. With Primo Levi, author of *Survival in Auschwitz* ([1947] 2008), Cohen warns that we should not repeat abuse in our unremarkable daily lives as we should not perpetrate violence on the larger landscape of politics. To be sure, the extraordinary, *un*domestic horror of the Nazi program is vivid in Cohen's work. In "Lovers" (*Let Us Compare Mythologies*, [1956] 2019), a kiss confronts the image of the gestapo extracting gold fillings from the teeth of the gassed dead. "Dance Me to the End of Love" (*Various Positions*, 1984) opens with the image of a "burning violin," a reference to the emaciated concentration camp inmates forced to play music as fellow inmates were force-marched into gas chambers of Zyklon B.

Yet Cohen neither rants against Nazis nor explains them. In *Flowers for Hitler* (1964), he does not think there's much to say about them beyond the human condition, in which self-absorption and cruelty flourish everywhere. Indeed, the poetry collection *Flowers for Hitler* opens with Primo Levi's warning about the ubiquity of our abuse, which Cohen explained in 1967: "The [Primo Levi] quotation is, 'Take care not to let it happen in your own homes.'... That's what *Flowers for Hitler* is all about. It's taking the mythology of the concentration camps and bringing it into the living room saying, 'This is what we do to each other'" (Burger 2014: 14).

In "The Failure of a Secular Life," from *Flowers for Hitler*, Cohen literally brings the concentration camp into the living room as he describes a Nazi torturer coming home from a hard day's work: "His wife hit him with an open nerve / and a cry the trade never heard. / He watched her real-life Dachau" (in Cohen 1994: 56). The camps were a horror. But the domestic Dachau was her cross. Or rather, it would be her cross were faith present. But this sort of domestic cruelty is the "failure of the secular life," one without commitment to God or persons. If "holy" is the bond with God and persons, the secular cannot help but abandon both as they are entwined.

The link between public horrors and quotidian abuse is with Cohen still half a century later in the 2014 song "Nevermind" (*Popular Problems*, with Patrick Leonard). He begins by describing the erasure of the people (and culture) who lose a war to the powers that run the planet. The winner inattentively, perhaps inadvertently, writes over the names that are "dust" to the victor and "blood" to the defeated.

And all of this
Expressions of

The sweet indifference
Some call love
The high indifference
Some call fate
But we had names
More intimate.

The erasure by the powerful is not the obvious horror of Nazi camps but the sin of indifference that we commit in passing, in simply not at/tending to those before us. It turns hearts into "swarms of flies," Cohen writes, and mouths into "bowls of lies." The cruelty of inattention is the import of Primo Levi's passage and of Cohen quoting it. This, both insist, is what we must not permit.

Cohen's presentation of the Holocaust as inseparable from quotidian cruelty was in part his response to the problem of writing about it at all. As Theodor Adorno set out in his 1955 essay, "Kulturkritik und Gesellchaft" ["Cultural Criticism and Society," 1955: vol. 10a, 30], making art about the Holocaust is impossible. Any attempt to capture or comment on it reproduces it as an aestheticized object, a simulacrum constructed out of artifice that drains the historical events of their horror. We are silenced between the difficulty of imagining such brutality from our perch within "normal" life and the difficulty of imagining normal life after such staggering cruelty.

Sandra Wynands suggests that Cohen tried to get beyond the problem of aestheticizing Auschwitz by flouting the expectable conventions of poetry so as not to make his writing "art" (1999). His technique, she suggests, was an *épater les bourgeois* style reminiscent of the late-nineteenth-century Decadent poets, who reveled in symbols of decay and perversion to show disgust with the commercialism and so-called "progress" of the day. Wynands holds that Cohen succeeded in forging a style sufficiently rebarbative to confront the Holocaust without aestheticizing it.

But any style, however initially outrageous, soon becomes acceptable and then nostalgia—a devolution Cohen understood. One also cannot avoid aestheticizing carnage by having "no style" as that too soon becomes a style. In the poem "Style" (*Flowers for Hitler*, in Cohen 1994: 68), Cohen makes this point, writing that he will forget such typical items of nostalgia as his mother's lawn and his childhood phone number. And then he adds, "I will forget my style / I will have no style." This is part his intention and part (self)mockery, a send-up of artists who proclaim that they have no style and so are the true and final exposers of things as they "really" are. Yet their nonstyle unavoidably becomes acceptable and then an item for nostalgia or kitsch.

So it may not have been flummoxing the bourgeoisie with an outrageous no-style that Cohen was after in *Flowers for Hitler*. Rather, he was interested in shattering the comforting binary between the "outrageous" and the "normal." The binary says those were extraordinary times; "we" don't do that sort of (Nazi) barbarism now. Cohen and Primo Levi held that we do and that we must write about it.

In insisting on a continuity between the gross brutality of the Holocaust and quotidian cruelty, Cohen shares something with both the Polish philosopher Zygmunt Bauman and Simone Weil, the French-Jewish philosopher and activist who in 1943 starved herself to death in England at age thirty-four, eating only the food she believed those in occupied France could get. In *Modernity and the Holocaust*, Bauman holds that the Nazi systematic murder of millions was not a barbaric exception to modernity but its outcome. "The truth is that every 'ingredient' of the Holocaust—all those things that rendered it possible—was normal ... in keeping with everything we know about our civilization" (Bauman 1989: 8). The seeds of the Holocaust are in our daily, modern living, where cruelties of all sorts are committed, as Levi and Cohen insisted.

Weil too saw our cruelty to others as the usual state of human affairs, motivated by our self-absorbed competition for survival. The exceptional moment, she wrote, is the "sacrament" of compassion, a meld of covenantal giving and Christ's donative love (1974: 95). We perform this sacrament not on our own but only when God moves through one person toward an afflicted other, when Christ acts *in* the giver (1951: 93). In this bold assertion of the entwined covenant, the bond between God and person literally forges bond among persons.

Compassion, Weil writes, "only Christ has done it" (1974: 94), a philosophic-poetic turn that could be mistaken for a Cohen lyric. Weil and Cohen understood that we cannot help but strive toward God and others, yet we bolt in fear of annihilation or we trade commitment for worldly gain. We are, Weil famously wrote, like a fly in a bottle straining to reach the light (of God and love) yet we remain ever behind the transparent capsule. Nonetheless, she concluded, "one must stay pressed against the glass" (1970: 292).

Cohen might put it differently: that we *do* stay pressed against the glass because covenant, relation, is the nature of our (solitary) existence. We remain, by God's design, pressed behind the bell jar we can't see, reaching for the love we flee from in self-protection from it.

With the intent to complicate the binary between the Nazi Holocaust and daily life and expose the "outrageous" self-absorption in "normal" living, *Flowers for Hitler* notes how quickly, after the systematic murder of millions, life returns to its ordinary contours—even buses run and movies are made ("A Migrating Dialogue," Cohen [1964] 1973: 86). This observation, Pawel Dobrosielski and Marcin Napiorkowski note, echoes the poem "Campo di Fiori" by Polish poet and Nobel prize winner Czesław Miłosz. The poem brings together two events, the destruction of the Warsaw Ghetto and the burning of philosopher and mathematician Giordano Bruno in the year 1600. "Even before the flames had died, observes Miłosz … life went back to normal, and merchants were selling such ordinary things as lemons and olives at the very same square the horror had taken place" (Dobrosielski and Napiorkowski 2014: Kindle Location 2829).

Cohen's indictment broadens the blame. He notices not only that the quotidian selling of lemons and olives erases extraordinary horror, as Milosz wrote, but that quotidian culture itself is horror-ful. In *Flowers for Hitler*, Wynands correctly observes (with echoes of Bauman), "disparate figures of contemporary Western culture [historical figures, cartoon characters] are listed as collaborators in the Nazi crimes … no peculiarly German form of authoritarianism or mentality produced the Holocaust but rather Western culture as a whole, including exponents of ostensibly 'innocent' popular culture" (1999: 203). Our modern daily lives cover up murder and are themselves murderous. This is Cohen, Weil, and Levi's intent.

Hannah Arendt made the inverse observation in *Eichmann in Jerusalem* (1963), which Cohen also takes up. Arendt was concerned not with the cruel in the quotidian but with the quotidian in extraordinary evil. Her subject was the 1961 trial of Adolph Eichmann, Hitler's key lieutenant in implementing the Holocaust. Arendt noted that exceptional evil is but the accumulation of commonplace acts committed by unexceptional people like Eichmann. Banality accrues into evil. Almost in call-and-response to Arendt, Cohen writes "All There Is to Know about Adolph Eichmann" (*Flowers for Hitler*, in *Cohen 1994: 53)*,

EYES:..Medium

HAIR:..Medium

WEIGHT:...Medium

HEIGHT:..Medium

DISTINGUISHING FEATURES...........None

NUMBER OF FINGERS:....................Ten

NUMBER OF TOES.........................Ten

INTELLIGENCE.............................Medium

What did you expect? Talons? Oversize incisors? Green saliva? Madness?

What Eichmann did was heinous, but he was ordinary. And we, Cohen continues, are capable of the heinous in the ordinary. By the time Cohen wrote *Flowers* in the early 1960s, Norman Ravvin notes (1997), Cohen understood that in the everyday lives we make for ourselves, "all things can be done / whisper museum ovens of / a war that Freedom won" ("It Uses Us!" *Flowers for Hitler*, in Cohen 1994: 51). The ovens that burned millions in Nazi camps end up in museums in countries that proclaim freedom. There, they try to catch the attention of museum-goers, passers-by, and remind them of the horror we do to each other. Two boys in *Favourite Game*, from the same period as *Flowers*, excite each other with stories of concentration camp terrors and torture a frog to death. The episode ends with the comment, "I suppose that's the way everything evil happens"—just from two guys horsing around (see also Erens 2018: 201). Even the self-sacrificing Edith of *Beautiful Losers* (1966) uses soap made from the flesh of Jews murdered in the Holocaust. There is no binary between exceptional evil and normal life. They subsist in each other. All things can be done in the human repertoire.

#

Much as Cohen understood the thrall that his confessions of infidelity inspired in fans, he knew that his *j'accuse* against our daily holocausts abetted his position as bad-boy poet, not unlike the "beat" poets and Jimmy Deans of the day. On love of God and women, he elliptically called himself "the poet of the two great intimacies" ("Commentary—My Wife and I," in Cohen 1994: 230). On the Holocaust, he wrote that his poems moved him "from the world of the golden-boy poet into the dung pile of the front-line writer" (https://books.google.com/books/about/Flowers_for_Hitler. html?id=jXA0AQAAQBAJ). With confidence in his self-assessment, he placed it on the back of *Flowers for Hitler*, apprising readers his literary place.

The book's first poem, "What I'm Doing Here," declares his purpose in writing. It is made from the meld of confession and indictment found again forty and fifty years later, in "On That Day" (*Dear Heather*, 2004) and "Almost Like the Blues" (*Popular Problems*, 2014, with Patrick Leonard). As we've seen, the narrator of "On That Day" mumbles "I wouldn't know" about the political crimes all around him, a confession of complacency unto abetting brutality. Then a different "I" charges us with: "did *you* report?" Are you, my audience, doing anything about it? In "Almost Like the Blues," the narrator similarly confesses to being absorbed with his "bad reviews" and then charges his audience with looking at extermination camps for their entertainment value: the story wasn't "boring at all." In "What I'm Doing Here," from the much earlier *Flowers*, Cohen is already making use of admitting and accusing. He writes (in Cohen 1994: 45),

> I do not know if the world has lied
> I have lied ...
> I have tortured ...
> I refuse the universal alibi ...
> I wait
> for each of *you* to confess.

Cohen, wrestling with the "slaughter bench" of our broken love and politics (Roth 2001: 10, 7; Hegel [1837] 2004: 21), was serious in confessing his complicity. But he was also aware of his confession-*cum*-indictment as an elixir for audience attention. Then again, he also knew that his attention-getting was yet one more sin of self-aggrandizing. We humans do not escape our created nature. *Huis clos*, no exit, once again.

Cohen was interested in the ontology of the cruel, in the capacities in human nature and God's design that underpin it. What undergirds the Holocaust, as with the rest of our self-interested brutality, is the way humanity is made. The will to evil, *yetzer ha'ra*, is a free radical, able to invade any love and circumstance.

Conclusion:
You Want It Darker
and *Thanks for the Dance*—
Cohen's Last Creed

Much of Cohen's artistry was devoted to our unavoidable breaches of covenant and to the harm and suffering they cause. At times, in songs like "Night Comes On" and "Closing Time," he feared that God had abandoned covenant as well. In grappling with these problems through the Abrahamic and other wisdom traditions, he contemplated many of the theodical questions sketched out in Chapter 1. To review the central ones:

Is our flight from covenantal commitment and consequent suffering an avoidable outcome of our free will, a condition of our moral agency? Could God, as Alvin Plantinga wrote, "have forestalled the occurrence of moral evil only by removing the possibility of moral good" (1974a: 30)? Is this, as John Peckham writes, the "rules of engagement" between God and a humanity whom God wishes to be capable of moral choice? Or is human wrongdoing the result of the absence of the good in the human will (Augustine, Aquinas) or the absence of wisdom in the human mind (Maimonides)? Is the pain resulting from evil meant to work as deterrent or rehabilitation? This is the suggestion of several punishment theodicies as they try to locate God's productive purpose in the misery we perpetrate and suffer. Alternately, are our hardships meant to teach us donation and generosity, the lessons of the cross, as cruciform theologians like Jürgen Moltmann and Marilyn McCord Adams propose—and as Cohen evoked frequently in his work? Are human tribulations training of sorts for more mature, righteous living, as John Hick posits in his soul-making theodicy?

The emerging God of process theology was not the God of Cohen's tradition, but process theodicy brings us to questions to which Cohen kept returning. While it does not hold God morally accountable for the world's evil, as God on this account develops with world and is not its controlling agent, it does hold God to be *metaphysically* responsible. The cosmos after all emerges from his primordial self-expression and from the primary direction or nature he gives to each entity. As God is responsible for this, he is responsible for the capacity and ease with which humanity's foundational nature bolts from covenantal commitment.

Throughout his life and his art, Cohen wrestled not only with the theodicies above but with the challenges to them. For instance, while human moral agency may require the freedom to choose evil, why do we choose it so often? Could God not have made us less prone to its worst excesses or constrained our choices to a narrowed range of possible wrongs? Could God not have made the human will less distorted and apt to choose evil; could our minds be more receptive to the wisdom that advances the good? How can suffering punish and deter when it is so broadly present in the world with little match between perpetrator and punishment? Finally, does any good *telos*—moral agency, donative righteousness, maturation of the soul—justify the bludgeoning we inflict upon each other?

Cohen asked and re-asked these questions through the poetic imagery of his work. He came to no answers, frustrated with himself, with human intimate and political relations, and often with God. Yet two points sifted down through his six decades of writing. Settling in his last song collections, they are something like a summation of his thought. First, God does not leave us, and we are unavoidably bound to him as we are to other persons. Second, God has made us with the capacity to make choices. We can choose to sustain or abandon commitment, and our vacillating decisions are what is sometimes called the human condition as God created it. There is no other God and no other creation, though we are limited in our understanding of them. These ideas are explained further in the passages below.

However much Cohen wrestled with God and the way he created us, Cohen's foundational frustration-*amid*-commitment endured into his last works. He neither solved nor resolved the discomfort of struggling always with this bond of "amid." But perhaps he came to some degree of comfort with the unavoidably uncomfortable project of living. The offer of covenant is ever-present, though we reach wildly for all manner of other things and so miss it. In "The Goal" (*Thanks for the Dance*, 2019), Cohen wrote, there is

No one to follow
And nothing to teach
Except that the goal
Falls short of the reach.

The goal and point of everything are near to us even as we reach and flail around it, losing the bonds that would give us love and peace.

To reckon with existence is to reckon with the God that made us needful of these bonds yet unable to sustain them. There is no other god to rage at or bind oneself to. Cohen's world, Thomas Marshall wrote in his study of Canadian poets, is one in which we must believe in God without understanding (Marshall 1979: 142). One poem in the 2006 *Book of Longing* reads:

Taxes
children
lost pussy
war
constipation
the living poet
in his harness
of beauty
offers the day back to g-d. (cited also in Simmons 2012: 460)

In the end, it comes back to God. This awe and need for God are not the musings only of an old man. Thirty years earlier, in "Who by Fire" (*New Skin for the Old Ceremony*, 1974), a younger Cohen faces the reality of the transcendent, who makes life possible and whose natural order also ends it. The song is Cohen's reworking of the *Unetanneh Tokef* prayer chanted on Yom Kippur, the Jewish Day of Atonement. After humanity has atoned for its wrongdoings, God determines who will flourish and who will die in the coming year: "who by fire, who by sword, who by water?" In Cohen's modern iteration, "And who in her lonely slip / who by barbiturate." We are, come what may, bound to God for our lives and deaths. In "Who by Fire," Cohen ends each verse by asking: "And who shall

I say is calling?" As always in Cohen's world of twined images and mobile pronouns, we must ask: who is this "I"? Possibly St. Peter, asking each of us who we are as we approach the gates of eternity. He may he asking for an identifying name or for whom we have been, our identifying actions, throughout life. The question "who shall I say in calling?" may also be ours: who is this God to whom we are unavoidably bound and who is *calling* us to account?

The mystery of our bondedness with God appears again a decade later in *Book of Mercy*, where Cohen writes, "You have sweetened your word on my lips. … You placed me in this mystery and you let me sing … You led me to this field where I can dance with a broken knee" ("You Have Sweetened Your Word," in Cohen 1994: 319). God's word is sweet but mysterious; we do not grasp it. And Cohen can dance, celebrate life and God, only in part, with the broken knee of our limited human comprehension of both. These motifs return twenty or so years later in *Book of Longing*'s "Takanawa Prince Hotel Bar" ([2006] 2007: 31), a bricolage of Jewish, Christian, Muslim, and Buddhist imagery describing the effort to near the divine. The effort may be called "awakening" in Buddhism, or entering the "furnace blue Heart" of Allah, or "slipping into the 27 Hells of my own religion" Judaism (a possible reference to William Blake's poem *Milton*, Elliot Wolfson 2006a: 140). In the late poem "Takanawa Prince," as in the 1984 *Book of Mercy*, all these efforts are made again on "bended knee," symbol of humility before awe that one cannot fully grasp.

Anger-amid-Covenant

Cohen's 2016 song collection *You Want It Darker* is his final testament to our necessary commitment to God. There is no alternative in living or dying. In considering this God, the ground for existence, one group of songs in *You Want It Darker* gives vent to Cohen's ire at God's inscrutable ways; a second group returns to covenant. "Leaving the Table" is of the first outraged group and begins:

> I'm leaving the table
> I'm out of the game
> I don't know the people
> In your picture frame

If I ever loved you, oh no, no
It's a crying shame
If I ever loved you
If I knew your name.

I'm not with you, Cohen almost pouts. I don't know your people or your name. The song may be read as anger at the women of his failed relationships, but the address to God shortly before death is inescapable. A later line reads: "Little by little / We're cutting the cord" to life. Cohen again evokes the "name," the Jewish reference to God of the unknowable tetragrammaton (YHVH) that appears in such songs as "Hallelujah" (*Various Positions*, 1984), "Love Itself" (*Ten New Songs*, 2001), and "Born in Chains" (*Popular Problems*, 2014). Here in "Leaving the Table," Cohen, fed up with the deal God has dealt in this game, rejects it. He's out of the game; he won't hang out with God's crowd (the people in the picture frame). As in "Hallelujah," he deems it "a shame" if he loved a God who never bothered to reveal his name. Why should he—humanity—stick around?

Cohen, at the end of his life, is still irate. He will not sentimentally let God off the hook for humanity's covenantal inadequacy that is God's creation. He, merely human, doesn't need an alibi for the way he is; that's on God's account. "Leaving the Table" continues:

"I don't need a reason
For what I became ...
I don't need a pardon, oh no no no
There's no one left to blame"
... except of course the ground for everything, God.

In "Traveling Light," from the same collection, Cohen is similarly irate and fed up possibly at women, certainly at God:

I guess I'm just
Somebody who
Has given up
On the me and you.

The cynicism in "It Seemed the Better Way," also from *You Want It Darker*, is both more pointed and more clearly directed at the transcendent. Cohen writes,

Seemed the better way
When first I heard him speak
Now it's much too late
To turn the other cheek.

God's donative vision seemed the better way at first but now it's "too late" for covenantal love and forgiveness. Of whom? Persons, God, or as often for Cohen, both. Cohen can't forgive God for humanity's covenant failures as they are grounded in God's design. He can't turn the other cheek even for God. The song continues: the truth about the God who spoke of love, death, and turning cheeks is "not the truth today." As in "Leaving the Table," Cohen is not buying God's line. He's out of the game. Why, God, did you tell us all that stuff about love and turning the other cheek when you made us unable to sustain it?

Songs of (Imperfect) Covenant

Cohen's complaint is as loud here as it was in "Night Comes On" (*Various Positions*, 1984) and "Closing Time" (*The Future*, 1992). Yet, while "Leaving the Table," "It Seemed the Better Way," and "Traveling Light" voice Cohen's anger, the album *You Want It Darker* returns to the reverence of *Book of Mercy*. The song "Treaty" serves as a bridge between the ire of "Leaving the Table" and acceptance of our flawed condition and covenant. Cohen begins with characteristic taunting:

I've seen you change the water into wine
I've seen you change it back to water too
I sit at your table every night
I try but I just don't get high with you.

These lines echo the disdain of "Leaving the Table." Cohen has seen God be miraculous as Jesus turned water into wine. But he has seen God withdraw his miracles as well. Why trust this God? Yet a few stanzas on, Cohen returns to his psalter. "Treaty" continues, "You were my ground, my safe and sound / You were my aerial." For all Cohen's frustration, God grounds him. The refrain of the song is not "I wish there was a treaty / between you and me" as if God and Cohen were enemies. It is rather, "I wish there was a treaty

/ between your love and mine." There is no question of the love between Cohen and God.

The insight of the following verse is as sharp as Cohen's "I needed so much to have nothing to touch" ("Night Comes On" 1984). In "Treaty," Cohen writes, "I'm sorry for the ghost I made you be / Only one of us was real and that was me." He was the only one he thought real, making God ephemeral, perhaps disposable. In the 1974 "Lover Lover Lover," Cohen had written, "I [the Father] never turned aside … it was you who covered up my face." In that song, God faults humanity for breaking covenant. Humanity does not take responsibility. In "Night Comes On" (1984) and "Closing Time" (1992), Cohen blames God for leaving. Humanity still does not take responsibility. In 2016, Cohen takes the fault. He admits to dismissing God, even if he doesn't understand why God made him able to do so. But God does not leave.

This brings Cohen to the song and psalm, "If I Didn't Have Your Love." Here, unlike in "Hallelujah" and "I'm Leaving the Table," he does not charge God with withholding his name. Cohen acknowledges that he has seen God's face:

> If the stars were all unpinned
> And a cold and bitter wind
> Swallowed up the world
> Without a trace
> Oh well that's where I would be
> What my life would seem to me
> If I couldn't lift the veil
> And see your face.

In Cohen's recurring conflation of images, this adoration could be for a woman, the "veil" perhaps the covering of the wedding day or of the Sabbath "bride," God's gift to us. But at the same time, the apocalyptic references to unpinned stars and a swallowed-up world evoke the landscape of the divine. Here, the veil of doubt and limits of human understanding are lifted, and it is God's "face" that Cohen has seen. We recall his recognition in 1976 that: "I can say 'to become close to Him is to feel His grace' because I have felt it" (Gnarowski 1976: 53).

Cohen knows that God's grace is present. "If I Didn't Have Your Love" continues,

If the sun would lose its light
And we lived an endless night …
That's how it would be
My life would seem to me
If I didn't have your love
To make it real.

The 2001 "A Thousand Kisses Deep" describes life when we sever relationship: nothing is left but the desperate effort to "live your life *as if* it's real." Here in "If I Didn't Have Your Love," Cohen has what makes it "real," love and God's presence.

However imperfect the bond, covenantal love makes life "real" because it is how we are really made. If such bonds were not foundational, their loss might be disappointing but not the abyss of grief expressed in "If I Didn't Have Your Love." If covenantal commitment were not central to our being, it might ornament life but would not bring the sense of groundedness and joy that finding love indeed brings—with a partner, community, God. Without it, Cohen writes in "If I Didn't Have Your Love," we are numb in a sunless world.

The song continues:

If the sea were sand alone
And the flowers made of stone
And no one that you hurt
Could ever heal
Well that's how broken I would be.

In one of his most self-aware lines since the 1984 "I needed so much to have nothing to touch," Cohen recognizes that God created us able not only to fail covenant but to heal and sustain it. Pointedly, the people Cohen himself hurt may have healed, which grants him a patch of grace. If they have healed and no longer blame him for abandoning them, perhaps he need not be so angry with God for making him able to abandon. As those he abandoned have healed, so too Cohen may heal his bond with God. This is the Moebius Strip covenant, wherein covenant among persons builds covenant with God. It's this sort of insight that made Kurt Cobain write, "Give me a Leonard Cohen afterworld / So I can sigh eternally" ("Pennyroyal Tea," *In Utero*, 2013, for the band Nirvana, cited in Hooton 2016).

The covenanted, committed Cohen of "If I Didn't Have Your Love" is the same angry man as in "Leaving the Table." But he has come to accept frustration and dismay *as part of* covenant. There is no covenant save a flawed one as humanity is flawed. It may be God's inscrutable plan, but there is no other plan. We are inescapably in and of it. This understanding is present also in the 2018 posthumous book *The Flame* and 2019 posthumous song collection, *Thanks for the Dance*, produced by Cohen's son, Adam. The songs were recorded in the same sessions as those in *You Want It Darker* (2016) and were completed by Adam with contributions from Daniel Lanois, Jennifer Warnes, Damien Rice, Beck Hanson, and Leslie Feist.

The eponymous title song is almost a lullaby in its childlike soothing. Cohen considers the limits of human relationship,

> So turn up the music
> Pour out the wine
> Stop at the surface
> The surface is fine
> We don't need to go any deeper.

The relationship described here is superficial. But Cohen doesn't criticize the woman he addresses for not giving enough, as he might have done when he wrote the embittered "A Thousand Kisses Deep." There, he is in despair that we do not go deeper. In "Thanks for the Dance," by contrast, Cohen finds that human relationships are imperfect and yet those inadequate bonds are the ones we may have. The song continues,

> And there's nothing to do
> But to wonder if you
> Are as hopeless as me
> And as decent.

The men and women of this hapless species are the only ones with whom to bond—much as there is no God to embrace other than the inscrutable one we (don't) know. The ineptitude of this mottled humanity does not mean we are not sometimes also decent.

Cohen does not back away from his theodicy, his charge that God made humanity as hobbled as it is. But he assents that humanity is made also to make choices even if self-absorption darkly colors them. We can choose to make God a ghost or real ("Treaty"). We can lift the veil and see his face ("If I Didn't Have Your Love"). We vacillate in our decisions, make bad ones, but sometimes also those that are decent. This is God's creation.

"You Want It Darker"— but There Is No Other "You"

I will close with a few remarks on the album's magisterial title song, "You Want It Darker." It begins with contempt in the mode of "Leaving the Table" and "Seemed the Better Way." Yet it ends with open-palmed faith. The first stanza reads,

> If you are the dealer, I'm out of the game
> If you are the healer, it means I'm broken and lame
> If thine is the glory then mine must be the shame.

Cohen confronts God: if you created this world, I'm out of your miserable creation. Why should I be broken in shame while you are in glory? Cohen then turns to his hallmark derision: "You want it darker / We kill the flame." This is a staggering idea. God for his unknown reasons wants life dark. How dark? A later verse reads: "I didn't know I had permission to murder and to maim / You want it darker." We, God's *dependent* creatures, grovel and do the dirty work of murdering and maiming. At times, we even kill God's own creatures in his name (Jonathan Sacks, cited in Field 2017). We were created able to do so. This is an inscrutable God.

It wasn't the first time Cohen leveled this charge. In one of his earliest works, "The Old Revolution" (*Songs from a Room*, 1969), he describes a prison for old revolutionaries who fought "on the side of the Ghost and the King." Simon Barker (2017) interestingly links the song to *Hamlet*, with its linchpin ghost of the murdered king. Yet the line reads also as the Holy Ghost and King of Kings, that is, God. The revolutionaries fought on the side of God, or thought they "had God on their side," as Bob Dylan's 1964 sardonic antiwar song has it. This reading takes shape in the refrain, "Into this furnace I ask you now to venture / you whom I cannot betray." Into the hellish furnace of war, one can ask only God to venture for God has bound himself to us. In return, God is the one whom we cannot betray. The God of "Old Revolution" is as perverse as the God of "You Want It Darker." In the cosmos of his creation, we do the dirty work of war. The soldier admits, "Now let me say I myself gave the order / to sleep and to search and to destroy." It's the old revolutionary who must wallow in butchery, who must search and destroy others. As in "You Want It Darker," in God's design, we kill the flame.

"You Want It Darker" continues probing life's grimness:

> There's a lover in the story
> But the story's still the same
> There's a lullaby for suffering
> And a paradox to blame
> But it's written in the scriptures
> And it's not some idle claim
> You want it darker
> We kill the flame.

God is our lover and lullaby, but since we, *his* creation, paradoxically cannot tolerate this intimacy, we bolt and suffer. This story is always and still the same: God our maker made us needy yet paradoxically lets us flee. It's known in public, in Scripture, God's proclamation to world. Only a perverse God wants it darker and makes his creatures kill the flame.

When Cohen comes to the song's refrain, he continues his taunt:

> Magnified, sanctified, be thy holy name
> Vilified, crucified, in the human frame
> A million candles burning for the help that never came.

The first line, "Magnified, sanctified, be thy holy name," is from the Hebrew prayer for the dead (*yitgadal v'yitkadash sh'mei raba*), used in Cohen's work for the first time three weeks before he died. He is sarcastic: *This* is the God we magnify and sanctify?—a God who allows vilification and crucifixion and whose help never comes? Why lay our vulnerable souls in his hands?

The second part of the refrain, however, puts an end to all this taunting. Sung by the cantor and choir of Cohen's childhood synagogue, it turns to openness and willing dependence on God: "*hineni, hineni*" [I am here, present]. "I'm ready, my lord." This is Cohen's pledge to God. It is also Abraham's response to

God at the *Akedah,* when he is asked to sacrifice his son Isaac (Gen. 22:1-19). He is open to God, ready before him. It is Moses' response to God at the burning bush (Exod. 3:1-4). And it is also Abraham's response to Isaac himself and to the angel who stops the sacrifice-that-wasn't-to-be. Abraham is present and open to them, to the *person* of Isaac as to the angelic and divine. Cohen, in invoking this "*hineni,*" assents to the interlocking commitments to God and person. Covenant with one is at once covenant with the other. This is God's creation. There are no other gods, the First and Second Commandments.

Staggeringly, as Moshe Halbertal notes in his preface, it is also God's response to humanity in Isa. 58:9: "Then you will call, and the LORD will answer; you will cry for help, and he will say: *Hineni,* Here am I." God is present, open and ready before humanity. He has committed himself. Three weeks before Cohen died, after a life of ricocheting between bond and breach, he answers God's "*hineni*" with his own.

The final lines of the song (not in *The Flame* printed compilation) rework the opening stanza. Rather than "If you are the dealer, I'm out of the game," Cohen writes, "If you are the dealer, *let* me out of the game," an acknowledgment of our necessary dependence on God, who determines whether we are in or out of the game of life. This is no longer an angry Cohen mocking God's perverse world. It is Cohen in covenant, who understands that God is the healer whom he sought and resisted throughout life—and that God is now taking him out of it.

The struggles of the covenant fail-er, prophet, and priest are done. It is God's turn. In the 1971 "Avalanche" (*Songs of Love and Hate*), God tells humanity to step up to the commitment of covenant, "It is your turn, beloved / It is your flesh that I wear." Here in "You Want It Darker" as in the 2019 "Listen to the Hummingbird" (*Thanks for the Dance*), Cohen returns the job to God. In "Hummingbird" he writes,

> Listen to the mind of God
> Which doesn't need to be
> Listen to the mind of God
> Don't listen to me.

Cohen does not solve his theodicy. He does not know why God made him, us, needy of relation and quick to bolt. Why do we fail to see and see *to* those nearby and half a world away, whose presence in the world makes us who we are? Absent solution, he had at age eighty-two a not-quite-content commitment to the inscrutable, provocative God, but commitment it is nonetheless in an open-ended struggle that reaches beyond this life. As Catherine Keller notes, "The case of the ancient future is not closed. Comfort ye my people" (Keller 2021: 168). The rest of "You Want It Darker" is an incantation: "*Hineni*," I'm here, ready, my Lord.

REFERENCES

"Acclaimed poet Irving Layton dies at 93" (2006), *Canadian Broadcasting Company* (CBC), January 5. Available online: https://www.cbc.ca/news/canada/acclaimed-poet-irving-layton-dies-at-93-1.619788 (accessed August 13, 2019).

Adams, M. (1992), "Redemptive Suffering: A Christian Solution to the Problem of Evil," in M. L. Peterson (ed.), *The Problem of Evil: Selected Readings*, 169–87, Notre Dame: University of Notre Dame Press.

Adorno, T. W. (1955), *Prismen: Kulturkritik und Gesellschaft*, Frankfurt am Main: Suhrkamp Verlag.

Alperowitz, G. (1990), "Building a Living Democracy," *Sojourners*, 19(6): 11–23.

Aquinas, T. (1264), *De Rationibus Fidei*, trans. J. Kenny, O. P. Available online: https://isidore.co/aquinas/english/Rationes.htm (accessed August 24, 2020).

Aquinas, T. ([1265–1273] 1948), *Summa Theologica 1–5*, trans. Fathers of the Dominican English Province, Westminster: Christian Classics.

Aquinas, T. (1989), *The Literal Exposition on Job: A Scriptural Commentary Concerning Providence*, trans. A. Damico, Atlanta: Scholars Press.

Aquinas, T. (1995), *On Evil*, trans. J. A. Oesterle and J. T. Oesterle, Notre Dame: University of Notre Dame Press.

Aquinas, T. ([1265–73] 2006), *Summa Theologiae*, in Brian Davies and Brian Leftow (eds.), *Thomas Aquinas: Summa Theologiae, Questions on God*, Cambridge: Cambridge University Press.

Arendt, H. (1963), *Eichmann in Jerusalem: A Report on the Banality of Evil*, New York: Viking.

"August 2, Leonard Cohen's Tel Aviv Concert Sells Out in a Day: Cohen plans to Donate All Proceeds to 'Israeli and Palestinian Groups Working for Coexistence'" (2009), *Ha'aretz*, August 2. Available online: https://www.haaretz.com/1.5085326 (accessed August 11, 2019).

Augustine ([391] 1953), *De vera religione*, in *Augustine: Earlier Writings*, trans. J. Burleigh, Philadelphia, PA: Westminster.

Augustine ([426] 1998), *The City of God against the Pagans*, trans. R. W. Dyson, Cambridge: Cambridge University Press.

Augustine ([388–395] 1955), *The Problem of Free Choice*, III.19.53, trans. Dom Mark Pontifex, New York: Newman Press.

Babich, B. (2013), *The Hallelujah Effect: Philosophical Reflections on Music, Performance Practice, and Technology*, Farnham: Ashgate.

Babich, B. (2014), "Hallelujah and Atonement," in J. Holt (ed.), *Leonard Cohen and Philosophy: Various Positions*, Kindle Locations 2273–495, Chicago: Open Court.

Barbour, I. (2000), *When Science Meets Religion: Enemies, Strangers, or Partners?*, San Francisco, CA: HarperSanFrancisco.

Barker, S. (2017), "'Even Damnation Is Poisoned with Rainbows': Conflict and Memory in *Hamlet* and 'The Old Revolution'," in P. Billingham (ed.), *Spirituality and Desire in Leonard Cohen's Songs and Poems: Visions from the Tower of Song*, 11–26, Newcastle upon Tyne: Cambridge Scholars.

Barth, K. (1960), *Church Dogmatics III/3*, trans. G. W. Bromiley and R. J. Ehrlich, ed. G. W. Bromiley and T. F. Torrance, Edinburgh: T&T Clark.

Bauman, Z. (1989), *Modernity and the Holocaust*, Ithaca, NY: Cornell University Press.

Bean, H. (2018), "Lecture on Vayakhel—Pekude," March 10, Ansche Chesed, New York.

Bellah, R. (2011), *Religion in Human Evolution*, Cambridge, MA: Harvard University Press.

Billingham, P. (2017a), "Crosses, Nails, and Lonely Wooden Towers: The *Leitmotif* of 'The Wounded Man' in Selected Songs of Leonard Cohen," in P. Billingham (ed.), *Spirituality and Desire in Leonard Cohen's Songs and Poems: Visions from the Tower of Song*, 27–42, Newcastle upon Tyne: Cambridge Scholars.

Billingham, P., ed. (2017b), *Spirituality and Desire in Leonard Cohen's Songs and Poems: Visions from the Tower of Song*, Newcastle upon Tyne: Cambridge Scholars.

Bird on a Wire (1974), [documentary film] Dir. Tony Palmer, UK: Machat.

Borowitz, E. (1990), *Exploring Jewish Ethics: Papers on Covenant Responsibility*, Detroit: Wayne State University Press.

Borowitz, E. (1991), *Renewing the Covenant: A Theology for the Postmodern Jew*, Philadelphia, PA: Jewish Publication Society.

Boucher, D. (2004), *Dylan and Cohen: Poets of Rock and Roll*, New York: Continuum.

Breslauer, S. D. (2006), "Toward a Theory of Covenant for Contemporary Jews," *Covenant*, 1(1). Available online: http://www.covenant.idc.ac.il/en/vol1/issue1/breslauer.html (accessed August 19, 2020).

Brueggemann, W. (2010), *Journey to the Common Good*, Louisville, KY: Westminster John Knox.

Buber, M. ([1923] 1958), *I and Thou*, trans. R. G. Smith, New York: Charles Scribner's.

Buber, M. ([1947] 1993), *Between Man and Man*, New York: Routledge.

Buber, M. ([1927] 2010), *I and Thou*, Eastford: Martino Fine Books.

Burger, J., ed. (2014), *Leonard Cohen on Leonard Cohen: Interviews and Encounters*, Chicago: Chicago Review Press.

Butler, J. (2006), *Gender Trouble: Feminism and the Subversion of Identity*, New York: Routledge.

Butler, J. (2011), *Bodies That Matter: On the Discursive Limits of Sex*, New York: Routledge.

Cacioppo, J., and S. Cacioppo (2014), "Social Relationships and Health: The Toxic Effects of Perceived Social Isolation," *Social and Personality Psychology Compass*, 8(2): 58–72.

Castelfranco, G. (2016), "Leonard Cohen Obituary," *GIGsoup*. Available online: https://gigsoupmusic.com/obituaries/gs-leonard-cohen-obituary/ (accessed August 19, 2020).

Celan, P. ([1952] 1993), *Mohn und Gedächtnis: Gedichte*, 12th ed., München: Deutsche Verlags-Anstalt. In English available online: http://mason.gmu.edu/~lsmithg/deathfugue.html (accessed April 20, 2020).

Cobb, J. B. Jr., and D. Griffin (1976), *Process Theology: An Introductory Exposition*, Philadelphia, PA: Westminster.

The Cloud of Unknowing (2001), trans. C. Spearing, London: Penguin Classics.

Cohen, D. (2016), "The Prayers of Leonard Cohen: If It Be Your Will" [lecture delivered at the Leonard Cohen Event, Amsterdam], August 14. Available online: https://www.leonardcohenfiles.com/doron-amsterdam.pdf (accessed January 6, 2020).

Cohen, L. (1961), *The Spice-Box of Earth*, London: Jonathan Cape.

Cohen, L. (1963), *The Favourite Game*, London: Secker and Warburg.

Cohen, L. ([1964] 1973), *Flowers for Hitler*, New York: Jonathan Cape.

Cohen, L. (1979), *Death of a Lady's Man*, London: Penguin Books.

Cohen, L. (1984), *Book of Mercy*, Toronto: McClelland & Stewart.

Cohen, L. (1988). *TV Interview and Performance of "Joan of Arc."* Available online: https://www.youtube.com/watch?v=xUxOOns1j1M (accessed August 21, 2020).

Cohen, L. ([1966] 1993), *Beautiful Losers*, New York: Vintage.

Cohen, L. (1994), *Stranger Music, Selected Poems and Songs*, New York: Vintage.

Cohen, L. ([2006] 2007), *Book of Longing*, New York: HarperCollins.

Cohen, L. (2009), *QTV Interview*. Available online: https://www.youtube.com/watch?v=ugh8Xe6hX7U (accessed August 19, 2020).

Cohen, L. (2011), *Poems and Songs*, ed. R. Faggen, New York: Everyman's Library/Penguin/Random House.

Cohen, L. (2012), *Performance of "Ain't No Cure for Love."* Available online: https://www.youtube.com/watch?v=b4R2-GlBd-c (accessed August 21, 2020).

Cohen, L. ([1966] 2018a), *Parasites of Heaven*, Toronto: McClelland & Stewart.

Cohen, L. (2018b), *The Flame*, London: Penguin.

Cohen, L. ([1956] 2019), *Let Us Compare Mythologies*, Edinburgh: Canongate.

Cowan, D. (2016), "Leonard Cohen's Life of Poetry and Song," *American Conservative*, December 16: 54–7. Available online: http://www.theamericanconservative.com/articles/leonard-cohens-life-of-poetry-and-song/ (accessed August 8, 2018).

Dabrowski, S. L. (2001), "TV Interview: *Swedish National Television*," in J. Burger (ed.), *Leonard Cohen on Leonard Cohen: Interviews and Encounters*, 439–77, Chicago: Chicago Review Press.

Dalziell, T., and P. Genoni (2018), "Mythmaking, Social Media and the Truth about Leonard Cohen's Last Letter to Marianne Ihlen," *The Conversation*, December 5. Available online: https://theconversation.com/mythmaking-social-media-and-the-truth-about-leonard-cohens-last-letter-to-marianne-ihlen-108082 (accessed August 11, 2019).

Dawkins, R. (1976), *The Selfish Gene*, Oxford: Oxford University Press.

Dennis, I. (2017), "Songs of Leonard Cohen: Postmodernity, The Victimary, Irony, A Blaze of Light," *Anthropoetics*, 23(1): 1–23. Available online: http://anthropoetics.ucla.edu/category/ap2301/ (accessed February 22, 2019).

Diamond, J. (2017), "Yahrzeit for a Life of Poetic Jewishness," *Jerusalem Post*, October 25. Available online: https://www.jpost.com/opinion/yahrzeit-for-a-life-of-poetic-jewishness-508439 (accessed July 10, 2020).

Dobrosielski, P., and M. Napiorkowski (2014), "Writing Poetry after Auschwitz," in J. Holt (ed.), *Leonard Cohen and Philosophy: Various Positions*, Kindle Locations 2745–928, Chicago: Open Court.

Dorman, L., and C. Rawlins (1990), *Leonard Cohen: Prophet of the Heart*, London: Omnibus Press.

Draper, P. (2001), "Pain and Pleasure: An Evidential Problem for Theists," in W. Rowe (ed.), *God and the Problem of Evil*, 180–202, Malden, MA: Blackwell.

Dudek, L. (1969), "The Writing of the Decade: Poetry in English," *Canadian Literature*, 41: 111–20.

Eastman, S. (2017), *Paul and the Person: Reframing Paul's Anthropology*, Grand Rapids, MI: Eerdmans.

Elliott, R. (2015), *The Late Voice: Time, Age and Experience in Popular Music*, London: Bloomsbury Academic.

Erens, P. (2018), "Old Ideas: Leonard Cohen's Legacy," *Virginia Quarterly Review*, 94(3): 196–205.

Esse, J.-L. (1997), "Interview with Leonard Cohen," trans. N. Halliwell, *Synergie, France-Inter*, October 6. Available online: https://www. leonardcohenfiles.com/finter.html (accessed March 3, 2020).

Evans, G. (1982), *Augustine on Evil*, Cambridge: Cambridge University Press.

Faggen, B. (2011), *Poems and Songs*, New York: Peguin.

Field, B. (2017), "You Want It Darker—Leonard Cohen's Most Jewish Album?" *Judaism Your Way*, January 13. Available online: http:// www.judaismyourway.org/want-darker-leonard-cohens-jewish-album/. (accessed March 6, 2019).

Footman, T. (2009), *Leonard Cohen, Hallelujah: A New Biography*, New Malden: Chrome Dreams.

Frankfort, H., and H. A. Frankfort (1959), *Before Philosophy*, Hammondsworth: Penguin.

Frye, N. (1971), "Leonard Cohen, Let Us Compare Mythologies (1956) Review," in N. Frye (ed.), *The Bush Garden: Essays on the Canadian Imagination*, 250, Toronto: House of Anansi Press.

Gans, E. (1982), "The Victim as Subject: The Esthetico-Ethical System of Rousseau's *Rêveries*," *Studies in Romanticism*, 21: 3–31.

Geller, S. (2000), "The God of the Covenant," in N. Porter (ed.), *One God or Many? Concepts of Divinity in the Ancient World*, vol. 1, 273–319, Chebeague: Transactions of the Casco Bay Assyriological Institute.

Geller, S. (2014), "The Religion of the Bible," in A. Berlin and M. Brettler (eds.), *The Jewish Study Bible*, 1979–97, New York: Oxford University Press.

Gitlin, T. (2002), "Grizzled Minstrels of Angst: Leonard Cohen and Bob Dylan, Forever Old," *American Scholar*, 71(2): 95–100.

Glaister, D. (2005), "Cohen Stays Calm as $5m Disappears," *The Guardian*, October 8. Available online: https://www.theguardian.com/ world/2005/oct/08/usa.topstories3 (accessed August 11, 2019).

Glazer, A. (2012), "Leonard Cohen and the Tosher Rebbe: On Exile as Redemption in Canadian Jewish Mysticism," *Canadian Jewish Studies*, 20: 149–89.

Glazer, A. (2017), *Tangle of Matter & Ghost: Leonard Cohen's Post-Secular Songbook of Mysticism(s) Jewish & Beyond*, Boston, MA: Academic Studies Press.

Gnarowski, M., ed. (1976), *Leonard Cohen: The Artist and His Critics*, Toronto: McGraw Hill Rayerson.

Godbout, J., and A. Caillé (1998), *The World of the Gift*, trans. D. Winkler, Montreal: McGill-Queen's University Press.

Goodman, L. (1991), *On Justice: An Essay in Jewish Philosophy*, New Haven, CT: Yale University Press.

Goodman, M. (2015), *Maimonides and the Book That Changed Judaism: Secrets of The Guide for the Perplexed*, Lincoln: University of Nebraska Press.

Grayston, D. (2009), "Monk Thomas Merton meets Leonard Cohen," reprinted in Todd, D. (2010), "Monk Thomas Merton meets Leonard Cohen," *Vancouver Sun*, November 28. Available online: https://vancouversun.com/news/staff-blogs/monk-thomas-merton-meets-leonard-cohen (accessed January 8, 2020). Original text "Thomas Merson and Leonard Cohen: Soul-Brothers and Spiritual Guides" available online: https://www.leonardcohenfiles.com/grayston2.pdf (accessed January 8, 2020).

Griffin, D. (1991), *Evil Revisited: Responses and Reconsiderations*, Albany: State University of New York Press.

Griffin, D. ([1976] 2004), *God, Power, and Evil: A Process Theodicy*, Philadelphia, PA: Westminster.

Halberstam, C. (2017), "Law in Biblical Israel," in C. Hayes (ed.), *The Cambridge Companion to Judaism and Law*, 19–47, New York: Cambridge University Press.

Halbertal, M. (2014), *Maimonides: Life and Thought*, trans. J. Linsider, Princeton, NJ: Princeton University Press.

Halbertal, M. (2017), "*Eikhah* and the Stance of Lamentation," in I. Ferber and P. Schwebel (eds.), *Lament in Jewish Thought*, 3–10, Berlin: De Gruyter.

Halbertal, M. (2020, July 1). Skype communication.

Halivni, D. W. (1996), *Book and the Sword: A Life of Learning in the Shadow of Destruction*, New York: Farrar, Straus & Giroux.

Hampson, S. (2007), "Leonard Cohen: Life of a Ladies' Man," *Globe and Mail*, May 26. Available online: https://www.theglobeandmail.com/arts/music/from-the-archives-leonard-cohen-life-of-a-ladies-man/article32811791/ (accessed March 4, 2019).

Hartman, D. (1976), *Maimonides: Torah and the Philosophic Quest*, Philadelphia, PA: Jewish Publication Society of America.

Haslam, T. (2017), "Mapping the Great Divide in the Lyrics of Leonard Cohen," *Rupkatha Journal*, 9(1): 1–10.

Hayes, C. (2012), *Introduction to the Bible*, New Haven, CT: Yale University Press.

Hegel, G. W. F. ([1837] 2004), *The Philosophy of History*, Mineola: Dover.

Hermes, W. (2019), "Leonard Cohen's Profound 'Thanks for the Dance' Is a Posthumous Grace Note," *Rolling Stone*, November 22. Available online: https://www.rollingstone.com/music/music-album-reviews/leonard-thanks-for-the-dance-916417/ (accessed December 19, 2019).

Heschel, A. J. (1997), *God in Search of Man*, New York: Farrar, Straus & Giroux.

Heschel, A. J. (2001), *The Prophets*, New York: Harper Perennial Classics.

Hesthamar, K. (2005), "Leonard Looks Back on the Past: Interview with Leonard Cohen." Available online: htttp://www.leonardcohenfiles.com/leonard2006.html (accessed August 7, 2018).

Hick, J. (2001), "An Irenaean Theodicy," in S. Davis (ed.), *Encountering Evil: Live Options in Theodicy*, 38–72, Louisville, KY: Westminster John Knox.

Hick, J. (2007), *Evil and the God of Love*, New York: Palgrave Macmillan.

Hirschfeld, M. (2018), *Aquinas and the Market*, Cambridge, MA: Harvard University Press.

Holt, J., ed. (2014), *Leonard Cohen and Philosophy: Various Positions*, Chicago: Open Court.

Hooton, C. (2016), "Leonard Cohen on Kurt Cobain's *Nirvana* Lyric Name-Check: 'I'm Sorry I Couldn't Have Spoken to the Young Man'," *The Independent*, November 11. Available online: https://www.independent.co.uk/arts-entertainment/music/news/leonard-cohen-on-kurt-cobains-nirvana-lyric-name-check-im-sorry-i-couldnt-have-spoken-to-the-young-a7410941.html (accessed August 21, 2020).

Horton, M. (2005), *Lord and Servant: A Covenant Christology*, Louisville, KY: Westminster John Knox.

Horton, M. (2007), *Covenant and Salvation: Union with Christ*, Louisville, KY: Westminster John Knox.

Howes, R. (2017), "Leonard Cohen and the Philosophical Voice of Learning," in P. Billingham (ed.), *Spirituality and Desire in Leonard Cohen's Songs and Poems: Visions from the Tower of Song*, 91–106, Newcastle upon Tyne: Cambridge Scholars.

Hume, H. ([1779] 1990), *Dialogues Concerning Natural Religion*, Part X, ed. M. Bell, New York: Penguin.

Hustak, A. (2016a), "Mr. Cohen, It Was a Privilege Knowing You," *Catholic Register*, November 16. Available online: https://www.catholicregister.org/item/23611-mr-cohen-it-was-a-privilege-knowing-you (accessed January 8, 2020).

Hustak, A. (2016b), "Remembering Leonard," *The Metropolitain*, November 12. Available online: http://themetropolitain.ca/fra/articles/view/1635 (accessed August 19, 2020).

Hutcheon, L. (1974), "*Beautiful Losers*: All the Polarities," *Canadian Literature*, 59: 42–56.

Hyde, L. (1983), *The Gift: Imagination and the Erotic Life of Property*, New York: Vintage Books.

IJzendoorn, M. van, J. Palacios, E. Sonuga-Barke, M. Gunnar, P. Vorria, R. McCall, L. Le Mare, M. Bakermans-Kranenburg, N. Dobrova-Krol, and F. Juffer (2011), "Children in Institutional Care: Delayed Development and Resilience," *Monographs of the Society for Research in Child Development*, 76(4): 8–30.

Inwagen, P. van (2006), *The Problem of Evil*, New York: Oxford University Press.

"It Was a Beautiful Slow Movie—The Story of Leonard Cohen and His Greatest Muse" (2018), *Christie's*, July 6. Available online: https://www.christies.com/features/Leonard-Cohen-and-his-greatest-muse-9305-1.aspx (accessed May 28, 2019).

Jacobson, R. (2000), "The Costly Loss of Praise," *Theology Today*, 57(3): 375–85.

Johnson, B. D. (1992), "Life of a Lady's Man: Leonard Cohen Sings of Love and Freedom," *Maclean's*, December 7: 63–4. Available online: https://archive.macleans.ca/article/1992/12/7/life-of-a-ladys-man#!&pid=62 (accessed August 17, 2020).

Johnson, B. D. (2005), "Up Close and Personal," *Maclean's*, August 22: 48–9. Available online: http://www.maartenmassa.be/LCdocs/magazines/2005-08-22_Macleans.pdf (accessed August 11, 2019).

Keller, C. (2021), *Facing Apocalypse: Climate, Democracy and Other Last Chances*, Ossining: Orbis.

King, P. (1983), "Leonard Cohen Mixes Movie-Making and Zen," *The Gazette*, July 16.

Kochen, M. (2008), "It Was Not for Naught That They Called It 'Hekdesh': Divine Ownership and the Medieval Charitable Foundation," in J. Fleishman (ed.), *The Bar-Ilan Conference Volume*, 131–42, Liverpool: Jewish Law Association.

Kopf, B. (1987), "Jennifer Warnes, Leonard Cohen: Lenny and *Jenny Sings Lenny*," *New Musical Express*, March 14. Available online: https://www.rocksbackpages.com/Library/Article/lenny-and-jenny-sings-lenny (accessed August 19, 2020).

Kubernik, H. (2014), *Leonard Cohen: Everybody Knows*, London: Backbeat Books.

Lang, K., and Robey E.-M. (2007, re-broadcast November 11, 2016). "Leonard Cohen, BalletBoyz, Contemporary war poetry," *Front Row*. BBC Radio 4. Available online: https://www.bbc.co.uk/programmes/b08118bn (accessed April 3, 2021).

Langlois, C. (2006), "Cohen's Age of Reason," *CARP magazine*:14–18. Available online: http://www.christinelanglois.com/wp-content/uploads/2009/04/leonard-cohen-ed9_leonard-cohen.pdf (accessed March 4, 2019).

Laugesen, K., L. Munksgård Baggesen, S. Jóhannesdóttir Schmidt, M. Glymour, M. Lasgaard, A. Milstein, H. Sørensen, N. Adler, and V. Ehrenstein (2018), "Social Isolation and All-Cause Mortality: A Population-Based Cohort Study in Denmark," *Scientific Reports*, 8(1): 4731.

Lebold, C. (2018), "From Existential Troubadour to Crooner of Light: Uses and Refractions of the Love Song in Leonard Cohen's Work," *Rock Music Studies*, 5(1): 1–19.

Lee, D. (1977), *Savage Fields: An Essay in Literature and Cosmology*, Toronto: Anansi.

Lee, J. (2010), "The Two Pillars Paradigm: Covenant as a Relational Concept in Response to the Contract-Based Economic Market," PhD diss., University of Edinburgh, Edinburgh.

Lee, J. (2011), *The Two Pillars of the Market: A Paradigm for Dialogue between Theology and Economics*, New York: Peter Lang.

Leibovitz, L. (2014a), *A Broken Hallelujah: Rock and Roll, Redemption, and the Life of Leonard Cohen*, New York: W. W. Norton.

Leibovitz, L. (2014b), "The Prophet in the Library: The Previously Undiscovered Speech That Launched Leonard Cohen's Career," *New Republic*, March 29. Available online: https://newrepublic.com/article/117177/leonard-cohens-previously-undiscovered-montreal-library-speech (accessed February 28, 2019).

Leigh-Hunt, N., D. Bagguley, K. Bash, V. Turner, S. Turnbull, N. Valtorta, and W. Caan (2017), "An Overview of Systematic Reviews on the Public Health Consequences of Social Isolation and Loneliness," *Public Health*, 152: 157–71.

"Leonard Cohen Awarded $9 million in Civil Suit" (2006), *CTV.ca*, 2 March. Available online: https://www.nme.com/news/music/leonard-cohen-53-1367727 (accessed August 11, 2019).

"Leonard Cohen Interviewed: 'I Didn't Have the Interior Authority to Tackle Some of My Greatest Songs'" (2015), *Uncut*, February 26. Available online: https://www.uncut.co.uk/features/leonard-cohen-i-didn-t-have-the-interior-authority-to-tackle-some-of-my-greatest-songs-18998/4#AauEVY5wVsI0q2Rb.99 (accessed March 4, 2019).

"Leonard Cohen's Temple of Song" (2016), *Globe and Mail*, November 18. Available online: https://www.theglobeandmail.com/arts/music/leonard-cohen-remembered-his-roots-and-remained-proud-of-his-jewishheritage/article32930044/ (accessed August 11, 2019).

"Leonard Cohen 'Unlikely' to Recover Stolen Millions: Funds Taken by Ex-manager Going to Be Hard to Recover" (2006), *NME*, March 3. Available online: https://www.nme.com/news/music/leonard-cohen-53-1367727 (accessed August 11, 2019).

Leonard Cohen: Zen and the Art of Songwriting (2009), [radio interview] National Public Radio, April 3, 10:13. Available online: https://www.npr.org/2009/04/03/102692227/leonard-cohen-zen-and-the-art-of-songwriting (accessed August 19, 2020).

Levinas, E. (1979), *Totality and Infinity: An Essay on Exteriority*, Dordrecht: Kluwer Academic.

Levinas, E. (1987), *Time and the Other*, trans. R. Cohen. Pittsburgh: Duquesne University Press.

Levinas, E. (1994a), *Beyond the Verse: Talmudic Readings and Lectures*, New York: Bloomsbury.

Levinas, E. (1994b), *Beyond the Verse: Talmudic Readings and Lectures*, trans. G. Mole, Bloomington: Indiana University Press.

Levinas, E. (1994c), *In the Time of the Nations*, trans. M. Smith, London: Athlone Press.

Levinas, E. (1994d), "Revelation in the Jewish Tradition," in E. Levinas, *Beyond the Verse: Talmudic Readings and Lectures*, 129–50, trans. G. Mole, Bloomington: Indiana University Press.

Levinas, E. (1996), *Proper Names*, trans. M. Smith, Stanford, CA: Stanford University Press.

Levi, P. ([1947] 2008), *Survival in Auschwitz*, New York: Classic House Books.

Lewis, C. S. (2001a), *Mere Christianity*, New York: HarperOne.

Lewis, C. S. (2001b), *The Problem of Pain*, New York: HarperOne.

Light, A. (2012), *The Holy or the Broken: Leonard Cohen, Jeff Buckley, and the Unlikely Ascent of Hallelujah*, New York: Simon & Schuster.

Lisle, T. de (2004), "Who Held a Gun to Leonard Cohen's Head?," *The Guardian*, September 16. Available online: https://www.theguardian.com/music/2004/sep/17/2 (accessed August 11, 2019).

London, D. DeF. (2012), "The Secret Chord: Leonard Cohen and the Ketuvim," https://deforestlondon.wordpress.com/2012/01/31/1041/ (accessed October 8, 2020).

Lumsden, S. (1970), "Leonard Cohen Wants the Unconditional Leadership of the World," *Winnipeg Free Press*, September 12. Available online: shttps://newspaperarchive.com/ca/manitoba/winnipeg/winnipeg-free-press/1970/09-12/page-93 (accessed August 19, 2020).

Lynskey, D. (2012), "Leonard Cohen: All I've Got to Put in a Song Is My Own Experience," *The Guardian*, January 9. Available online: https://www.theguardian.com/music/2012/jan/19/leonard-cohen (accessed August 12, 2019).

Mackie, J. (1992), "Evil and Omnipotence," in Michael Peterson (ed.), *The Problem of Evil: Selected Readings*, 89–101, Notre Dame: University of Notre Dame Press.

Macklem, K., C. Gillis, and B. Johnson (2005), "Devasted," *Maclean's*, August 22. Available online: http://www.maartenmassa.be/LCdocs/magazines/2005-08-22_Macleans.pdf (accessed August 11, 2019).

Maimonides, M. ([1190] 1956), *Guide for the Perplexed*, trans. A. H. Freidlander, New York: Dover.

Maimonides, M. ([1190] 2008), *The Guide for the Perplexed*, trans. A. M. Friedlander, New York: Barnes & Noble.

Marianne & Leonard: Words of Love (2019), [documentary film] Dir. Nick Broomfield, Kyle Gibbon, Shani Hinton, Marc Hoeferlin, USA: Roadside Attractions.

Marshall, T. (1979), "A History of Us All: Leonard Cohen," in T. Marshall, *Harsh and Lovely Land: The Major Canadian Poets and the Making of a Canadian Tradition*, 135–43, Vancouver: University of British Columbia Press.

Martin, G. (1991), *NME*, 19 October.

Maslin, J. (2012), "Time Passes, but a Song's Time Doesn't: 'The Holy or the Broken' by Alan Light," *New York Times Book Review*, December 9. Available online: https://www.nytimes.com/2012/12/10/books/the-holy-or-the-broken-by-alan-light.html (accessed August 10, 2019).

Mauss, M. ([1923] 1990), *The Gift: The Form and Reason for Exchange in Archaic Society*, trans. W. D. Halls, London: Routledge.

Meister, C. (2012), *Evil: A Guide for the Perplexed*, New York: Bloomsbury Academic.

Měsíc, J. (2015), "Leonard Cohen, the Priest of a Catacomb Religion," *Moravian Journal of Literature and Film*, 6(1): 29–47.

Měsíc, J. (2016), "Leonard Cohen: The modern troubadour," *American and British Studies Annual*, 9: 134–46.

Měsíc, J. (2018), "The Nature of Love in the Work of Leonard Cohen," *Journal of Popular Romance Studies*, October 4. Available online: http://jprstudies.org/2018/10/the-nature-of-love-in-the-work-of-leonard-cohenby-jiri-mesic/ (accessed November 4, 2018).

Meyer, H. (1954), *The Philosophy of St. Thomas Aquinas*, trans. F. Eckhoff, St. Louis: B. Herder Book.

Moltmann-Wendel, E. (1995), *I Am My Body: A Theology of Embodiment*, New York: Continuum.

Moltmann, J. (1993a), *The Crucified God: The Cross of Christ as the Foundation and Criticism of Christian Theology*, trans. R. A. Wilson and John Bowden, Minneapolis, MN: Fortress Press.

Moltmann, J. (1993b), *The Trinity and the Kingdom: The Doctrine of God*, trans. M. Kohl, Minneapolis, MN: Fortress Press.

Mount, E. Jr. (1999), *Covenant, Community and the Common Good: An Interpretation of Christian Ethics*, Cleveland, OH: The Pilgrim Press.

Nadel, I. (1996), *Various Positions: A Life of Leonard Cohen*, New York: Pantheon.

Narvaez, D. (2014), *Neurobiology and the Development of Human Morality: Evolution, Culture, and Wisdom*, New York: W. W. Norton.

Nelson, C., N. Fox, and C. Zeanah (2014), *Romania's Abandoned Children: Deprivation, Brain Development, and the Struggle for Recovery*, Cambridge, MA: Harvard University Press.

Nicolet, V. (2014), "Leonard Cohen's Use of the Bible: Transformation of the Sacred," *Biblical Reception*, 3: 223–39.

O'Kane, J., M. Medley, and B. Wheeler (2016), "Closing Time: The
Canadian Arts Community Remembers Leonard Cohen," *Globe and
Mail*, November 11. Available online: https://www.theglobeandmail.
com/arts/music/closing-time-the-canadian-arts-community-remembers-
leonard-cohen/article32815894/ (accessed August 10, 2019).

Ondaatje, M. (1970), *Leonard Cohen*, Toronto: McClelland & Stewart.

O'Neil, M. (2015), "Leonard Cohen, Singer of the Bible," *Cross Currents*,
65(1): 91–99.

Oord, T. (2015), *The Uncontrolling Love of God: An Open and
Relational Account of Providence*, Downers Grove, IL: IVP Academic.

Pacey, D. (1976), "The Writer and His Public," in C. Klinck, A. Bailey, C.
Bissell, R. Daniells, N. Frye, and D. Pacey (eds.), *Literary History of
Canada: Canadian Literature in English (Second Edition) Volume II*,
3–21, Toronto: University of Toronto Press.

Pally, M. (2014), "The Hebrew Bible Is a Problem Set," in R. Schieder
(ed.), *Die Gewalt des einen Gottes: Die Monotheismus-Debatte
[The Violence of the One God: The Monotheism Debate]*, 218–48,
Berlin: Berlin University Press.

Pally, M. (2016), *Commonwealth and Covenant: Economics, Politics, and
Theologies of Relationality*, Grand Rapids, MI: Eerdmans.

Pally, M. (2020), "Philosophical Questions and Biological Findings: Part
I: Human Cooperativity, Competition, and Aggression," *Zygon*.

Pantell, M., H. Rehkopf, D. Jutte, S. Syme, J. Balmes, and N. Adler
(2013), "Social Isolation: A Predictor of Mortality Comparable to
Traditional Clinical Risk Factors," *American Journal of Public Health*,
103(11): 2056–62.

Peckham, J. (2018), *Theodicy of Love: Cosmic Conflict and the Problem
of Evil*, Grand Rapids, MI: Baker.

Phillips, D. Z. (2001), "Theism without Theodicy," in S. Davis (ed.),
Encountering Evil: Live Options in Theodicy, 145–61, Louisville,
KY: Westminster John Knox.

Pinnock, S. (2002), *Beyond Theodicy: Jewish and Christian Continental
Thinkers Respond to the Holocaust*, Albany: State University of
New York Press.

Plantinga, A. (1974a), *God, Freedom, and Evil*, Grand Rapids, MI:
Eerdmans.

Plantinga, A. (1974b), *The Nature of Necessity*, Oxford: Clarendon.

Pleshoyano, A. (2013), "Leonard Cohen's Poiesis Toward the Unified
Heart Where all Bounds Fade Away," in K. Kachappilly (ed.), *Mystic
Musings in Art and Poetry*, 13–38, New Delhi: Christian World
Imprints.

Porter, J. (1990), *The Recovery of Virtue: The Relevance of Aquinas for
Christian Ethics*, Louisville, KY: Westminster John Knox.

Posner, N. (2017), "That's How the Light Gets In," *Queens Quarterly*, 124(4): 510–25.

Purdham, M. (2012), "Who is the Lord of the World? Leonard Cohen's Beautiful Losers and the Total Vision," *Canadian Literature*, 212: 86–102.

Raab, C. (2017), "How the Light Gets In," *Commonweal*, 144(8): 15–17.

Rahner, K. (1969), *The Unity of Spirit and Matter in the Christian Understanding of Faith*, London: Darton Longman & Todd.

Ravvin, N. (1997), "Writing around the Holocaust: Uncovering the Ethical Centre of Leonard Cohens Beautiful Losers?," in N. Ravvin, *A House of Words: Jewish Writing, Identity and Memory*, 22–31, Montreal: McGill-Queens University Press.

Remnick, D. (2016), "How the Light Gets In/Leonard Cohen Makes It Darker," *New Yorker*, October 17. Available online: https://www.newyorker.com/magazine/2016/10/17/leonard-cohen-makes-it-darker (accessed August 8, 2018).

Reynolds, A. (1990), *Leonard Cohen: A Remarkable Life*, London: Omnibus.

Rice, R. (2014), *Suffering and the Search for Meaning*, Downers Grove, IL: IVP Academic.

Riches, S. (2014), "Leonard Cohen on Romantic Love," in J. Holt (ed.), *Leonard Cohen and Philosophy: Various Positions*, Kindle Locations 2109–2272, Chicago: Open Court.

Rodin, S. (1997), *Evil and Theodicy in the Theology of Karl Barth*, New York: Peter Lang.

Rohter, L. (2009), "Leonard Cohen on the Road, for Reasons Practical and Spiritual," *New York Times*, February 25. Available online: https://www.nytimes.com/2009/02/25/arts/25iht-25cohe.20413789.html (accessed August 11, 2019).

Rosemann, P. (2018), "Leonard Cohen, Philosopher," *Maynooth Philosophical Papers*, 9: 1–20.

Rosenzweig, F. ([1921] 1971), *The Star of Redemption*, trans. W. W. Hallo, New York: Holt, Rinehart and Winston.

Rosenzweig, F. ([1921] 2005), *The Star of Redemption*, trans. B. E. Galli, Madison: University of Wisconsin Press.

Roth, J. K. (2001), "A Theodicy of Protest," in S. Davis (ed.), *Encountering Evil: Live Options in Theodicy*, 1–20, Louisville, KY: Westminster John Knox.

Sarna, N. (1966), *Understanding Genesis*, New York: Schocken Books.

Schudel, M. (2016), "Leonard Cohen, Singer-Songwriter of Love, Death and Philosophical Longing, Dies at 82," *Washington Post*, November 11. Available online: https://www.washingtonpost.com/entertainment/music/leonard-cohen-singer-songwriter-of-love-death-and-philosophical-longing-dies-at-82/2016/11/10/1e6bf036-a779-11e6-8042-f4d111c862d1_story.html (accessed August 12, 2019).

Scobie, S. (1978), *Leonard Cohen*, Vancouver: Douglas & McIntyre.

Scott, M. (2015), *Pathways in Theodicy: An Introduction to the Problem of Evil*, Minneapolis, MN: Fortress Press.

Shepherd, A. (2014), *The Gift of the Other: Levinas, Derrida, and a Theology of Hospitality*, Cambridge: Lutterworth Press, James Clarke, https://doi.org/10.2307/j.ctt1cgf0nw.

Siemerling, W. (1994a), *Discoveries of the Other: Alterity in the Work of Leonard Cohen, Hubert Aquin, Michael Ondaatje, and Nicole Brossard*, Toronto: University of Toronto Press.

Siemerling, W. (1994b), "A Political Constituency That Really Exists in the World: An Interview with Leonard Cohen," in M. Fournier and K. Norris (eds.), *Take This Waltz: A Celebration of Leonard Cohen*, 154–69, Ste. Anne de Bellevue: Muses'.

Simmons, S. (2012), *I'm Your Man: The Life of Leonard Cohen*, New York: HarperCollins.

Simmons, S. (2014), "The Silence between Two Thoughts." Available online: http://sylviesimmons.com/the-silence-between-two-thoughts/ (accessed August 13, 2019).

Smith, J. K. A. (2000), *The Fall of Interpretation: Philosophical Foundations for a Creational Hermeneutic*, Downers Grove, IL: InterVarsity.

Sounes, H. (2001), *Down the Highway: The Life of Bob Dylan*, New York: Grove.

Stackhouse, M. (1997), *Covenant and Commitments: Faith, family, and economic life*, Louisville, KY: Westminister John Knox.

Steinskog, E. (2010), "Queering Cohen: Cover Versions as Subversions of Identity," in G. Plasketes (ed.), *Play it Again: Cover Songs in Popular Music*, 139–52, Farnham: Ashgate.

Stern, M. (1980), *Greek and Latin Authors on Jews and Judaism: From Tacitus to Simplicius*, Jerusalem: Academy of Sciences and Humanities.

Swinton, J. (2007), *Raging with Compassion: Pastoral Responses to the Problem of Evil*, Grand Rapids, MI: Eerdmans.

Tanner, K. (2010), "In the Image of the Invisible," in C. Boesel and C. Keller (eds.), *Apophatic Bodies: Negative Theology, Incarnation, and Relationality*, 117–35, New York: Fordham University Press.

Toda, F. (1984), "Five Years with the Length of Five Years: Echoes of Wordsworth in the Words of Leonard Cohen," *Atlantis*, 6(1/2): 69–74.

Todd, D. (2010), "Leonard Cohen: The Theology of Love," *Vancouver Sun*, November 27. Available online: https://vancouversun.com/news/staff-blogs/leonard-cohen-the-theology-of-love (accessed January 8, 2020).

Todd, D. (2016), "Leonard Cohen: Jewish, Buddhist and Christian, too," *Vancouver Sun*, November 25. Available online: http://vancouversun.com/opinion/columnists/douglas-todd-leonard-cohen-jewishbuddhist-and-christian-too (accessed March 6, 2019).

Vitello, P. (2014), "Joshu Sasaki, 107, Tainted Zen Master," *The New York Times*, August 4. Available online: https://www.nytimes.com/2014/08/05/us/joshu-sasaki-a-zen-master-tarnished-by-abuse-claims-dies-at-107.html (accessed August 12, 2019).

Waddell, R., E. Nagy, M. Peters, M. Herrera, A. Donahue, A. Ben-Yehuda, and M. Concepcion (2010), "Money Makers," *Billboard*, Febraury 25. Available online: https://www.billboard.com/articles/news/959249/money-makers-page-1 (accessed August 11, 2019).

Walzer, M. (1985), *Exodus and Revolution*, New York: Basic Books.

Weil, S. (1951), *Waiting for God*, New York: HarperCollins.

Weil, S. (1970), *The First and Last Notebooks*, London: Oxford University Press.

Weil, S. (1974), *Gateway to God*, D. Raper (ed.), London: Collins, Fontana Books.

Weinandy, T. (2000), *Does God Suffer?*, Notre Dame, IN: University of Notre Dame Press.

Wegter-McNelly, K. (2011), *The Entangled God: Divine Relationality and Quantum Physics*, New York: Routledge.

Whitehead, A. N. ([1929] 1978), *Process and Reality: An Essay in Cosmology*, New York: Free Press.

Wiesel, E. (1978), *Legends of our Time*, New York: Avon.

Wills, B. (2014), "Clouds of Unknowing," in J. Holt (ed.), *Leonard Cohen and Philosophy: Various Positions*, Kindle Locations 3864–4021, Chicago: Open Court.

Wolfson, E. (2006a), "New Jerusalem Glowing: Songs and Poems of Leonard Cohen in a Kabbalistic Key," *Kabbalah: Journal for the Study of Jewish Mystical Texts*, 15: 103–53.

Wolfson, E. (2006b), *Venturing Beyond: Law and Morality in Kabbalistic Mysticism*, New York: Oxford University Press.

Wolfson, E. (2014), *Giving beyond the Gift: Apophasis and Overcoming Theomania*, New York: Fordham University Press.

Worrall, S. (2008), "Leonard Cohen: Out of the Monastery and Back on the Road," *The Independent*, June 15. Available online: https://www.independent.co.uk/arts-entertainment/music/features/leonard-cohen-out-of-the-monastery-and-back-on-the-road-845789.html (accessed July 1, 2020).

Wynands, S. (1999), "The Representation of the Holocaust in *Flowers for Hitler*," *Essays on Canadian Writing*, 69: 198–209.

Zizioulas, J. (1975), "Human Capacity and Incapacity: A Theological Exploration of Personhood," *Scottish Journal of Theology*, 28: 401–48.

INDEX

Adams, M. 28, 148
Adorno, T. W. 71, 142
Amos 5:21-24 45, 70
anger-amid-commitment 98, 100,
    148
apocalypse, apocalpytic 50, 135,
    138, 153
Aquinas, T. 1, 15, 20, 22–6, 31,
    35–7, 39, 95, 147
Arendt, H. 144
Augustine 1, 4, 18, 22–3, 25, 53,
    62, 147

Babich, B. 28, 82, 93, 95, 105, 107,
    110, 120, 139
Barbour, I. 34
Barth, K. 25
Bauman, Z. 143–4
Beautiful Losers 8, 50, 65, 66, 67,
    73, 93, 111, 130, 145
Billingham, P. 1, 72, 93, 94, 117
Blue Alert 11
bond
    broken 50, 62, 69, 74, 76, 87,
        90, 94, 104, 107, 112, 125–6,
        129–30, 132, 149
    covenantal 77, 97
    entwined 68, 84
    with God and other persons 3, 6,
        17, 24, 32, 41, 43–6, 48, 50,
        54, 56, 59, 67, 70, 73, 75–6,
        82, 87–8, 90–1, 94, 98, 100,
        104, 117, 123, 126, 129, 135,
        137, 141, 143, 154–5
    with humanity 2, 17
    I-Thou, 105

Lurianic 89
    reciprocal 2, 11, 23, 41, 62
    sustained 75, 79, 81, 97,
        101, 104
Book of Longing 12, 51, 56, 62,
    149, 150
Book of Mercy 3, 10, 56–9, 65, 70,
    72, 76, 78, 89, 90, 91, 121,
    132, 150, 152
Borowitz, E. 48
Broomfield, N. 56, 108–10, 171
Buber, M. 35, 37, 47, 84, 105
Buddhism, Buddhist 10, 25, 50, 55,
    93, 100, 110, 150

*Can't Forget: A Souvenir of the
    Grand Tour* 3
Celan, P. 53
Christian imagery 6, 93–4, 150
Christianity, Christian tradition 25,
    44, 52, 55, 93, 96, 97, 99, 101
2 Chron. 28:8-15 44
commitment
    broken 11, 27, 45, 68, 71, 73,
        84, 90, 96, 107, 124, 130,
        132–3, 137, 139
    covenantal 2, 6, 28, 33, 40–1,
        46, 49, 55, 98, 147–8, 154
    Moebius Strip 49
    reciprocal 23, 41, 45, 47
    to God and other persons 3–4,
        19, 27, 56, 65, 68, 84, 114,
        141, 150, 158
    with humanity 2, 90
community 42–4, 54, 64, 154
concentration camp 140–1, 145

convenant
  artistic expression 56, 69, 94,
    121, 131, 132, 150, 152, 158
  breach of 2, 3, 4, 5, 6, 11, 20, 25,
    28, 32, 52, 61, 63, 70–2, 74–7,
    81–2, 85, 90, 100, 103–4, 115,
    121, 123–6, 129, 130–6, 139–
    40, 147–9, 151–3, 155, 158
  community/network 43, 54,
    64–6, 103
  covenant, human relationship
    104–5, 121, 123, 126, 130
  covenant, love 95, 97, 154
  covenant, nature of 33, 40–3
  covenant, Moebius Strip
    (entwined nature) 43–6, 50,
    59, 66, 81–2, 85, 143, 154
  covenant, politics 133–7, 140,
    144
  covenant, reciprocity of 17, 19,
    20, 23, 41–2, 48, 55, 90, 95,
    103
  covenant, tradition and thought
    5, 17, 24, 32, 42, 54, 62, 68,
    94–5, 97
creation 19, 22–3, 28–9, 31, 33,
  35–7, 45–6, 58, 75–8, 94, 126,
  148, 151, 156–8
crooner 116–17
cross 31, 59, 82, 85, 95–7, 99, 122,
  134, 141, 147
crucifixion, crucified 27–8, 71, 82,
  94–5, 98–100, 135, 157

Dawkins, R. 74
Dennis, I. 71, 83, 104, 114
Dear Heather 11, 131–3, 146
Death of a Ladies' Man 9, 81, 107,
  113, 116
Death of a Lady's Man 9, 54, 108,
  112, 113
divine
  female 125–6
  plan xvii, 30

suffering 27–8
Deut. 14:22 44
Deut. 15:1-2 44
Deut. 15:12-14 45
Deut. 20:10 44
Deut. 23:15-16 45
Deut. 24:19-22 44

Eastman, S. 38
evil 4, 15–26, 28–31, 34, 76–7,
  139, 144–8
evil-as-absence 23, 25
exile, exiler 51–2, 59, 61–62, 67,
  70, 94
Exod. 3:1-4 158
Exod. 3:2 96
Exod. 4:10 98
Exod. 19:2 42
Exod. 21:2 45
Exod. 22:21 44
Exod. 22:25 45
Exod. 32 45
Exod. 32:9-14 97
Exod. 33:18-23 119
Exod. 34:6 4

Famous Blue Raincoat 10
Flowers for Hitler 8, 53, 141–6
Frye, N. 7, 94, 111–12

Gen. 1 22
Gen. 1:1 16
Gen. 2:7 35-36
Gen. 3 18
Gen. 6–8 45
Gen. 6–9 34
Gen. 6:17 xvii
Gen. 12:3 3, 41
Gen. 22:1–2 xiv
Gen. 22:1-19 90, 129, 158
Gen. 22:7–8 xv
Gen. 24 109
Gen. 26:4 3, 41
Gen. 28:14 3, 42

Gen. 32:22-31 59, 94
Gen. 32:25-31 65
Gen. 37:12-28 26
Genesis Rabbah 22:6 62, 139
Glazer, A. 1-3, 51-2, 70
God's image 20, 35
Griffin, D. 21, 30-1

Halbertal, M. xiii, 23, 70, 74-5, 158
Haslam, T. 49, 57
Hegel, G. W. F. 21, 146
Heschel, A. J. 46
Hick, J. 28-29, 52
Holocaust 27, 30, 53, 71, 77,
    140-6
Hos. 2 27
Hos. 6:6 45
Hos. 11:1 27
human flourishing 39, 49
Hume, H. 16, 126
Hutcheon, L. 50, 66

I'm Your Man 10-12, 103, 109-10,
    117, 124, 133, 135
Irenaeus 29

Jer. 5:19 15
Jer. 12:1 15
Jer. 26:14-15 xv
Jewish imagery 88, 90, 94, 122,
    150
Jewish tradition 2, 33, 35, 37, 44,
    52, 56, 74-5, 78, 94, 96, 101,
    122
Jewish philosophers 23, 26,
    45, 143
Josh. 9 44
Josh. 9:18 44
Judaism 4, 25, 44, 49, 55-6, 78, 90,
    96, 150

Kabbalah, Lurianic 54, 82, 88, 91,
    97, 119, 121, 129
2 Kgs 6:22-23 44

Langlois, C. 110-11, 118
Lebold, C. 81, 107, 116-17
Let Us Compare Mythologies 7-8,
    91-2, 141
Lev. 6:2-3 44
Lev. 19:34 44
Lev. 23:22 44
Lev. 25:4-6 44
Lev. 25:8-13 44
Levinas, E. 37, 42, 46-7, 84
Levi, P. 141-4
Live Songs 39, 72

Mackie, J. 21
Maimonides, M. 23-5, 147
Marianne & Leonard: Words of
    Love 56, 108-10, 171
Měsíc 2, 50, 54, 70, 83, 94, 100,
    104
Mic. 7:2-7 45
Moebius Strip 42-4, 46, 49-50, 59,
    68, 81, 84-6, 154
Moltmann, J. 27-8, 148
moral agency, moral agent 4,
    18-22, 26, 29, 147-8
More Best of Leonard Cohen 109
Muslim 33, 93, 150

Narvaez, D. 39
New Skin for the Old Ceremony
    8-9, 27, 54, 69, 75, 85, 97,
    112, 116-17, 119, 124, 131-2,
    139, 149
Num. 5:6 44

Old Ideas 12, 43, 69, 73, 79, 97,
    107, 114, 139

Pacey, D. 50
Pally, M. 42-3, 56, 74
Parasites of Heaven 8
Peckham, J. 15, 19, 147
Plantinga, A. 4, 19, 20, 147
Poems and Songs 12

politics 2, 9, 66, 129, 132–5,
    137–9, 141, 146
Popular Problems 13, 59, 70, 94,
    118, 126, 130, 138, 141,
    146, 151
Prov. 21:3 45
Ps. 3:4 3
Ps. 10:1 15
Ps. 11 15
Ps. 22:1 85
Ps. 38:9 56
Ps. 42:2 58
Ps. 51:17 45, 77, 90
Ps. 74:14 16
Ps. 115:3 19
Ps. 135:6 19
Ps. 137:5 62
Pss. 7:4-5 44
Pss. 10:4-5 15
Pss. 17:5-7 3
Pss. 94:3-7 15
Purdham, M. 65–7, 73

Rahner, K. 100–1
Recent Songs 9, 52, 67–8, 86, 98,
    100, 106–7, 138
relational xvii, 32, 38, 40, 43, 48,
    51, 61, 66, 74
Rosenzweig, F. 42, 45–6

Sabbath 55, 88–90, 153
sex 2, 7, 51, 54, 66, 68, 88, 105,
    107, 111, 113, 115, 119, 121,
    123, 125, 135
Siemerling, W. 64, 82–5
Simmons, S. 2, 5, 8–9, 11, 49, 51,
    62, 93, 105, 108–9, 112, 114,
    122, 149
sin 23, 26, 28–9, 32, 63, 76, 126,
    142, 146
Songs from a Room 4, 8, 58, 99,
    129, 156
Songs of Leonard Cohen 5, 7–8, 63,
    67, 85, 93, 108, 111, 116, 126

Songs of Love and Hate 9, 69, 72,
    106, 118, 158
*Stranger Music, Selected Poems and
    Songs* 10, 109, 112
Sufism 2, 25, 50, 53, 93

Talmud 2, 6, 42, 54–5, 62
telos 2, 38–9, 41, 43, 50, 65, 94,
    115, 148
Ten New Songs 11, 36, 61, 68,
    72–3, 84, 86–7, 104, 126, 131,
    137, 151
Thanks for the Dance 6, 13, 62,
    67, 106, 115, 131, 147, 149,
    155, 158
The Cloud of Unknowing 52
The Favourite Game 8, 63–4,
    111, 122
The Flame 13, 91, 118, 155, 158
The Future 10, 54, 73, 78, 109,
    114, 125, 129–30, 135, 152
The Spice Box of Earth 8, 71, 88,
    101, 137
theodicy
    Cohen's 4–5, 15–17, 32–3, 61–2,
        71–2, 75, 85, 100, 104, 115,
        123, 155, 158
    cruciform 27–8, 31, 52, 97
    evil-as-negation 23, 25
    free will 4, 19, 22
    process 30–1, 148
    soul-making 28–30, 52, 97, 148
Tikkun olam 53
Tour of 1979 134
Trinitiy, Trinitarian 6, 28, 37, 129,
    133, 135, 137, 140
troubadour 104, 116–17

Various Positions 10, 50, 56–8, 76,
    78–9, 82, 89, 109, 119, 121–2,
    124, 141, 151–2

Weil, S. 143–4
Whitehead, A. N. 30–1

Wiesel, E. 77
wisdom 18, 23–5, 110, 147–8
Wolfson, E. 2, 52–4, 62, 87, 94,
    100, 150
Wynands, S. 142, 144

You Want It Darker 6, 13, 61–2,
    74, 93, 147, 150–2, 155–9

CPSIA information can be obtained
at www.ICGtesting.com
Printed in the USA
BVHW062133241121
622494BV00002B/8